SUPER COOKERY

Low Fat & Salads

p

This is a Parragon Book
This edition published in 2001

Parragon
Queen Street House
4 Queen Street
Bath BA1 1HE, UK

Printed in China

Note

Cup measurements used in this book are for American cups.
Tablespoons are assumed to be 15 ml. Unless otherwise stated,
milk is assumed to be full fat, eggs are medium and pepper is
freshly ground black pepper.

Contents

Introduction

No-one who has more than a passing interest in their health can be unaware of the problems associated with a diet that contains too much fat. A high level of fat consumption is implicated in obesity – and all that that entails – coronary disease, diabetes and even cancer. The message that we should all cut down on the fat in our diets is reinforced every time we go shopping, and it is almost impossible to walk around a supermarket without being beset on all sides by labels proclaiming low-fat this, reduced-fat that and no-fat the other.

Cutting the amount of fat in our diets is, of course, an effective way to lose weight, simply because it will reduce the number of calories we consume, as well as reducing the likelihood that we will contract a serious disease. However, before we cut fat out of our lives completely, it is important to remember that we all need to include a certain amount of fat in our daily intake of food if our bodies are to function properly. Essential fatty acids are needed to build cell membranes and for other vital bodily functions. Our brain tissue, nerve sheaths and bone marrow need fat, for example, and we all need fat to protect vital organs such as our liver, kidneys and heart.

Nutritionists suggest that we should aim to cut our intake of fat to 27-30 per cent of our total daily calorie intake. If your average diet totals 2000 calories, this will mean eating no more than about 75 g/2¼ oz of fat a day. As a guide, bear in mind that most people consume about 40 per cent of their daily calories in the form of fat. Remember, however, that if you are being treated for any medical condition, you must discuss with your family doctor the changes you propose making in your diet before you begin your new regime.

When you are thinking about reducing your intake of fat, it is important to know that fats can be broadly divided into saturated and unsaturated fat. Saturated fats are those that are solid at room temperature, and they are found mainly in animal products – butter and cheese, high-fat meats (sausages, pâté, streaky bacon), cakes, chocolate, potato crisps, biscuits, coconut and hydrogenated (hardened) vegetable or fish oils. Unsaturated fats are healthier – but they are still fats. Your target should be a reduction to 8 per cent of your daily calories in the form of saturated facts, with the remainder in the form of unsaturated fats. These are usually liquid at room temperature and come from vegetable sources – olive oil, ground nut oil, sunflower oil, safflower oil and corn oil. Remember, though, that oil is only another name for liquid fat. Using oil instead of margarine or butter to fry onions or garlic will do nothing to reduce your overall intake of fat.

INGREDIENTS

One of the simplest and most beneficial changes you can make in your diet is to change from full-fat milk, cream, cheese and yogurt to a low- or reduced-fat equivalent. Semi-skimmed milk, for example, has all the nutritional benefits of whole milk but 10 g/⅓ oz of fat per pint compared with 23 g/¼ oz of fat per pint in whole milk. Use skimmed milk to make custards and sauces and you will not notice the difference in flavour. Low-fat yogurt or fromage frais mixed with chopped chives is a delicious and healthy alternative to butter or sour cream.

Most vegetables are naturally low in fat and can be used to make a meal of meat or fish go further. Recent nutritional research indicates that we should all aim to eat five portions of fresh fruit and vegetables every day because they contain what are known as antioxidant vitamins, including beta carotene (which creates vitamin A in the body) and vitamins C and E. The antioxidant vitamins in vegetables are thought to help prevent a number of degenerative illnesses (including cancer, heart disease, arthritis and even ageing of the skin) and to protect the body from the harmful effects of pollution and ultraviolet light, which can damage the body's cells. Phytochemicals, which occur naturally in plants, are thought to be instrumental in the fight against cancer.

Steaming is the best way to cook vegetables to preserve their goodness. Boiling can, for example, destroy up to three-quarters of the vitamin C present in green vegetables. If you have to boil, cook the vegetables as quickly as possible and avoid over-cooking, which also destroys the carotene.

If you have time, it is a good idea to make your own stock to use as the basis of casseroles and soups. The ready-made stocks and stock cubes that are available from shops are often high in salt and artificial flavourings. Instead, use fresh herbs and spices in the water in which vegetables have been cooked or in which dried mushrooms have been soaked. Liquids in which meat and fish of various kinds have been cooked should be saved, too. Chill the liquid in the refrigerator and you will easily be able to remove and discard the fat, which will have risen to the top of the container and solidified.

Pasta, noodles, pulses and grains can all be used in the low-fat diet, and they are useful for bulking out dishes. Pasta is available in a wide range of shapes, and it is excellent for boosting your carbohydrate intake. Inadequate intake of carbohydrate can result in fatigue and poor energy levels. Wholemeal (whole wheat) pasta is also particularly high in fibre, which helps to speed the passage of waste material through the digestive system. Stir cooked brown rice into soups and casseroles to thicken them, or mix one part red lentils with three parts lean minced (ground) beef to make a smaller amount of meat go further. Before you buy, check that noodles and pasta have not been enriched with egg. Look out instead for wholemeal (whole wheat) or rice varieties.

EQUIPMENT

Good quality non-stick pans and cookware will directly reduce the amount of fat needed for cooking, and are easier to clean. Use plastic implements or wooden spoons with non-stick pans so that you do not scratch the surface.

A ridged frying pan (skillet) makes it possible to cook with the minimum amount of fat or oil, because the fat drips down between the ridges rather than being absorbed by the food. When you are stir-frying, use a small amount of oil. Keep the heat constant and the food moving to ensure quick, even cooking. Use a non-stick wok, which will help you cut down still further on the amount of oil you need to use in cooking.

Use a perforated spoon to remove food from the frying pan (skillet), so that cooking juices are left behind. Absorbent kitchen paper is useful for draining surface oil and fat from food that has just been cooked, and it can also be used to mop up fat that rises to the top during cooking. Use plain, unpatterned paper so that no dye is transferred to the food.

COOKING METHODS

The way we cook our food is one of the most important factors in ensuring a healthy and low-fat diet. In general, steaming is the best way to cook vegetables to preserve their goodness. Boiling can, for example, destroy up to three-quarters of the vitamin C present in green vegetables. This guide will help you to choose the healthiest way to cook your dish, while maintaining optimum flavour and colour.

Frying. This is the most fat-rich method of cooking. Yet, surprisingly deep-frying the food absorbs less fat than shallow-frying. To cut down on fat intake buy a good quality, non-stick frying pan as you will need less fat, and use a vegetable oil, high in polyunsaturates. The preferred method is to stir-fry, as you require little oil as the food is cooked quickly over a high heat.

Grilling. This is a good alternative to frying, producing a similar crisp and golden coating while remaining moist and tender inside. Ingredients with a delicate texture and which can easily dry out, such as white fish or chicken breasts, will require brushing with oil. Marinating can reduce the need for oil. Always cook on a rack, so that the fat drains away.

Poaching. This is ideal for foods with a delicate texture of subtle flavour, such as chicken and fish but is fat free. Instead of water try alternative liquids such as stock, wine and acidulated water, flavoured with herbs and vegetable. The cooking liquid can make the basis of a nutritious and flavoursome sauce.

Steaming. This is also fat-free and is becoming a popular method of cooking meat, fish, chicken and vegetables. Ingredients maintain their colour, flavour and texture, fewer nutrients are leached out. An additional advantage is that when meat is steamed, the fat melts and drips into the cooking liquid – this should not then be used for gravy.

Braising and stewing. Slow cooking techniques produce succulent dishes that are especially welcome in winter. Trim all visible fat from the meat and always remove the skin from the chicken.

Roasting. Fat is an integral part of this cooking technique, and without it meat or fish would dry out. Try standing meat on a rack over a roasting tray so that the fat drains off. Do not use the meat juices for gravy.

Baking. Many dishes are fat free. Foil-wrapped parcels of meat or fish are always delicious. Add fruit juice or wine instead of oil or butter for a moist texture.

Microwaving. Food cooked in this way rarely requires additional fat.

MAKING SALADS

The popular definition of a salad is a dish of raw or cold cooked foods, usually served with a dressing or seasoning to add flavour. Traditionally they are used as a side dish accompaniment to a main course or as a starter. However, several different salads, carefully balanced, can make an excellent main course for a casual meal in the summer. On their own, individual salads are ideal to use as a starter for a more formal occasion or perfect for a light lunch.

More substantial salad dishes can be devised, however, with the addition of cooked or semi-cooked vegetables, and ingredients such as cooked meats can be included. Using cooked vegetables in a salad adds gentle flavour and the mixing of hot and cold ingredients adds interest to the dish. Another idea that is gaining in popularity is to combine vegetables with fruit to make a range of contrasting savoury and sweet tastes in a salad. Other ingredients often incorporated in salad dishes include dried fruits, nuts and seeds.

Salads are generally of high nutritional value. They are not, however, necessarily low in fat content, owing to the rich dressings, sauces and mayonnaises that are sometimes used to give them flavour. If you are following a low fat diet, then look at the ingredients in the dressings given with the recipes in this book and chose low fat alternatives such as butter and margarine instead of oils.

STORE CUPBOARD

Rice and pasta

There are a good variety of rices to choose from for incorporating in salads. Try long-grain, basmati, Italian arborio or wild rice. Brown rice is a good source of vitamin B1 and fibre. Keep a good selection of pasta, preferably in small shapes, such as rigatoni, farfalle, or fusili, and of course, macaroni and spaghetti.

Legumes

As they provide a valuable source of protein, stock up on red kidney beans, cannellini beans and chick peas to use in salads.

Nuts and seeds

As well as adding protein, vitamins and useful healthy fats to the diet, nuts such as hazelnuts, walnuts, pine kernels, and seeds such as sesame, sunflower and poppy add flavour and texture to salads.

Oils and fats

Oils are useful for adding subtle flavourings to food. Use extra-virgin olive oil for salad dressings or try hazelnut and walnut oils for a superb flavour. All fats and oils are high in calories; butter and margarine are lower-fat options.

Vinegars

Red or white wine vinegar, tarragon, sherry or balsamic vinegars will all add their own subtle flavours to salad dishes.

Soups & Starters

Many favourite snacks and starters – especially those that we buy ready-prepared on supermarket shelves and in cans – are surprisingly high in fat. Next time, before you buy, think instead about making some of the appetizing recipes on the following pages – they will get your meal off to a wonderful low-fat start.

Soups are a traditional first course, but, served with crusty bread, they can also be a satisfying meal in their own right. Although it does take a little longer, consider making your own stock by using the liquid left after cooking vegetables and the juices from fish and meat that have been used as the base of casseroles. Use a potato to thicken your soups rather than stirring in the traditional thickener of flour and water – or, worse, flour and fat.

Also included here are a delicious range of salads; if you are following a low-fat diet check the ingredients, in particular the dressing, and replace those high in fat with lower-fat options.

Chicken & Asparagus Soup

Serves 4

INGREDIENTS

225 g/8 oz fresh asparagus
850 ml/1¹/₂ pints/3³/₄ cups fresh
  chicken stock
150 ml/5 fl oz/²/₃ cup dry white
  wine

1 sprig each fresh parsley, dill
  and tarragon
1 garlic clove
60 g/2 oz/¹/₃ cup vermicelli
  rice noodles

350 g/12 oz lean cooked chicken,
  finely shredded
salt and white pepper
1 small leek

1 Wash the asparagus and trim away the woody ends. Cut each spear into pieces 4 cm/1¹/₂ inches long.

2 Pour the stock and wine into a large saucepan and bring to the boil.

3 Wash the herbs and tie them with clean string. Peel the garlic clove and add, with the herbs, to the saucepan together with the asparagus and noodles. Cover and simmer for 5 minutes.

4 Stir in the chicken and plenty of seasoning. Simmer gently for a further 3-4 minutes or until heated through.

5 Trim the leek, slice it down the centre and wash under running water to remove any dirt. Shake dry and shred finely.

6 Remove the herbs and garlic and discard.

7 Ladle the soup into warm bowls, sprinkle with shredded leek and serve at once.

VARIATION

You can use any of your favourite herbs in this recipe, but choose those with a subtle flavour so that they do not overpower the asparagus. Small, tender asparagus spears give the best results and flavour.

COOK'S TIP

Rice noodles contain no fat and are an ideal substitute for egg noodles.

Beef, Water Chestnut & Rice Soup

Serves 4

INGREDIENTS

350 g/12 oz lean beef (such as
    rump or sirloin)
1 litre/1¾ pints/1 quart fresh
    beef stock
1 cinnamon stick, broken
2 star anise
2 tbsp dark soy sauce

2 tbsp dry sherry
3 tbsp tomato purée (paste)
115 g/4 oz can water chestnuts,
    drained and sliced
175 g/6 oz/3 cups cooked white
    rice
1 tsp zested orange rind

6 tbsp orange juice
salt and pepper

TO GARNISH:
strips of orange rind
2 tbsp chives, snipped

1 Carefully trim away any fat from the beef. Cut the beef into thin strips and then place into a large saucepan.

2 Pour over the stock and add the cinnamon, star anise, soy sauce, sherry, tomato purée (paste) and water chestnuts. Bring to the boil, skimming away any surface scum with a flat ladle. Cover the pan and simmer gently for about 20 minutes or until the beef is tender.

3 Skim the soup with a flat ladle to remove any scum again. Remove and discard the cinnamon and star anise. Blot the surface with absorbent kitchen paper to remove any fat.

4 Stir in the rice, orange rind and juice. Season with salt and pepper to taste. Heat through for 2–3 minutes before ladling into warm bowls. Serve the soup garnished with strips of orange rind and snipped chives.

VARIATION

Omit the rice for a lighter soup that is an ideal starter for an Oriental meal of many courses. For a more substantial soup that would be a meal in its own right, add diced vegetables such as carrot, (bell) pepper, sweetcorn or courgette (zucchini).

Winter Beef & Vegetable Soup

Serves 4

INGREDIENTS

60 g/2 oz/⅓ cup pearl barley
1.2 litres/2 pints/5 cups fresh
   beef stock
1 tsp dried mixed herbs

225 g/8 oz lean rump or sirloin
   beef
1 large carrot, diced
1 leek, shredded
1 medium onion, chopped

2 sticks celery, sliced
salt and pepper
2 tbsp fresh parsley, chopped,
   to garnish
crusty bread, to serve

1 Place the pearl barley in a large saucepan. Pour over the stock and add the mixed herbs. Bring to the boil, cover and simmer for 10 minutes.

2 Trim any fat from the beef and cut the meat into thin strips.

3 Skim away any scum that has risen to the top of the stock.

4 Add the beef, carrot, leek, onion and celery to the pan. Bring back to the boil, cover and simmer

for about 20 minutes or until the meat and vegetables are just tender.

5 Skim away any remaining scum that has risen to the top of the soup with a flat ladle. Blot the surface with absorbent kitchen paper to remove any fat. Season with salt and pepper to taste.

6 Ladle the soup into warm bowls and sprinkle with freshly chopped parsley. Serve accompanied with plenty of crusty bread.

VARIATION

This soup is just as delicious made with lean lamb or pork fillet. A vegetarian version can be made by omitting the beef and beef stock and using vegetable stock instead. Just before serving, stir in 175 g/ 6 oz fresh bean curd (tofu), drained and diced. An even more substantial soup can be made by adding other root vegetables, such as swede or turnip, instead of, or as well as, the carrot.

Mediterranean-Style Fish Soup

Serves 4

INGREDIENTS

1 tbsp olive oil
1 large onion, chopped
2 garlic cloves, finely chopped
425 ml/15 fl oz/1³/₄ cups fresh
    fish stock
150 ml/5 fl oz/²/₃ cup dry white
    wine
1 bay leaf
1 sprig each fresh thyme,
    rosemary and oregano

450 g/1 lb firm white fish fillets
    (such as cod, monkfish or
    halibut), skinned and cut into
    2.5 cm/1 inch cubes
450 g/1 lb fresh mussels,
    prepared
400 g/14 oz can chopped
    tomatoes

225 g/8 oz peeled prawns
    (shrimp), thawed if frozen
salt and pepper
sprigs of thyme, to garnish

TO SERVE:
lemon wedges
4 slices toasted French bread,
    rubbed with cut garlic clove

1 Heat the oil in a large pan and gently fry the onion and garlic for 2–3 minutes until just softened.

2 Pour in the stock and wine and bring to the boil. Tie the bay leaf and herbs together with clean string and add to the saucepan together with the fish and mussels. Stir well, cover and simmer for 5 minutes.

3 Stir in the tomatoes and prawns (shrimp) and continue to cook for a further 3–4 minutes until piping hot and the fish is cooked through.

4 Discard the herbs and any mussels that have not opened. Season and ladle into warm bowls. Garnish with sprigs of thyme and serve with lemon wedges and toasted bread.

COOK'S TIP

Traditionally, the toasted bread is placed at the bottom of the bowl and the soup spooned over the top. For convenience, look out for prepared, cooked shellfish mixtures, which you could use instead of fresh fish. Simply add to the soup with the tomatoes in step 3.

Tuscan Bean & Vegetable Soup

Serves 4

INGREDIENTS

1 medium onion, chopped
1 garlic clove, finely chopped
2 celery sticks, sliced
1 large carrot, diced
400 g/14 oz can chopped
   tomatoes
150 ml/5 fl oz/²⁄₃ cup Italian dry
   red wine

1.2 litres/2 pints/5 cups fresh
   vegetable stock
1 tsp dried oregano
425 g/15 oz can mixed beans
   and pulses
2 medium courgettes
   (zucchini), diced
1 tbsp tomato purée (paste)

salt and pepper

TO SERVE:
low-fat pesto sauce
crusty bread

1 Place the onion, garlic, celery and carrot in a large saucepan. Stir in the tomatoes, red wine, vegetable stock and oregano.

2 Bring the vegetable mixture to the boil, cover and leave to simmer for 15 minutes. Stir the beans and courgettes (zucchini) into the mixture, and continue to cook, uncovered, for a further 5 minutes.

3 Add the tomato purée (paste) to the mixture and season well with salt and pepper to taste. Then heat through, stirring occasionally, for 2–3 minutes, but do not allow the mixture to boil again.

4 Ladle the soup into warm bowls and top with a spoonful of low-fat pesto on each portion. Serve the soup accompanied with plenty of fresh crusty bread.

VARIATION

For a more substantial soup, add 350 g/12 oz diced lean cooked chicken or turkey with the tomato purée (paste) in step 3.

Lentil, Pasta & Vegetable Soup

Serves 4

INGREDIENTS

1 tbsp olive oil
1 medium onion, chopped
4 garlic cloves, finely chopped
350 g/12 oz carrot, sliced
1 stick celery, sliced

225 g/8 oz/1 ¼ cups red lentils
600 ml/1 pint/2 ½ cups fresh
   vegetable stock
700 ml/1 ¼ pint/scant 3 cups
   boiling water

150 g/5 ½ oz/scant 1 cup pasta
150 ml/5 fl oz/⅔ cup natural
   low-fat fromage frais
   (unsweetened yogurt)
salt and pepper
2 tbsp fresh parsley, chopped,
   to garnish

1 Heat the oil in a large saucepan and gently fry the prepared onion, garlic, carrot and celery, stirring gently, for 5 minutes until the vegetables begin to soften.

2 Add the lentils, stock and boiling water. Season with salt and pepper to taste, stir and bring back to the boil. Simmer, uncovered, for 15 minutes until the lentils are completely tender. Allow to cool for 10 minutes.

3 Meanwhile, bring another saucepan of water to the boil and cook the pasta according to the instructions on the packet. Drain well and set aside.

4 Place the soup in a blender and process until smooth. Return to a saucepan and add the pasta. Bring back to a simmer and heat for 2–3 minutes until piping hot. Remove from the heat and stir in the fromage frais (yogurt). Season if necessary.

5 Serve sprinkled with chopped parsley.

COOK'S TIP

Avoid boiling the soup once the fromage frais (yogurt) has been added. Otherwise it will separate and become watery, spoiling the appearance of the soup.

Creamy Sweetcorn Soup

Serves 4

INGREDIENTS

1 large onion, chopped
1 large potato, peeled and diced
1 litre/1³/₄ pints/1 quart
    skimmed milk
1 bay leaf
¹/₂ tsp ground nutmeg
salt and pepper

450 g/1 lb sweetcorn kernels,
    canned or frozen, drained
    or thawed
1 tbsp cornflour (cornstarch)
3 tbsp cold water
4 tbsp natural low-fat fromage
    frais (unsweetened yogurt)

TO GARNISH:
100 g/3¹/₂ oz lean ham, diced
2 tbsp fresh chives, snipped

1 Place the onion and potato in a large pan and pour over the milk. Add the bay leaf, nutmeg and half the sweetcorn. Bring to the boil, cover and simmer for 15 minutes until the potato is softened. Stir occasionally and keep the heat low so that the milk does not burn on the bottom of the pan.

2 Discard the bay leaf and leave the liquid to cool for 10 minutes.

Transfer to a blender and process for a few seconds. Or, rub through a sieve.

3 Pour the smooth liquid into a pan. Blend the cornflour (cornstarch) with the water to make a paste and stir it into the soup.

4 Bring the soup back to the boil, stirring until it thickens, and add the remaining sweetcorn. Heat through for 2–3 minutes until piping hot.

5 Remove from the heat and season with salt and pepper to taste. Stir in the fromage frais (yogurt). Ladle the soup into warm bowls and serve sprinkled with the diced ham and snipped chives.

VARIATION

For a more substantial soup, add 225 g/8 oz flaked white crab meat or peeled prawns (shrimp) in step 4.

22

Tomato & Red Pepper Soup

Serves 4

INGREDIENTS

2 large red (bell) peppers
1 large onion, chopped
2 sticks celery, trimmed and
    chopped
1 garlic clove, crushed

600 ml/1 pint/2½ cups fresh
    vegetable stock
2 bay leaves
2 x 400 g/14 oz cans plum
    tomatoes

salt and pepper
2 spring onions (scallions), finely
    shredded, to garnish
crusty bread, to serve

1 Preheat the grill (broiler) to hot. Halve and deseed the (bell) peppers, arrange them on the grill (broiler) rack and cook, turning occasionally, for 8–10 minutes until softened and charred.

2 Leave to cool slightly, then carefully peel off the charred skin. Reserving a small piece for garnish, chop the (bell) pepper flesh and place in a large saucepan.

3 Mix in the onion, celery and garlic. Add the stock and the bay leaves. Bring to the boil, cover and simmer for 15 minutes. Remove from the heat.

4 Stir in the tomatoes and transfer to a blender. Process for a few seconds until smooth. Return to the saucepan.

5 Season to taste and heat for 3–4 minutes until piping hot. Ladle into warm bowls and garnish with the reserved (bell) pepper cut into strips and the spring onion (scallion). Serve with crusty bread.

COOK'S TIP

If you prefer a coarser, more robust soup, lightly mash the tomatoes with a wooden spoon and omit the blending process in step 4.

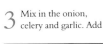

Carrot, Apple & Celery Soup

Serves 4

INGREDIENTS

900 g/2 lb carrots, finely diced
1 medium onion, chopped
3 sticks celery, diced
1 litre/1¾ pints/1 quart fresh
    vegetable stock

3 medium-sized eating
    (dessert) apples
2 tbsp tomato purée (paste)
1 bay leaf
2 tsp caster (superfine) sugar

¼ large lemon
salt and pepper
celery leaves, washed and
    shredded, to garnish

1 Place the carrots, onion and celery in a large saucepan and add the stock. Bring to the boil, cover and simmer for 10 minutes.

2 Meanwhile, peel, core and dice 2 of the eating (dessert) apples. Add the pieces of apple, tomato purée (paste), bay leaf and caster (superfine) sugar to the saucepan and bring to the boil. Reduce the heat, half cover and allow to simmer for 20 minutes. Remove and discard the bay leaf.

3 Meanwhile, wash, core and cut the remaining apple into thin slices, leaving on the skin. Place the apple slices in a small saucepan and squeeze over the lemon juice. Heat gently and simmer for 1–2 minutes until tender. Drain and set aside.

4 Place the carrot and apple mixture in a blender or food processor and blend until smooth. Alternatively, press the carrot and apple mixture through a sieve with the back of a wooden spoon.

5 Gently re-heat the soup if necessary and season with salt and pepper to taste. Ladle the soup into warm bowls and serve topped with the reserved apple slices and shredded celery leaves.

COOK'S TIP

Soaking light coloured fruit in lemon juice helps to prevent it from turning brown.

Chilled Prawn & Cucumber Soup

Serves 4

INGREDIENTS

1 cucumber, peeled and diced
400 ml/14 fl oz/1²/₃ cups fresh
 fish stock, chilled
150 ml/5 fl oz/²/₃ cup tomato
 juice
150 ml/5 fl oz/²/₃ cup low-fat
 natural (unsweetened) yogurt

150 ml/5 fl oz/²/₃ cup low-fat
 fromage frais (or double the
 quantity of yogurt)
125 g/4¹/₂ oz peeled prawns
 (shrimp), thawed if frozen,
 roughly chopped
few drops Tabasco sauce

1 tbsp fresh mint, chopped
salt and white pepper
ice cubes, to serve

TO GARNISH:
sprigs of mint
cucumber slices
whole peeled prawns (shrimp)

1 Place the diced cucumber in a blender or food processor and work for a few seconds until smooth. Alternatively, chop the cucumber finely and push through a sieve.

2 Transfer the cucumber to a bowl. Stir in the stock, tomato juice, yogurt, fromage frais (if using) and prawns (shrimp), and mix well. Add the Tabasco sauce and season with salt and pepper to taste.

3 Stir in the chopped mint, cover and chill for at least 2 hours.

4 Ladle the soup into glass bowls and add a few ice cubes. Serve garnished with sprigs of fresh mint, cucumber slices and whole peeled prawns (shrimp).

VARIATION

Instead of prawns (shrimp), add white crab meat or minced chicken. For a vegetarian version of this soup, omit the prawns (shrimp) and add an extra 125 g/4¹/₂ oz finely diced cucumber. Use fresh vegetable stock instead of fish stock.

Celery, Stilton & Apple Soup

Serves 4

INGREDIENTS

50 g/1³/₄ oz/4 tbsp butter
2 shallots, chopped
3 celery sticks, chopped
1 garlic clove, crushed
2 tbsp plain (all-purpose) flour

600 ml/1 pint/2¹/₂ cups
   vegetable stock
300 ml/¹/₂ pint/1¹/₄ cups milk
150 g/5¹/₂ oz/1¹/₂ cups blue Stilton
   cheese, crumbled, plus extra
   to garnish

2 tbsp walnut halves, roughly
   chopped
150 ml/¹/₄ pint/²/₃ cup natural
   (unsweetened) yogurt
salt and pepper
chopped celery leaves, to garnish

1 Melt the butter in a large saucepan and sauté the shallots, celery and garlic for 2–3 minutes, stirring, until softened.

2 Add the flour and cook for 30 seconds.

3 Gradually stir in the vegetable stock and milk and bring to the boil.

4 Reduce the heat to a gentle simmer and add the crumbled blue Stilton cheese and walnut halves. Cover and leave to simmer for 20 minutes.

5 Stir in the natural (unsweetened) yogurt and heat for a further 2 minutes without boiling.

6 Season the soup, then transfer to a warm soup tureen or individual serving bowls, garnish with chopped celery leaves and extra crumbled blue Stilton cheese and serve at once.

COOK'S TIP

As well as adding protein, vitamins and useful fats to the diet, nuts add important flavour and texture to vegetarian meals.

VARIATION

Use an alternative blue cheese, such as Dolcelatte or Gorgonzola, if preferred or a strong vegetarian Cheddar cheese, grated.

Spicy Chicken Noodle Soup

Serves 4

INGREDIENTS

2 tbsp tamarind paste
4 red Thai chillies, finely chopped
2 cloves garlic, crushed
2.5 cm/1-inch piece Thai ginger,
    peeled and very finely chopped
4 tbsp fish sauce

2 tbsp palm sugar or caster
    (superfine) sugar
8 lime leaves, roughly torn
1.2 litres/2 pints/5 cups chicken stock
350 g/12 oz boneless chicken breast
100 g/3½ oz carrots, very thinly sliced
350 g/12 ozsweet potato, diced

100 g/3½ oz baby corn cobs, halved
3 tbsp fresh coriander (cilantro),
    roughly chopped
100 g/3½ oz cherry tomatoes, halved
150 g/5½ oz flat rice noodles
fresh coriander (cilantro),
    chopped,to garnish

1 Place the tamarind paste, Thai chillies, garlic, Thai ginger, fish sauce, sugar, lime leaves and chicken stock in a large preheated wok and bring to the boil, stirring constantly. Reduce the heat and cook for about 5 minutes.

2 Using a sharp knife, thinly slice the chicken. Add the chicken to the wok and cook for a further 5 minutes, stirring the mixture well.

3 Reduce the heat and add the carrots, sweet potato and baby corn cobs to the wok. Leave to simmer, uncovered, for 5 minutes, or until the vegetables are just tender and the chicken is completely cooked through.

4 Stir in the coriander (cilantro), cherry tomatoes and noodles. Leave the soup to simmer for about 5 minutes, or until the noodles are tender. Garnish and serve hot.

COOK'S TIP

Tamarind paste is produced from the seed pod of the tamarind tree. It adds both a brown colour and tang to soups and gravies. If unavailable, dilute molasses (dark muscovado) sugar or treacle with lime juice.

Chilli Fish Soup

Serves 4

INGREDIENTS

15 g/¹/₂ oz Chinese dried mushrooms
2 tbsp sunflower oil
1 onion, sliced
100 g/3¹/₂ oz/1¹/₂ cups mangetout
(snow peas)100 g/3¹/₂ oz/1¹/₂

cups bamboo shoots
3 tbsp sweet chilli sauce
1.2 litres/2 pints/5 cups fish or
vegetable stock
3 tbsp light soy sauce

2 tbsp fresh coriander (cilantro)
450 g/1 lb cod fillet, skinned and
cubed

1 Place the mushrooms in a large bowl. Pour over enough boiling water to cover and leave to stand for 5 minutes. Drain the mushrooms thoroughly. Using a sharp knife, roughly chop the mushrooms.

2 Heat the sunflower oil in a preheated wok. Add the onion to the wok and stir-fry for 5 minutes, or until softened.

3 Add the mangetout (snow peas), bamboo shoots, chilli sauce, stock and soy sauce to the wok and bring to the boil.

4 Add the coriander (cilantro) and cubed fish to the wok. Leave to simmer for 5 minutes or until the fish is cooked through.

5 Transfer the soup to warm bowls, garnish with extra coriander (cilantro) if wished and serve hot.

VARIATION

Cod is used in this recipe as it is a meaty white fish. For real luxury, use monkfish tail instead.

COOK'S TIP

There are many different varieties of dried mushrooms, but shiitake are best. They are not cheap, but a small amount will go a long way.

Hot & Sour Mushroom Soup

Serves 4

INGREDIENTS

2 tbsp tamarind paste	2 tbsp palm sugar or caster	225 g/8 oz button mushrooms,
4 red Thai chilies, very finely chopped	(superfine) sugar8 lime leaves,	halved
2 cloves garlic, crushed	roughly torn	350 g/12 oz shredded white cabbage
2.5 cm/1 inch piece of Thai ginger,	1.2 litres/2 pints/5 cups vegetable	100 g/3½ oz fine green beans, halved
peeled and very finely chopped	stock	3 tbsp fresh coriander (cilantro),
4 tbsp fish sauce	100 g/3½ oz carrots, very	roughly chopped
	thinly sliced	100 g/3½ oz cherry tomatoes, halved

1 Place the tamarind paste, Thai chilies, garlic, Thai ginger, fish sauce, palm or caster (superfine) sugar, lime leaves and stock in a large preheated wok. Bring the mixture to the boil, stirring occasionally.

2 Reduce the heat and add the carrots, mushrooms, cabbage and green beans. Leave the soup to simmer, uncovered, for about 10 minutes, or until the vegetables are just tender.

3 Stir the coriander (cilantro) and cherry tomatoes into the mixture in the wok and heat through for 5 minutes.

4 Transfer the soup to warm bowls and serve hot.

COOK'S TIP

Tamarind is one of the ingredients that gives Thai cuisine its special sweet and sour flavour.

VARIATION

Instead of the white cabbage, try using Chinese leaves for a sweeter flavour. Add the Chinese leaves with the coriander (cilantro) and cherry tomatoes in step 3.

Chicken & Leek Soup

Serves 6

INGREDIENTS

350 g/12 oz boneless chicken	1.2 litres/2 pints/5 cups chicken	salt and white pepper
350 g/12 oz leeks	stock	cooked rice and diced red (bell)
30 g/1 oz/2 tbsp butter	1 bouquet garni sachet	peppers (optional)
	8 pitted prunes, halved	

1 Using a sharp knife, cut the chicken and leeks into 2.5cm/1-inch pieces.

2 Melt the butter in a large saucepan, add the chicken and leeks and fry for 8 minutes, stirring occasionally.

3 Add the chicken stock and bouquet garni sachet to the mixture in the pan, and season with salt and pepper to taste.

4 Bring the soup to the boil and simmer over a gentle heat for 45 minutes.

5 Add the pitted prunes with some cooked rice and diced (bell) peppers (if using), and simmer for 20 minutes. Remove the bouquet garni sachet and discard. Pour the soup into a warm tureen or individual bowls and serve.

COOK'S TIP

If you have time, make the chicken stock yourself, using the recipe on page 5. Alternatively, you can buy good fresh stock from supermarkets.

COOK'S TIP

Instead of the bouquet garni sachet, you can use a bunch of fresh, mixed herbs, tied together with string. Choose herbs such as parsley, thyme and rosemary.

Thai Chicken Noodle Soup

Serves 4–6

INGREDIENTS

1 sheet of dried egg noodles from a 250 g/9 oz pack
1 tbsp oil
4 skinless, boneless chicken thighs, diced
1 bunch spring onions (scallions), sliced

2 garlic cloves, chopped
2 cm/³/₄ inch piece fresh ginger root, finely chopped
850 ml/1¹/₂ pints/3³/₄ cups chicken stock
200 ml/7 fl oz/scant 1 cup coconut milk

3 tsp red Thai curry paste
3 tbsp peanut butter
2 tbsp light soy sauce
1 small red (bell) pepper, chopped
60 g/2 oz/¹/₂ cup frozen peas
salt and pepper

1 Put the noodles in a shallow dish and soak in boiling water following the instructions on the packet.

2 Heat the oil in a large saucepan or wok, add the chicken, and fry for 5 minutes, stirring until lightly browned. Add the white part of the spring onions (scallions), the garlic and ginger and fry for 2 minutes, stirring. Add the stock, coconut milk, curry paste, peanut butter and soy sauce. Season with

salt and pepper to taste. Bring to the boil, stirring, then simmer for 8 minutes, stirring occasionally. Add the red (bell) pepper, peas and green spring onion (scallion) tops and cook for 2 minutes.

3 Add the drained noodles and heat through. Spoon into individual bowls and serve with a spoon and fork.

VARIATION

Green Thai curry paste can be used instead of red curry paste for a less fiery flavour.

Chicken Consommé

Serves 8–10

INGREDIENTS

1.75 litres/3 pints/8 cups chicken stock	150 ml/¼ pint/⅔ cup medium sherry 4 egg whites plus egg shells	125 g/4 oz cooked chicken, sliced thinly salt and pepper

1 Place the chicken stock and sherry in a large saucepan and heat gently for 5 minutes.

2 Add the egg whites and the egg shells to the chicken stock and whisk until the mixture begins to boil.

3 Remove the pan from the heat and allow the mixture to subside for 10 minutes. Repeat this process three times. This allows the egg white to trap the sediments in the chicken stock to clarify the soup. Let the consommé cool for 5 minutes.

4 Carefully place a piece of fine muslin (cheesecloth) over a clean saucepan. Ladle the soup over the muslin and strain into the saucepan.

5 Repeat this process twice, then gently re-heat the consommé. Season with salt and pepper to taste then add the cooked chicken slices. Pour the soup into a warm serving dish or individual bowls.

6 Garnish the consommé with any of the suggestions in the Cook's Tip, right.

COOK'S TIP

Consommé is usually garnished with freshly cooked pasta shapes, noodles, rice or lightly cooked vegetables. Alternatively, you could garnish it with omelette strips, drained first on paper towels.

Chicken Wonton Soup

Serves 4-6

INGREDIENTS

FILLING:
350 g/12 oz minced (ground) chicken
1 tbsp soy sauce
1 tsp grated, fresh ginger root
1 garlic clove, crushed
2 tsp sherry

2 spring onions (scallions), chopped
1 tsp sesame oil
1 egg white
$^1\!/_2$ tsp cornflour (cornstarch)
$^1\!/_2$ tsp sugar
about 35 wonton wrappers

SOUP:
1.5 litres/$2^3\!/_4$ pints/6 cups chicken
   stock
1 tbsp light soy sauce
1 spring onion (scallion), shredded
1 small carrot, cut into very thin slices

1 Combine all the ingredients for the filling and mix well.

2 Place a small spoonful of the filling in the centre of each wonton wrapper.

3 Dampen the edges and gather up the wonton wrapper to form a pouch enclosing the filling.

4 Cook the filled wontons in boiling water for 1 minute or until they float to the top.

5 Remove with a slotted spoon. Bring the chicken stock to the boil.

6 Add the soy sauce, spring onion (scallion), carrot and wontons to the soup. Simmer gently for 2 minutes then serve.

VARIATION

Substitute the chicken for minced (ground) pork.

COOK'S TIP

Look for wonton wrappers in Chinese or oriental supermarkets. Fresh wrappers can be found in the chilled compartment and they can be frozen if you wish. Wrap in cling film (plastic wrap) before freezing.

Rosy Melon & Strawberries

Serves 4

INGREDIENTS

¹/₄ honeydew melon	150 ml/5 fl oz/²/₃ cup rosé wine	175 g/6 oz small strawberries,
¹/₂ Charentais or Cantaloupe melon	2–3 tsp rose water	washed and hulled
		rose petals, to garnish

1 Scoop out the seeds from both melons with a spoon. Then carefully remove the skin, taking care not to remove too much flesh.

2 Cut the melon flesh into thin strips and place in a bowl. Pour over the wine and sufficient rose water to taste. Mix together gently, cover and leave to chill in the refrigerator for at least 2 hours.

3 Halve the strawberries and carefully mix into the melon. Allow the melon and strawberries to stand at room temperature for about 15 minutes for the flavours to develop – if the melon is too cold, there will be little flavour.

4 Arrange on individual serving plates and serve sprinkled with a few rose petals, if wished.

COOK'S TIP

Rose water is a distillation of rose petals. It is generally available from large pharmacies and leading supermarkets as well as from more specialist food suppliers.

VARIATION

It does not matter whether the rosé wine is sweet or dry – although sweet wine contains more calories. Experiment with different types of melon. Varieties such as 'Sweet Dream' have whitish-green flesh, while Charentais melons, which have orange flesh, go better with a dry wine. If you wish, soak the strawberries in the wine with the melon, but always allow the fruit to return to room temperature before serving.

Italian Platter

Serves 4

INGREDIENTS

125 g/4½ oz reduced-fat
   Mozzarella cheese, drained
60 g/2 oz lean Parma ham
   (prosciutto)
400 g/14 oz can artichoke
   hearts, drained
4 ripe figs

1 small mango
few plain Grissini (bread sticks),
   to serve

DRESSING:
1 small orange

1 tbsp passata (sieved tomatoes)
1 tsp wholegrain mustard
4 tbsp low-fat natural
   (unsweetened) yogurt
fresh basil leaves
salt and pepper

1 Cut the cheese into 12 sticks, 6.5 cm/2½ inches long. Remove the fat from the Parma ham (prosciutto) and slice the meat into 12 strips.

2 Carefully wrap a strip of Parma ham (prosciutto) around each stick of cheese and arrange them neatly on a large serving platter.

3 Halve the artichoke hearts and cut the figs into quarters. Arrange

them on the serving platter in groups.

4 Peel the mango, then slice it down each side of the large, flat central stone. Slice the flesh into strips and arrange them so that they form a fan shape on the serving platter.

5 To make the dressing, pare the rind from half of the orange using a vegetable peeler. Cut the rind into small strips and place them in a bowl.

Extract the juice from the orange and add it to the bowl containing the rind.

6 Add the passata (sieved tomatoes), mustard, yogurt and seasoning to the bowl and mix together. Shred the basil leaves and mix them into the dressing.

7 Spoon the dressing into a small dish and serve with the Italian Platter, accompanied with Grissini (bread sticks).

Breakfast Muffins

Serves 4

INGREDIENTS

2 wholemeal muffins	4 medium eggs	4 tbsp fresh vegetable stock
8 rashers lean back bacon, rinds removed	2 large tomatoes	salt and pepper
	2 large flat mushrooms	1 small bunch fresh chives, snipped, to garnish

1 Preheat the grill (broiler) to medium. Cut the muffins in half and lightly toast them for 1–2 minutes on the open side. Set aside and keep warm.

2 Trim off all visible fat from the bacon and grill for 2–3 minutes on each side until cooked through. Drain on absorbent kitchen paper and keep warm.

3 Place 4 egg-poaching rings in a frying pan (skillet) and pour in enough water to cover the base of the pan. Bring to the boil and reduce the heat to a simmer. Break one egg into each ring and poach for 5–6 minutes until set.

4 Cut the tomatoes into 8 thick slices and arrange on a piece of kitchen foil on the grill (broiler) rack. Grill (broil) for 2–3 minutes until just cooked. Season to taste.

5 Peel and thickly slice the mushrooms. Place in a saucepan with the stock, bring to the boil, cover and simmer for 4–5 minutes until cooked. Drain and keep warm.

6 To serve, arrange the tomato and mushroom slices on the toasted muffins and top each with 2 rashers of bacon. Arrange an egg on top of each and sprinkle with a little pepper. Garnish and serve at once.

VARIATION

Omit the bacon for a vegetarian version and use more tomatoes and mushrooms instead. Alternatively, include a grilled (broiled) low-fat tofu (bean curd) or Quorn burger.

Cheesy Ham & Celery Savoury

Serves 4

INGREDIENTS

4 sticks celery
12 thin slices of lean ham
1 bunch spring onions (scallions)
175 g/6 oz low-fat soft cheese
   with garlic and herbs

6 tbsp low-fat natural
   (unsweetened) yogurt
4 tbsp Parmesan cheese, freshly
   grated
celery salt and pepper

TO SERVE:
tomato salad
crusty bread

1 Wash the celery, remove the leaves and slice the celery sticks into 3 equal portions.

2 Cut any visible fat off the ham and lay the slices on a chopping board. Place a piece of celery on each piece of ham and roll up. Place 3 ham and celery rolls in each of 4 small, heatproof dishes.

3 Trim the spring onions (scallions), then finely shred both the white and green parts. Sprinkle the spring onions (scallions) over the ham and celery rolls and season with celery salt and pepper.

4 Mix together the soft cheese and yogurt and spoon over the ham and celery rolls.

5 Preheat the grill (broiler) to medium. Sprinkle each portion with 1 tablespoon of grated Parmesan cheese and grill (broil) for 6–7 minutes until hot and the cheese has formed a crust. If the cheese starts to brown too quickly, lower the grill (broiler) setting slightly.

6 Serve with a tomato salad and crusty bread.

COOK'S TIP

Parmesan is useful in low-fat recipes because its intense flavour means you need to use only a small amount.

Parsleyed Chicken & Ham Pâté

Serves 4

INGREDIENTS

225 g/8 oz lean, skinless
    chicken, cooked
100 g/3½ oz lean ham, trimmed
small bunch fresh parsley
1 tsp lime rind, grated

2 tbsp lime juice
1 garlic clove, peeled
125 ml/4½ fl oz/½ cup low-fat
    natural fromage frais
    (unsweetened yogurt)

salt and pepper
1 tsp lime zest, to garnish

TO SERVE:
wedges of lime
crisp bread

1 Dice the chicken and ham and place in a blender or food processor. Add the parsley, lime rind and juice, and garlic and process well until finely minced. Alternatively, finely chop the chicken, ham, parsley and garlic and place in a bowl. Mix gently with the lime rind and juice.

2 Transfer the mixture to a bowl and mix in the fromage frais (yogurt). Season with salt and pepper to taste, cover and leave to chill in the refrigerator for about 30 minutes.

3 Transfer the pâté to individual serving dishes and garnish with lime zest.

4 Serve the parsleyed chicken and ham pâtés with lime wedges and crisp bread.

VARIATION

This pâté can be made equally successfully with other kinds of minced, lean, cooked meat such as turkey, beef and pork. Alternatively, replace the chicken and ham with peeled prawns (shrimp) and/or white crab meat or with canned tuna in brine, drained. Remember that removing the skin from poultry reduces the fat content of any dish.

Spinach Cheese Moulds

Serves 4

INGREDIENTS

100 g/3½ oz fresh spinach leaves
300 g/10½ oz skimmed milk soft
   cheese
2 garlic cloves, crushed

sprigs of fresh parsley, tarragon
   and chives, finely chopped
salt and pepper

TO SERVE:
salad leaves and fresh herbs
pitta bread

1 Trim the stalks from the spinach leaves. Rinse the leaves under running water. Pack the leaves into a saucepan while still wet, cover and cook for 3–4 minutes until wilted – they will cook in the steam from the wet leaves (do not overcook). Drain well and pat dry with absorbent kitchen paper.

2 Base-line 4 small pudding basins or individual ramekin dishes with baking parchment. Line the basins or ramekins with spinach leaves so that the leaves overhang the edges if they are large enough to do so.

3 Place the cheese in a bowl and add the garlic and herbs. Mix together thoroughly and season to taste.

4 Spoon the cheese and herb mixture into the basins or ramekins and pull over the overlapping spinach to cover the cheese, or lay extra leaves to cover the top. Place a greaseproof (waxed) paper circle on top of each dish and weigh

down with a 100 g/3½ oz weight. Leave to chill in the refrigerator for 1 hour.

5 Remove the weights and peel off the paper. Loosen the moulds (molds) gently by running a small palette knife (spatula) around the edges of each dish and turn them out on to individual serving plates. Serve with a mixture of salad leaves and fresh herbs, and warm pitta bread.

Soufflé Omelette

Serves 4

INGREDIENTS

175 g/6 oz cherry tomatoes
225 g/8 oz mixed mushrooms
(such as button, chestnut,
shiitake, oyster and wild
mushrooms)

4 tbsp fresh vegetable stock
small bunch fresh thyme
4 medium eggs, separated
4 medium egg whites
4 tsp olive oil

25 g/1 oz rocket (arugula) leaves
salt and pepper
fresh thyme sprigs, to garnish

1 Halve the tomatoes and place them in a pan. Wipe the mushrooms with kitchen paper, trim if necessary and slice if large. Place in the pan.

2 Add the stock and thyme to the pan, and season to taste with salt and pepper. Bring to the boil, cover and simmer for 5–6 minutes until tender. Drain, remove the thyme and discard, and keep the mixture warm.

3 Meanwhile, whisk the egg yolks with 8 tablespoons of water until frothy. In a clean, grease-free bowl, mix the 8 egg whites until stiff and dry.

4 Spoon the egg yolk mixture into the egg whites and, using a metal spoon, fold the whites and yolks into each other until well mixed. Take care not to knock out too much of the air.

5 For each omelette, brush a small omelette pan with 1 teaspoon of oil and heat until hot. Pour in a quarter of the egg mixture and cook for 4–5 minutes or until the mixture has set.

6 Preheat the grill (broiler) to medium and finish cooking the omelette for 2–3 minutes.

7 Transfer the omelette to a warm serving plate. Fill the omelette with a few rocket (arugula) leaves, and a quarter of the mushroom and tomato mixture. Flip over the top of the omelette, garnish with sprigs of thyme and serve.

Grilled Rice & Tuna Peppers

Serves 4

INGREDIENTS

60 g/2 oz/¹⁄₃ cup wild rice
60 g/2 oz/¹⁄₃ cup brown rice
4 assorted medium (bell) peppers
200 g/7 oz can tuna fish in brine,
    drained and flaked

325 g/11¹⁄₂ oz can sweetcorn
    kernels (with no added sugar
    or salt), drained
100 g/3¹⁄₂ oz reduced-fat
    Cheddar cheese, grated
1 bunch fresh basil leaves,
    shredded

2 tbsp dry white breadcrumbs
1 tbsp Parmesan cheese,
    freshly grated
salt and pepper
fresh basil leaves, to garnish
crisp salad leaves, to serve

1 Place the 2 rices in different saucepans, cover with water and cook according to the instructions on the packet. Drain well.

2 Meanwhile, preheat the grill (broiler) to medium. Halve the (bell) peppers, remove the seeds and stalks and arrange the peppers on the grill (broiler) rack, cut side down. Cook for 5 minutes, turn over and cook for a further 4–5 minutes.

3 Transfer the cooked rice to a mixing bowl and add the flaked tuna and drained sweetcorn. Gently fold in the grated Cheddar. Mix in the basil leaves and season to taste.

4 Divide the tuna and rice mixture into 8 equal portions. Pile each portion into each cooked (bell) pepper half. Mix together the breadcrumbs and Parmesan cheese and sprinkle the mixture over each (bell) pepper.

5 Place the (bell) peppers back under the grill (broiler) for 4–5 minutes until hot and golden-brown. Serve immediately, garnished with fresh basil leaves and accompanied with fresh, crisp salad leaves.

Baked Potatoes with a Spicy Filling

Serves 4

INGREDIENTS

4 baking potatoes, each about
    300 g/10½ oz
1 tbsp vegetable oil (optional)
400 g/14 oz can chick-peas
    (garbanzo beans), drained

1 tsp ground coriander
1 tsp ground cumin
4 tbsp fresh coriander (cilantro),
    chopped

150 ml/5 fl oz/⅔ cup low-fat
    natural (unsweetened) yogurt
salt and pepper
salad, to serve

1 Preheat the oven to 200°C/400°F/Gas Mark 6. Scrub the potatoes and pat them dry with absorbent kitchen paper. Prick them all over with a fork, brush with oil (if using) and season.

2 Place the potatoes on a baking sheet (cookie sheet) and bake for 1–1¼ hours or until cooked through. Leave to cool for 10 minutes.

3 Meanwhile, mash the chick-peas (garbanzo beans) with a fork or potato masher. Stir in the spices and half the chopped coriander (cilantro). Cover and set aside.

4 Halve the cooked potatoes and scoop the flesh into a bowl, keeping the shells intact. Mash the flesh until smooth and gently mix into the chick-pea (garbanzo bean) mixture with the yogurt. Season well.

5 Fill the potato shells with the potato and chick-pea (garbanzo bean) mixture. Return the potatoes to the oven and bake for 10–15 minutes until heated through. Serve sprinkled with the remaining chopped coriander (cilantro) and a fresh salad.

COOK'S TIP

For an even lower fat version of this recipe, bake the potatoes without oiling them first.

Spinach Crêpes with Curried Crab

Serves 4

INGREDIENTS

115 g/4 oz buckwheat flour
1 large egg, beaten
300 ml/¹/₂ pint/1¹/₄ cups
   skimmed milk
125 g/4¹/₂ oz frozen spinach,
   thawed, well-drained and
   chopped
2 tsp vegetable oil

FILLING:
350 g/12 oz white crab meat
1 tsp mild curry powder
1 tbsp mango chutney
1 tbsp reduced-calorie
   mayonnaise
2 tbsp low-fat natural
   (unsweetened) yogurt

2 tbsp fresh coriander (cilantro),
   chopped

TO SERVE:
green salad
lemon wedges

1 Sift the flour into a bowl and remove any husks that remain in the sieve (strainer).

2 Make a well in the centre of the flour and add the egg. Gradually whisk in the milk, then blend in the spinach. Transfer the batter to a jug and let stand for 30 minutes.

3 To make the filling, mix together all the ingredients, except the coriander (cilantro), in a bowl, cover and chill.

4 Whisk the batter. Brush a small crêpe pan with a little oil, heat until hot and pour in enough batter to cover the base thinly. Cook for 1–2 minutes until set, turn over and cook for 1 minute until golden. Transfer to a warmed plate. Repeat to make 8 pancakes, layering them on the plate with baking parchment.

5 Stir the coriander (cilantro) into the crab mixture. Fold each pancake into quarters. Open one fold and fill with the crab mixture. Serve warm, with a green salad and lemon wedges.

VARIATION

Try lean diced chicken in a light white sauce or peeled prawns (shrimp) instead of the crab.

Crispy Potato Skins

Serves 4

INGREDIENTS

4 large baking potatoes
2 tbsp vegetable oil
4 tsp salt
150 ml/¼ pint/⅔ cup soured
   cream and 2 tbsp chopped
   chives, to serve
snipped chives, to garnish

BEAN SPROUT SALAD:
50 g/1¾ oz/½ cup bean sprouts
1 celery stick, sliced
1 orange, peeled and segmented
1 red dessert (eating)
   apple, chopped
½ red (bell) pepper, chopped
1 tbsp chopped parsley
1 tbsp light soy sauce
1 tbsp clear honey
1 small garlic clove, crushed

BEAN FILLING:
100 g/3½ oz/1½ cups canned,
   mixed beans, drained
1 onion, halved and sliced
1 tomato, chopped
2 spring onions
   (scallions), chopped
2 tsp lemon juice
salt and pepper

1 Scrub the potatoes and put on a baking tray (cookie sheet). Prick the potatoes all over with a fork and rub the oil and salt into the skin.

2 Cook in a preheated oven at 200°C / 400°F/Gas Mark 6 for 1 hour or until soft.

3 Cut the potatoes in half lengthwise and

scoop out the flesh, leaving a 1 cm/½ inch thick shell. Put the shells, skin side uppermost, in the oven for 10 minutes until crisp.

4 Mix the ingredients for the bean sprout salad in a bowl, tossing in the soy sauce, honey and garlic to coat.

5 Mix the ingredients for the bean filling in a bowl.

6 Mix the soured cream and chives in another bowl.

7 Serve the potato skins hot, with the two salad fillings, garnished with snipped chives, and the sour cream and chive sauce.

Lentil Pâté

Serves 4

INGREDIENTS

1 tbsp vegetable oil, plus extra for greasing	½ tsp ground coriander	2 tbsp milk
1 onion, chopped	850 ml/1½ pints/1¼ cups vegetable stock	2 tbsp mango chutney
2 garlic cloves, crushed	175 g/6 oz/¾ cup red lentils	2 tbsp chopped parsley
1 tsp garam masala	1 small egg	plua extra to garnish
		salad leaves and warm toast, to serve

1 Heat the oil in a large saucepan and sauté the onion and garlic for 2–3 minutes, stirring. Add the spices and cook for a further 30 seconds.

2 Stir in the stock and lentils and bring the mixture to the boil. Reduce the heat and simmer for 20 minutes until the lentils are cooked and softened. Remove the pan from the heat and drain off any excess moisture.

3 Put the mixture in a food processor and add the egg, milk, mango chutney and parsley. Blend until smooth.

4 Grease and line the base of a 450 g/1 lb loaf tin (pan) and spoon the mixture into the tin (pan), levelling the surface. Cover and cook in a preheated oven at 200°C/400°F/Gas Mark 6 for 40–45 minutes or until firm to the touch.

5 Allow the pâté to cool in the tin (pan) for 20 minutes, then transfer to the refrigerator to cool completely.

6 Turn out the pâté on to a serving plate, slice and garnish with chopped parsley. Serve with salad leaves and warm toast.

VARIATION

Use other spices, such as chilli powder or Chinese five-spice powder, to flavour the pâté and add tomato relish or chilli relish instead of the mango chutney, if you prefer.

Roasted Vegetables on Muffins

Serves 4

INGREDIENTS

1 red onion, cut into eight

1 aubergine (eggplant), halved
   and sliced

1 yellow (bell) pepper, sliced

1 courgette (zucchini), sliced

4 tbsp olive oil

1 tbsp garlic vinegar

2 tbsp vermouth

2 garlic cloves, crushed

1 tbsp chopped thyme

2 tsp light brown
   sugar

4 muffins, halved

salt and pepper

SAUCE:

2 tbsp butter

1 tbsp flour

150 ml/$\frac{1}{4}$ pint/$\frac{2}{3}$ cup milk

85 ml/3 fl oz vegetable stock

75 g/2$\frac{3}{4}$ oz/$\frac{3}{4}$ cup vegetarian
   Cheddar, grated

1 tsp wholegrain mustard

3 tbsp chopped mixed herbs

1 Arrange the vegetables in a shallow ovenproof dish. Mix together the oil, vinegar, vermouth, garlic, thyme and sugar and pour over the vegetables. Leave to marinate for 1 hour.

2 Transfer the vegetables to a baking tray (cookie sheet). Cook in a pre-heated oven at 200°C/400°F/Gas Mark 6 for 20–25 minutes or until the vegetables have softened.

3 Meanwhile, make the sauce. Melt the butter in a small pan and add the flour. Cook for 1 minute and remove from the heat. Stir in the milk and stock and return the pan to the heat. Bring to the boil, stirring, until thickened. Stir in the cheese, mustard and mixed herbs and season well.

4 Preheat the grill (broiler) to high. Cut the muffins in half and grill

for 2–3 minutes until golden brown, then remove and arrange on a serving plate.

5 Spoon the roasted vegetables on to the muffins and pour the sauce over the top. Serve immediately.

Sardines with Olives & Tomatoes

Serves 4

INGREDIENTS

12 fresh sardines, gutted and cleaned	15 g/¹/₂ oz butter	TO GARNISH:
fresh basil leaves	1 tbsp olive oil	plum tomatoes, sliced
4 plum tomatoes	2 tbsp lemon juice	olives, sliced
8 pitted black olives	salt and pepper	1 fresh basil sprig

1 Season the sardines inside and out with salt and pepper to taste. Insert 1-2 basil leaves inside the cavity of each fish. Using a sharp knife, make a few slashes in the body of each fish.

2 Cut the tomatoes and olives into slices and transfer to a large bowl. Tear 4 basil leaves into small pieces and toss together with the tomatoes and olives.

3 Divide the tomato and olive mixture among

4 large sheets of kitchen foil, and place 3 sardines on top of each portion.

4 Melt the butter and oil together in a small pan. Stir in the lemon juice and pour the mixture over.

5 Carefully wrap up the fish in the foil. Barbecue (grill) the fish over medium hot coals for 15–20 minutes until the fish is cooked through.

6 Transfer the fish to individual serving plates and remove the foil.

Garnish the fish with slices of tomato and olive, and with a fresh sprig of basil. Serve at once.

COOK'S TIP

Slashing the body of the fish helps the flesh to absorb the flavours. It is particularly important if you do not have time to allow the fish to marinate before cooking.

Bacon & Scallop Skewers

Makes 4

INGREDIENTS

grated rind and juice of 1/2 lemon	12 scallops	1 yellow (bell) pepper
4 tbsp sunflower oil	1 red (bell) pepper	6 rashers smoked streaky bacon
1/2 tsp dried dill	1 green (bell) pepper	

1 Mix together the lemon rind and juice, oil and dill in a non-metallic dish. Add the scallops and mix thoroughly to coat in the marinade. Leave to marinate for 1–2 hours.

2 Cut the red, green and yellow (bell) peppers in half and deseed them. Cut the (bell) pepper halves into 2.5 cm/1 inch pieces and then set aside until required.

3 Carefully remove the rind from the bacon. Stretch the bacon rashers with the back of a knife, then cut each bacon rasher in half.

4 Remove the scallops from the marinade, reserving any excess marinade. Wrap a piece of bacon around each scallop.

5 Thread the bacon-wrapped scallops on to skewers, alternating with the (bell) pepper pieces.

6 Barbecue (grill) the bacon and scallop skewers over hot coals for about 5 minutes, basting with the marinade.

7 Transfer the bacon and scallop skewers to serving plates and serve at once.

VARIATION

Peel 4–8 raw prawns (shrimp) and add them to the marinade with the scallops. Thread them on to the skewers alternately with the scallops and (bell) peppers.

Salt & Pepper Prawns

Serves 4

INGREDIENTS

2 tsp salt
1 tsp black pepper
2 tsp Szechuan peppercorns
1 tsp sugar

450 g/1 lb peeled raw tiger prawns
(shrimp)
2 tbsp groundnut oil
1 red chilli, deseeded and finely
chopped

1 tsp freshly grated ginger
3 cloves garlic, crushed
spring onions (scallions), sliced, to
garnish
prawn (shrimp) crackers, to serve

1 Grind the salt, black pepper and Szechuan peppercorns in a pestle and mortar. Mix the salt and pepper mixture with the sugar and set aside until required.

2 Rinse the prawns (shrimp) under cold running water and pat dry with absorbent kitchen paper.

3 Heat the oil in a preheated wok. Add the prawns (shrimp), chilli, ginger and garlic and stir-fry for 4–5 minutes, or until the prawns (shrimp) are cooked through.

4 Add the salt and pepper mixture to the wok and stir-fry for 1 minute.

5 Transfer to warm serving bowls and garnish with spring onions (scallion). Serve hot with prawn (shrimp) crackers.

COOK'S TIP

Szechuan peppercorns are also known as farchiew. These wild reddish-brown peppercorns from the Szechuan region of China add an aromatic flavour to a dish.

COOK'S TIP

Tiger prawns (shrimps) are widely available and are not only colourful and tasty, but they have a meaty texture, too. If cooked tiger prawns (shrimp) are used, add them with the salt and pepper mixture in step 4 – if the cooked prawns (shrimp) are added any earlier they will toughen up and be inedible.

Herb & Garlic Shrimp

Serves 4

INGREDIENTS

350 g/12 oz raw prawns
  (shrimp), peeled
2 tbsp chopped, fresh parsley

4 tbsp lemon juice
2 tbsp olive oil
65 g/2¼ oz butter

2 cloves garlic, chopped
salt and pepper

1 Place the prepared prawns (shrimp) in a shallow, non-metallic dish with the parsley, lemon juice and salt and pepper to taste. Leave the prawns (shrimp) to marinate in the herb mixture for at least 30 minutes.

2 Heat the oil and butter in a small pan with the garlic until the butter melts. Stir to mix thoroughly.

3 Remove the prawns (shrimp) from the marinade with a perforated spoon and add them to the pan containing the garlic butter. Stir the prawns

(shrimp) into the garlic butter until well coated, then thread the prawns (shrimp) on to skewers.

4 Barbecue (grill) the kebabs (kabobs) over hot coals for 5–10 minutes, turning the skewers occasionally, until the prawns (shrimp) turn pink and are cooked through. Brush the prawns (shrimp) with the remaining garlic butter during the cooking time.

5 Transfer the herb and garlic prawn (shrimp) kebabs (kabobs) to serving plates. Drizzle over any of

the remaining garlic butter and serve at once.

VARIATION

If raw prawns (shrimp) are unavailable, use cooked prawns (shrimp) but reduce the cooking time. Small cooked prawns (shrimp) can also be cooked in a kitchen foil parcel istead of on the skewers. Marinate and toss the cooked prawns (shrimp) in the garlic butter, wrap in kitchen foil and cook for about 5 minutes, shaking the parcels once or twice.

Meat & Poultry

The increased interest in healthy eating means
that most supermarkets and butchers now offer
special cuts of lean meat. Although they are often
slightly more expensive than standard cuts, it is
worth buying this meat and spending a little extra
time cooking it carefully to enhance the flavour.
You will not need to buy as much if you combine
the meat with thoughtfully chosen
and prepared vegetables.

Look out, too, for packs of low- or reduced-fat
minced (ground) meat in your local supermarket,
and include it in burgers or serve it in a flavour-
filled sauce with rice or your favourite pasta.

Cut any visible fat from beef and pork before
you cook it. Chicken and turkey are lower in fat
than red meats, and you can make them even
healthier by removing the skin. Duck is a rich meat
with a distinctive flavour, and you need only a
small amount to create apparently extravagant,
flavourful dishes that are also healthy.

Pan-Cooked Pork with Fennel & Aniseed

Serves 4

INGREDIENTS

4 lean pork chops, 125 g/ 4¹/₂ oz each	¹/₂ tsp aniseed	2 tbsp Pernod
60 g/2 oz/¹/₃ cup brown rice, cooked	1 tbsp olive oil	salt and pepper
1 tsp orange rind, grated	1 fennel bulb, trimmed and thinly sliced	fennel fronds, to garnish
4 spring onions (scallions), trimmed and finely chopped	450 ml/16 fl oz/2 cups unsweetened orange juice	cooked vegetables, to serve
	1 tbsp cornflour (cornstarch)	

1 Trim away any excess fat from the pork chops. Using a small, sharp knife, make a slit in the centre of each chop to create a pocket.

2 Mix the rice, orange rind, spring onions (scallions), salt and pepper to taste and aniseed together in a bowl. Press the mixture into the pocket of each chop, then press gently to seal.

3 Heat the oil in a frying pan (skillet) and fry the pork chops on each side for 2–3 minutes until lightly browned.

4 Add the sliced fennel and orange juice to the pan, bring to the boil and simmer for 15–20 minutes until the meat is tender and cooked through. Remove the pork and fennel with a slotted spoon and transfer to a serving plate.

5 Blend the cornflour (cornstarch) and Pernod together in a small bowl. Add the cornflour (cornstarch) mixture to the pan and stir into the pan juices. Cook for 2–3 minutes, stirring, until the sauce thickens.

6 Pour the Pernod sauce over the pork chops, garnish with fennel fronds and serve with a selection of cooked vegetables.

Pork Stroganoff

Serves 4

INGREDIENTS

350 g/12 oz lean pork fillet
1 tbsp vegetable oil
1 medium onion, chopped
2 garlic cloves, crushed
25 g/1 oz plain (all-purpose)
    flour
2 tbsp tomato purée (paste)

425 ml/15 fl oz/1¾ cups fresh
    chicken or vegetable stock
125 g/4½ oz button mushrooms,
    sliced
1 large green (bell) pepper,
    deseeded and diced
½ tsp ground nutmeg

4 tbsp low-fat natural
    (unsweetened) yogurt, plus
    extra to serve
salt and pepper
white rice, freshly boiled, to serve
ground nutmeg and chopped
    parsley, to garnish

1 Trim away any excess fat and silver skin from the pork, then cut the meat into slices about 1 cm/½ inch thick.

2 Heat the oil in a large frying pan (skillet) and gently fry the pork, onion and garlic for 4–5 minutes until lightly browned.

3 Stir in the flour and tomato purée (paste), pour in the stock and stir to mix thoroughly.

4 Add the mushrooms, (bell) pepper, seasoning and nutmeg. Bring to the boil, cover and simmer for 20 minutes or until the pork is tender and cooked through.

5 Remove the saucepan from the heat and stir in the yogurt.

6 Garnish the boiled rice with chopped parsley. Spoon extra yogurt on top of the pork and mushrooms and dust with a little ground nutmeg.

COOK'S TIP

You can buy ready-made meat, vegetable and fish stocks from leading supermarkets. Although more expensive they are better nutritionally than stock cubes which are high in salt and artificial flavourings. However, home-made stock is best of all.

Pan-Cooked Pork Medallions with Apples & Cider

Serves 4

INGREDIENTS

8 lean pork medallions, about
50 g/1³⁄₄ oz each
2 tsp vegetable oil
1 medium onion, finely sliced
1 tsp caster (superfine) sugar
1 tsp dried sage

150 ml/5 fl oz/²⁄₃ cup dry (hard)
cider
150 ml/5 fl oz/²⁄₃ cup fresh
chicken or vegetable stock
1 green-skinned apple
1 red-skinned apple

1 tbsp lemon juice
salt and pepper
fresh sage leaves, to garnish
freshly cooked vegetables, to
serve

1 Discard the string from the pork and trim away any excess fat. Re-tie with clean string and set aside until required.

2 Heat the oil in a frying pan (skillet) and gently fry the onion for 5 minutes until softened. Add the sugar and cook for 3–4 minutes until golden.

3 Add the pork to the pan and cook for 2 minutes on each side until browned. Add the sage, cider and stock. Bring to the boil and then simmer for 20 minutes.

4 Meanwhile, core and cut each apple into 8 wedges. Toss the apple wedges in lemon juice so that they do not turn brown.

5 Add the apples to the pork and mix gently. Season and cook for 3–4 minutes until tender.

6 Remove the string from the pork and serve immediately, garnished with fresh sage and accompanied with freshly cooked vegetables.

COOK'S TIP

If pork medallions are not available, buy 400g/14 oz pork fillet and slice it into evenly-sized medallions yourself.

Red Roast Pork with Peppers

Serves 4

INGREDIENTS

450 g/1 lb lean pork fillets
6 tbsp dark soy sauce
2 tbsp dry sherry
1 tsp five-spice powder
2 garlic cloves, crushed

2.5 cm/1 inch piece root (fresh)
    ginger, finely chopped
1 large red (bell) pepper
1 large yellow (bell) pepper
1 large orange (bell) pepper
4 tbsp caster (superfine) sugar
2 tbsp red wine vinegar

TO GARNISH:
spring onions (scallions),
    shredded
fresh chives, snipped

1 Trim away excess fat and silver skin from the pork and place in a shallow dish.

2 Mix together the soy sauce, sherry, five-spice powder, garlic and ginger. Spoon over the pork, cover and marinate in the refrigerator for at least 1 hour.

3 Preheat the oven to 190°C/375°F/Gas Mark 5. Drain the pork, reserving the marinade.

Place the pork on a roasting rack over a roasting tin (pan). Cook in the oven, occasionally basting with the marinade, for 1 hour or until cooked through.

4 Meanwhile, halve and deseed the (bell) peppers. Cut each (bell) pepper half into 3 equal portions. Arrange them on a baking sheet (cookie sheet) and bake alongside the pork for the last 30 minutes of the cooking time.

5 Place the caster (superfine) sugar and vinegar in a small saucepan and heat gently until the sugar dissolves. Bring to the boil and simmer for 3–4 minutes, until syrupy.

6 As soon as the pork is cooked, remove it from the oven and brush liberally with the sugar syrup. Leave to stand for 5 minutes, then slice and arrange on a warm serving platter with the (bell) peppers. Garnish and serve.

Pork with Ratatouille Sauce

Serves 4

INGREDIENTS

4 lean, boneless pork chops, about 125 g/4$^{1}/_{2}$ oz each	SAUCE:	100 g/3$^{1}/_{2}$ oz button mushrooms
1 tsp dried mixed herbs	1 medium onion	400 g/14 oz can chopped
salt and pepper	1 garlic clove	tomatoes
baked potatoes, to serve	1 small green (bell) pepper	2 tbsp tomato purée (paste)
	1 small yellow (bell) pepper	1 tsp dried mixed herbs
	1 medium courgette (zucchini)	1 tsp caster (superfine) sugar

1 To make the sauce, peel and chop the onion and garlic. Deseed and dice the (bell) peppers. Trim and dice the courgette (zucchini). Wipe and halve the mushrooms.

2 Place all of the vegetables in a saucepan and stir in the chopped tomatoes and tomato purée (paste). Add the dried herbs, sugar and plenty of seasoning. Bring to the boil, cover and simmer for 20 minutes.

3 Meanwhile, preheat the grill (broiler) to medium. Trim away any excess fat from the chops, then season on both sides and rub in the dried mixed herbs. Cook the chops for 5 minutes, then turn over and cook for a further 6–7 minutes or until cooked through.

4 Drain the chops on absorbent kitchen paper and serve accompanied with the sauce and baked potatoes.

COOK'S TIP

This vegetable sauce could be served with any other grilled (broiled) or baked meat or fish. It would also make an excellent alternative filling for the Spinach Crêpes

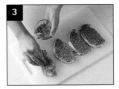

Beef & Orange Curry

Serves 4

INGREDIENTS

1 tbsp vegetable oil
225 g/8 oz shallots,
   halved
2 garlic cloves, crushed
450 g/1 lb lean rump or sirloin
   beef, trimmed and cut into
   2 cm/^{3}/4 inch cubes
3 tbsp curry paste

450 ml/16 fl oz/2 cups fresh
   beef stock
4 medium oranges
2 tsp cornflour (cornstarch)
salt and pepper
2 tbsp fresh coriander (cilantro),
   chopped, to garnish
basmati rice, freshly boiled, to serve

RAITA:
1/2 cucumber, finely diced
3 tbsp fresh mint, chopped
150 ml/5 fl oz/^{2}/3 cup low-fat
   natural (unsweetened) yogurt

1 Heat the oil in a large saucepan. Gently fry the shallots, garlic and the cubes of beef for 5 minutes, stirring occasionally, until the beef is evenly browned all over.

2 Blend together the curry paste and stock. Add the mixture to the beef and stir to mix. Bring to the boil, cover and simmer for 1 hour or until the meat is tender.

3 Meanwhile, grate the rind of one orange. Extract the juice from the orange and from a second orange. Peel the two remaining oranges, removing as much pith as possible. Slice between each segment and remove the flesh.

4 Blend the cornflour (cornstarch) with the orange juice. At the end of the cooking time, stir the

orange rind into the beef along with the orange and cornflour (cornstarch) mixture. Bring to the boil and simmer, stirring, for 3–4 minutes until the sauce thickens. Season and stir in the orange segments.

5 To make the raita, mix the cucumber with the mint and stir in the yogurt. Season. Garnish the curry and serve with rice and the raita.

Pan-Seared Beef with Ginger, Pineapple & Chilli

Serves 4

INGREDIENTS

4 lean beef steaks (such as rump,
   sirloin or fillet),
   100 g/3$\frac{1}{2}$ oz each
2 tbsp ginger wine
2.5 cm/1 inch piece root (fresh)
   ginger, finely chopped
1 garlic clove, crushed
1 tsp ground chilli

1 tsp vegetable oil
salt and pepper
red chilli strips, to garnish

TO SERVE:
freshly cooked noodles
2 spring onions (scallions),
   shredded

RELISH:
225 g/8 oz fresh pineapple
1 small red (bell) pepper
1 red chilli
2 tbsp light soy sauce
1 piece stem ginger in syrup,
   drained and chopped

1 Trim any excess fat from the beef. Using a meat mallet or covered rolling pin, pound the steaks until 1 cm/$\frac{1}{2}$ inch thick. Season on both sides and place in a shallow dish.

2 Mix the ginger wine, root (fresh) ginger, garlic and chilli and pour over the meat. Cover and chill for 30 minutes.

3 To make the relish, peel and finely chop the pineapple and place it in a bowl. Halve, deseed and finely chop the (bell) pepper and chilli. Stir into the pineapple together with the soy sauce and stem ginger. Cover and chill.

4 Brush a grill (broiler) pan with the oil and heat until hot. Drain the beef and add to the pan, pressing down to seal. Lower the heat and cook for 5 minutes. Turn the steaks over and cook for 5 minutes.

5 Drain the steaks on kitchen paper and transfer to serving plates. Garnish with chilli strips, and serve with noodles, spring onions (scallions) and the relish.

Beef & Tomato Gratin

Serves 4

INGREDIENTS

350 g/12 oz lean beef, minced
(ground)
1 large onion, finely chopped
1 tsp dried mixed herbs
1 tbsp plain (all-purpose) flour
300 ml/¹/₂ pint/1¹/₄ cups
beef stock

1 tbsp tomato purée (paste)
2 large tomatoes, thinly sliced
4 medium courgettes (zucchini),
thinly sliced
2 tbsp cornflour (cornstarch)
300 ml/¹/₂ pint/1¹/₄ cups skimmed
milk

150 ml/5 fl oz/²/₃ cup low-fat
natural fromage frais
(unsweetened yogurt)
1 medium egg yolk
4 tbsp Parmesan cheese, freshly
grated
salt and pepper

1 Preheat the oven to 190°C/375°F/Gas Mark 5. In a large pan, dry-fry the beef and onion for 4–5 minutes until browned.

2 Stir in the herbs, flour, stock and tomato purée (paste), and season. Bring to the boil and simmer for 30 minutes until thickened.

3 Transfer the beef mixture to an ovenproof gratin dish. Cover with a layer of the sliced tomatoes and then add a layer of sliced courgettes (zucchini). Set aside until required.

4 Blend the cornflour (cornstarch) with a little milk in a small bowl. Pour the remaining milk into a saucepan and bring to the boil. Add the cornflour (cornstarch) mixture and cook, stirring, for 1–2 minutes until thickened. Remove from the heat and beat in the fromage frais (yogurt) and egg yolk. Season well.

5 Place the dish on to a baking sheet (cookie sheet) and spread the white sauce over the layer of courgettes (zucchini). Sprinkle with grated Parmesan and bake in the oven for 25–30 minutes until golden-brown. Serve immediately.

Sweet & Sour Venison Stir-Fry

Serves 4

INGREDIENTS

1 bunch spring onions (scallion)	1 tbsp vegetable oil	2 tbsp dry sherry
1 red (bell) pepper	1 clove garlic, crushed	2 tsp clear honey
100 g/3½ oz mangetout (snow peas)	2.5 cm/1 inch piece root (fresh) ginger, finely chopped	225 g/8 oz can pineapple pieces in natural juice, drained
100 g/3½ oz baby sweetcorn cobs	3 tbsp light soy sauce, plus extra for serving	25 g/1 oz beansprouts
350 g/12 oz lean venison steak	1 tbsp white wine vinegar	freshly cooked rice, to serve

1 Trim the spring onions (scallions) and cut into 2.5 cm/1 inch pieces. Halve and deseed the (bell) pepper and cut it into 2.5 cm/1 inch pieces. Top and tail the mangetout (snow peas) and trim the baby corn.

2 Trim the excess fat from the meat and cut it into thin strips. Heat the oil in a large frying pan (skillet) or wok until hot and stir-fry the meat, garlic and ginger for 5 minutes.

3 Add the spring onion (scallion), (bell) pepper, mangetout (snow peas) and baby corn to the pan, then add the soy sauce, vinegar, sherry and honey. Stir-fry for 5 minutes, keeping the heat high.

4 Carefully stir in the pineapple pieces and beansprouts and cook for a further 1–2 minutes to heat through. Serve with freshly cooked rice and extra soy sauce for dipping.

VARIATION

For a quick and nutritious meal-in-one, cook 225 g/8 oz egg noodles in boiling water for 3–4 minutes. Drain well and add to the pan in step 4, together with the pineapple and beansprouts. Stir well to mix. You will have to add an extra 2 tbsp soy sauce with the pineapple and beansprouts so that the stir-fry does not dry out.

Venison & Garlic Mash

Serves 4

INGREDIENTS

8 medallions of venison,
75 g/2³/₄ oz each
1 tbsp vegetable oil
1 red onion, chopped
150 ml/5 fl oz/²/₃ cup fresh beef
stock
150 ml/5 fl oz/²/₃ cup red wine

3 tbsp redcurrant jelly
100 g/3¹/₂ oz no-need-to-soak
dried, pitted prunes
2 tsp cornflour (cornstarch)
2 tbsp brandy
salt and pepper
patty pans, to serve (optional)

GARLIC MASH:
900 g/2 lb potatoes, peeled and
diced
¹/₂ tsp garlic purée (paste)
2 tbsp low-fat natural fromage
frais (unsweetened yogurt)
4 tbsp fresh parsley, chopped

1 Trim off any excess fat from the meat and season with salt and pepper on both sides.

2 Heat the oil in a pan and fry the medallions with the onions on a high heat for 2 minutes on each side until brown.

3 Lower the heat and pour in the stock and wine. Add the redcurrant jelly and prunes and stir until the jelly melts. Bring to the boil, cover and simmer for 10 minutes until cooked through.

4 Meanwhile, make the garlic mash. Place the potatoes in a saucepan and cover with water. Bring to the boil and cook for 8–10 minutes until tender. Drain.

5 Mash the potatoes until smooth. Add the garlic purée (paste), fromage frais (yogurt) and parsley and blend thoroughly. Season, set aside and keep warm.

6 Remove the medallions from the pan with a slotted spoon and keep warm.

7 Blend the cornflour (cornstarch) with the brandy in a small bowl and add to the pan juices. Heat, stirring, until thickened. Season to taste. Serve the venison with the sauce and garlic mash.

Venison Meatballs with Sherried Kumquat Sauce

Serves 4

INGREDIENTS

450 g/1 lb lean venison, minced (ground)
1 small leek, finely chopped
1 medium carrot, finely grated
½ tsp ground nutmeg

1 medium egg white, lightly beaten
salt and pepper

TO SERVE:
freshly cooked pasta or noodles
freshly cooked vegetables

SAUCE:
100 g/3½ oz kumquats
15 g/½ oz caster (superfine) sugar
150 ml/5 fl oz/⅔ cup water
4 tbsp dry sherry
1 tsp cornflour (cornstarch)

1 Place the venison in a mixing bowl together with the leek, carrot, seasoning and nutmeg. Add the egg white and bind the ingredients together with your hands until the mixture is well moulded and firm.

2 Divide the mixture into 16 equal portions. Using your fingers, form each portion into a small round ball.

3 Bring a large saucepan of water to the boil. Arrange the meatballs on a layer of baking parchment in a steamer or large sieve (strainer) and place over the boiling water. Cover and steam for 10 minutes until cooked through.

4 Meanwhile, make the sauce. Wash and thinly slice the kumquats. Place them in a saucepan with the sugar and water and bring to the boil. Simmer for 2–3 minutes until just tender.

5 Blend the sherry and cornflour (cornstarch) together and add to the pan. Heat through, stirring, until the sauce thickens. Season to taste.

6 Drain the meatballs and transfer to a serving plate. Spoon over the sauce and serve.

Fruity Lamb Casserole

Serves 4

INGREDIENTS

450 g/1 lb lean lamb, trimmed
    and cut into 2.5 cm/1 inch
    cubes
1 tsp ground cinnamon
1 tsp ground coriander
1 tsp ground cumin
2 tsp olive oil

1 medium red onion, finely
    chopped
1 garlic clove, crushed
400 g/14 oz can chopped
    tomatoes
2 tbsp tomato purée (paste)
125 g/4¹/₄ oz no-soak dried
    apricots

1 tsp caster (superfine) sugar
300 ml/¹/₂ pint/1¹/₄ cups
    vegetable stock
salt and pepper
1 small bunch fresh coriander
    (cilantro), to garnish
brown rice, steamed couscous or
    bulgar wheat, to serve

1 Preheat the oven to 180°C/350°F/Gas Mark 4. Place the meat in a mixing bowl and add the spices and oil. Mix thoroughly so that the lamb is well coated in the spices.

2 Heat a non-stick frying pan (skillet) for a few seconds until it is hot, then add the spiced lamb. Reduce the heat and cook for 4–5 minutes, stirring, until browned all over.

Using a slotted spoon, remove the lamb and transfer to a large ovenproof casserole.

3 In the same frying pan (skillet), cook the onion, garlic, tomatoes and tomato purée (paste) for 5 minutes. Season to taste. Stir in the apricots and sugar, add the stock and bring to the boil.

4 Spoon the sauce over the lamb and mix well.

Cover and cook in the oven for 1 hour, removing the lid for the last 10 minutes.

5 Roughly chop the coriander (cilantro) and sprinkle over the casserole to garnish. Serve with brown rice, steamed couscous or bulgar wheat.

Lamb, Pepper & Couscous

Serves 4

INGREDIENTS

2 medium red onions, sliced

juice of 1 lemon

1 large red (bell) pepper, deseeded and thickly sliced

1 large green (bell) pepper, deseeded and thickly sliced

1 large orange (bell) pepper, deseeded and thickly sliced

pinch of saffron strands

cinnamon stick, broken

1 tbsp clear honey

300 ml/$\frac{1}{2}$ pint/1$\frac{1}{4}$ cups vegetable stock

2 tsp olive oil

350 g/12 oz lean lamb fillet, trimmed and sliced

1 tsp Harissa paste

200 g/7 oz can chopped tomatoes

425 g/15 oz can chick-peas (garbanzo beans), drained

350 g/12 oz precooked couscous

2 tsp ground cinnamon

salt and pepper

1 Toss the onions in the lemon juice and transfer to a saucepan. Mix in the (bell) peppers, saffron, cinnamon stick and honey. Pour in the stock, bring to the boil, cover and simmer for 5 minutes.

2 Meanwhile, heat the oil in a frying pan (skillet) and gently fry the lamb for 3–4 minutes until browned all over.

3 Using a slotted spoon, drain the lamb and transfer it to the pan with the onions and peppers. Season and stir in the Harissa paste, tomatoes and chick-peas (garbanzo beans). Mix well, bring back to the boil and simmer, uncovered, for 20 minutes.

4 Meanwhile, soak the couscous, following the instructions on the packet. Bring a saucepan of

water to the boil. Transfer the couscous to a steamer or sieve (strainer) lined with muslin (cheesecloth) and place over the pan of boiling water. Cover and steam as directed.

5 Transfer the couscous to a warm serving platter and dust with ground cinnamon. Remove and discard the cinnamon stick. Spoon the stew over the couscous to serve.

Hot Pot Chops

Serves 4

INGREDIENTS

4 lean, boneless lamb leg steaks, about 125 g/4$^{1}/_{2}$ oz each	1 medium carrot, thinly sliced	salt and pepper
1 small onion, thinly sliced	1 medium potato, thinly sliced	fresh rosemary, to garnish
	1 tsp olive oil	freshly steamed green
	1 tsp dried rosemary	vegetables, to serve

1 Preheat the oven to 180°C/350°F/Gas Mark 4. Using a sharp knife, trim any excess fat from the lamb steaks.

2 Season both sides of the steaks with salt and pepper to taste and arrange them on a baking sheet (cookie sheet).

3 Alternate layers of sliced onion, carrot and potato on top of each lamb steak.

4 Brush the tops of the potato lightly with oil, season well with salt and pepper to taste and then sprinkle with a little dried rosemary.

5 Bake the hot pot chops in the oven for 25–30 minutes until the lamb is tender and cooked through.

6 Drain the lamb on absorbent kitchen paper and transfer to a warmed serving plate. Garnish with fresh rosemary and serve accompanied with a selection of green vegetables.

VARIATION

This recipe would work equally well with boneless chicken breasts. Pound the chicken slightly with a meat mallet or covered rolling pin so that the pieces are the same thickness throughout.

Minty Lamb Burgers

Serves 4

INGREDIENTS

350 g/12 oz lean lamb, minced (ground)
1 medium onion, finely chopped
4 tbsp dry wholemeal breadcrumbs
2 tbsp mint jelly
salt and pepper

TO SERVE:
4 wholemeal baps, split
2 large tomatoes, sliced
small piece of cucumber, sliced
lettuce leaves

RELISH:
4 tbsp low-fat natural fromage frais (unsweetened yogurt)
1 tbsp mint jelly, softened
5 cm/2 inch piece of cucumber, finely diced
1 tbsp fresh mint, chopped

1 Place the lamb in a large bowl and mix in the onion, breadcrumbs and jelly. Season well, then mould the ingredients together with your hands to form a firm mixture.

2 Divide the mixture into 4 and shape each portion into a round measuring 10 cm/4 inches across. Place the rounds on a plate lined with baking parchment and leave to chill for 30 minutes.

3 Preheat the grill (broiler) to medium. Line a grill (broiler) rack with baking parchment, securing the ends under the rack, and place the burgers on top. Cook for 8 minutes, then turn over the burgers and cook for a further 7 minutes or until cooked through.

4 Meanwhile, make the relish. Mix together the fromage frais (unsweetened yogurt), mint jelly, cucumber and freshly chopped mint in a bowl. Cover and leave to chill in the refrigerator until required.

5 Drain the burgers on absorbent kitchen paper. Serve the burgers inside the baps with sliced tomatoes, cucumber, lettuce and relish.

Jerk Chicken

Serves 4

INGREDIENTS

4 chicken portions	5 cm/2 inch piece root (fresh)	pinch ground cinnamon
1 bunch spring onions (scallions),	ginger, peeled and roughly	pinch ground cloves
trimmed	chopped	4 tbsp white wine vinegar
1–2 Scotch Bonnet chillies,	1/2 tsp dried thyme	3 tbsp light soy sauce
deseeded	1/2 tsp paprika	pepper
1 garlic clove	1/4 tsp ground allspice	

1 Rinse the chicken portions and pat them dry on absorbent kitchen paper. Place them in a shallow dish.

2 Place the spring onions (scallions), chillies, garlic, ginger, thyme, paprika, allspice, cinnamon, cloves, wine vinegar, soy sauce and pepper to taste in a food processor and process to make a smooth mixture.

3 Pour the spicy mixture over the chicken. Turn the chicken portions over so that they are well coated in the marinade. Transfer the chicken to the refrigerator and leave to marinate for up to 24 hours.

4 Remove the chicken from the marinade and barbecue (grill) over medium hot coals for about 30 minutes, turning the chicken over and basting occasionally with any remaining marinade, until the chicken is cooked through.

5 Transfer the chicken portions to individual serving plates and serve at once.

COOK'S TIP

As Jamaican cuisine becomes increasingly popular, you will find jars of ready-made jerk marinade, which you can use when time is short. Allow the chicken to marinate for as long as possible for maximum flavour.

Favourite Barbecued Chicken

Serves 4

INGREDIENTS

8 chicken wings or 1 chicken cut into 8 portions	3 tbsp brown fruity sauce	1 tbsp olive oil
3 tbsp tomato purée (paste)	1 tbsp white wine vinegar	1 clove garlic, crushed (optional)
	1 tbsp clear honey	salad leaves, to serve

1 Remove the skin from the chicken if you want to reduce the fat in the dish.

2 To make the barbecue glaze, place the tomato purée (paste), brown fruity sauce, white wine vinegar, honey, oil and garlic in a small bowl. Stir all of the ingredients together until they are thoroughly blended.

3 Brush the barbecue (grill) glaze over the chicken and barbecue (grill) over hot coals for 15–20 minutes. Turn the chicken portions over occasionally and baste frequently with the barbecue (grill) glaze. If the chicken begins to blacken before it is cooked, raise the rack if possible or move the chicken to a cooler part of the barbecue (grill) to slow down the cooking.

4 Transfer the barbecued (grilled) chicken to warm serving plates and serve with a selection of fresh salad leaves.

VARIATION

This barbecue (grill) glaze also makes a very good baste to brush over pork chops.

COOK'S TIP

When poultry is cooked over a very hot barbecue (grill) the heat immediately seals in all of the juices, leaving the meat succulent. For this reason you must make sure that the coals are hot enough before starting to barbecue (grill).

Indian Charred Chicken

Serves 4

INGREDIENTS

4 chicken breasts, skinned and boned	1/2 tsp ground cumin	CUCUMBER RAITA:
2 tbsp curry paste		1/4 cucumber
1 tbsp sunflower oil	TO SERVE:	salt
1 tbsp light muscovado sugar	naan bread	150 ml/5 fl oz/2/3 cup natural
1 tsp ground ginger	green salad leaves	yogurt
		1/4 tsp chilli powder

1 Place the chicken breasts between sheets of baking parchment or cling film (plastic wrap). Pound them with the flat side of a meat mallet or rolling pin to flatten them.

2 Mix together the curry paste, oil, sugar, ginger and cumin in a small bowl. Spread the mixture over both sides of the chicken and set aside until required.

3 To make the raita, peel the cucumber and scoop out the seeds with a spoon. Grate the cucumber flesh, sprinkle with salt, place in a sieve and leave to stand for 10 minutes. Rinse off the salt and squeeze out any moisture by pressing the cucumber with the base of a glass or back of a spoon.

4 To make the raita, mix the cucumber with the yogurt and stir in the chilli powder. Leave to chill until required.

5 Transfer the chicken to an oiled rack and barbecue (grill) over hot coals for 10 minutes, turning once.

6 Warm the naan bread at the side of the barbecue. Serve the chicken with the naan bread and raita and accompanied with fresh green salad leaves.

COOK'S TIP

Flattening the chicken breasts makes them thinner so that they cook more quickly.

Tricolour Chicken & Spinach Lasagne

Serves 4

INGREDIENTS

350 g/12 oz frozen chopped
   spinach, thawed and drained
$^1/_2$ tsp ground nutmeg
450 g/1 lb lean, cooked chicken
   meat, skinned and diced
4 sheets no-pre-cook lasagne
   verde
$1^1/_2$ tbsp cornflour (cornstarch)

425 ml/15 fl oz/1$^3/_4$ cups
   skimmed milk
4 tbsp Parmesan cheese,
   freshly grated
salt and pepper

TOMATO SAUCE:
400 g/14 oz can chopped tomatoes

1 medium onion, chopped
1 garlic clove, crushed (minced)
150 ml/5 fl oz/$^2/_3$ cup white wine
3 tbsp tomato purée (paste)
1 tsp dried oregano

1 Preheat the oven to 200°C/400°F/Gas Mark 6. To make the tomato sauce, place the tomatoes in a pan and stir in the onion, garlic, wine, tomato purée (paste) and oregano. Bring to the boil and simmer for 20 minutes until thick. Season.

2 Drain the spinach again and spread it out on kitchen paper to absorb any excess water. Layer the spinach in the base of an ovenproof dish. Sprinkle with nutmeg and season.

3 Arrange the chicken over the spinach and spoon over the tomato sauce. Arrange the lasagne over the tomato sauce.

4 Blend the cornflour (cornstarch) with a little of the milk to make a paste. Pour the remaining milk into a pan and stir in the cornflour (cornstarch) paste. Heat for 2–3 minutes, stirring, until the sauce thickens. Season well.

5 Spoon the sauce over the lasagne and transfer the dish to a baking sheet (cookie sheet). Sprinkle the grated cheese over the sauce and bake for 25 minutes until golden.

Chicken Pasta Bake
with Fennel & Raisins

Serves 4

INGREDIENTS

2 bulbs fennel	60 g/2 oz/$^1\!/_3$ cup raisins	2 tbsp Parmesan cheese, grated
2 medium red onions, shredded	225 g/8 oz lean, boneless cooked	salt and pepper
1 tbsp lemon juice	chicken, skinned and shredded	
125 g/4$^1\!/_2$ oz button mushrooms	375 g/13 oz low-fat soft cheese	
1 tbsp olive oil	with garlic and herbs	
225 g/8 oz penne (quills)	125 g/4$^1\!/_2$ oz low-fat Mozzarella	
	cheese, thinly sliced	

1 Preheat the oven to 200°C/400°F/Gas Mark 6. Trim the fennel, reserving the green fronds for garnishing, and slice the bulbs thinly. Coat the onions in the lemon juice. Quarter the mushrooms.

2 Heat the oil in a large frying pan (skillet) and fry the fennel, onion and mushrooms for 4–5 minutes, stirring, until just softened. Season and

transfer the vegetable mixture to a large bowl.

3 Bring a pan of lightly salted water to the boil and cook the penne (quills) according to the instructions on the packet until 'al dente' (just cooked). Drain and mix the pasta with the vegetables.

4 Stir the raisins and chicken into the pasta mixture. Soften the soft

cheese by beating it, then mix into the pasta and chicken – the heat from the pasta should make the cheese melt slightly.

5 Put the mixture into an ovenproof dish and transfer to a baking sheet (cookie sheet). Arrange the Mozzarella on top and sprinkle with the Parmesan. Bake for 20–25 minutes until golden. Garnish with fennel fronds and serve.

Baked Southern-Style Chicken & Chips

Serves 4

INGREDIENTS

4 baking potatoes, each	½ tsp paprika pepper	6 tbsp dry white breadcrumbs
225 g/8 oz	½ tsp dried thyme	salt and pepper
1 tbsp sunflower oil	8 chicken drumsticks, skin	
2 tsp coarse sea salt	removed	TO SERVE:
2 tbsp plain (all-purpose) flour	1 medium egg, beaten	low-fat coleslaw salad
pinch of cayenne pepper	2 tbsp cold water	sweetcorn relish

1 Preheat the oven to 200°C/400°F/Gas Mark 6. Wash and scrub the potatoes and cut each into 8 equal portions. Place in a clean plastic bag and add the oil. Seal and shake well to coat.

2 Arrange the potato wedges, skin side down, on a non-stick baking sheet (cookie sheet), sprinkle over the sea salt and bake in the oven for 30–35 minutes until they are tender and golden-brown.

3 Meanwhile, mix the flour, cayenne, paprika, thyme and salt and pepper to taste together on a plate. Press the chicken drumsticks into the seasoned flour to lightly coat all over.

4 On one plate mix together the egg and water. On another plate sprinkle the breadcrumbs. Dip the chicken drumsticks first in the egg and then in the breadcrumbs. Place on a non-stick baking sheet (cookie sheet).

5 Bake the chicken drumsticks alongside the potato wedges for 30 minutes, turning after 15 minutes, until they are tender and cooked through.

6 Drain the potato wedges thoroughly on absorbent kitchen paper to remove any excess fat. Serve the potato wedges with the chicken, accompanied by low-fat coleslaw and sweetcorn relish, if wished.

Lime Chicken Skewers with Mango Salsa

Serves 4

INGREDIENTS

4 boneless chicken breasts,
    skinned, about 125 g/
    4¹/₂ oz each
3 tbsp lime marmalade
1 tsp white wine vinegar
¹/₂ tsp lime rind, finely grated
1 tbsp lime juice

salt and pepper

TO SERVE:
lime wedges
boiled white rice, sprinkled with
    chilli powder

SALSA:
1 small mango
1 small red onion
1 tbsp lime juice
1 tbsp fresh coriander (cilantro),
    chopped

1 Slice the chicken breasts into thin pieces and thread on to 8 skewers so that the meat forms an S-shape down each skewer.

2 Preheat the grill (broiler) to medium. Arrange the chicken kebabs (kabobs) on the grill (broiler) rack. Mix together the marmalade, vinegar, lime rind and juice. Season with salt and pepper to taste. Brush the dressing over the chicken and grill (broil) for 5 minutes. Turn the chicken over, brush with the dressing again and grill (broil) for a further 4-5 minutes or until the chicken is cooked through.

3 Meanwhile, prepare the salsa. Peel the mango and slice the flesh off the smooth, central stone. Dice the flesh into small pieces and place in a small bowl.

4 Peel and finely chop the onion and mix into the mango, together with the lime juice and chopped coriander (cilantro). Season with salt and pepper to taste, cover and chill until required.

5 Serve the chicken kebabs (kabobs) with the salsa, accompanied with wedges of lime and boiled white rice sprinkled with chilli powder.

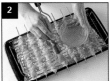

Sage Chicken & Rice

Serves 4

INGREDIENTS

1 large onion, chopped
1 garlic clove, crushed
2 sticks celery, sliced
2 carrots, diced
2 sprigs fresh sage
300 ml/$\frac{1}{2}$ pint/1 $\frac{1}{4}$ cups chicken
   stock
350 g/12 oz boneless, skinless
   chicken breasts

225 g/8 oz/1 $\frac{1}{3}$ cups mixed
   brown and wild rice
400 g/14 oz can chopped
   tomatoes
dash of Tabasco sauce
2 medium courgettes (zucchini),
   trimmed and thinly sliced
100 g/3 $\frac{1}{2}$ oz lean ham, diced
salt and pepper

fresh sage, to garnish

TO SERVE:
salad leaves
crusty bread

1 Place the onion, garlic, celery, carrots and sprigs of fresh sage in a large saucepan and pour in the chicken stock. Bring to the boil, cover the pan and simmer for 5 minutes.

2 Cut the chicken into 2.5 cm/1 inch cubes and stir into the pan with the vegetables. Cover the pan and continue to cook for a further 5 minutes.

3 Stir in the rice and chopped tomatoes. Add a dash of Tabasco sauce to taste and season well. Bring to the boil, cover and simmer for 25 minutes.

4 Stir in the sliced courgettes (zucchini) and diced ham and continue to cook, uncovered, for a further 10 minutes, stirring occasionally, until the rice is just tender.

5 Remove and discard the sprigs of sage. Garnish with a few sage leaves and serve with a fresh salad and fresh crusty bread.

COOK'S TIP

If you do not have fresh sage, use 1 tsp of dried sage in step 1.

Chilli Chicken & Sweetcorn Meatballs

Serves 4

INGREDIENTS

450 g/1 lb lean chicken, minced (ground)

4 spring onions (scallions), trimmed and finely chopped

1 small red chilli, deseeded and finely chopped

2.5 cm/1 inch piece root (fresh) ginger, finely chopped

100 g/3 1/2 oz can sweetcorn (no added sugar or salt), drained

salt and white pepper

boiled jasmine rice, to serve

TO GARNISH:

spring onions (scallions) and red (bell) pepper, chopped

SAUCE:

150 ml/5 fl oz/2/3 cup fresh chicken stock

100 g/3 1/2 oz cubed pineapple in natural juice, drained, with 4 tbsp reserved juice

1 medium carrot, cut into thin strips

1 small red (bell) pepper, deseeded and diced

1 small green (bell) pepper, deseeded and diced

1 tbsp light soy sauce

2 tbsp rice vinegar

1 tbsp caster (superfine) sugar

1 tbsp tomato purée (paste)

2 tsp cornflour (cornstarch) mixed to a paste with 4 tsp cold water

1 To make the meatballs, place the chicken in a bowl and add the spring onions (scallion), chilli, ginger, seasoning and sweetcorn. Mix together.

2 Divide the mixture into 16 portions and form each into a ball. Bring a pan of water to the boil.

Arrange the meatballs on a sheet of baking parchment in a steamer or large sieve (strainer), place over the water, cover and steam for 10–12 minutes.

3 To make the sauce, pour the stock and pineapple juice into a pan and bring to the boil. Add

the carrot, (bell) peppers and pineapple, cover and simmer for 5 minutes. Stir in the other ingredients and heat through, stirring, until thickened. Season.

4 Drain the meatballs and transfer to a serving plate. Garnish and serve with rice and the sauce.

Crispy-Topped Stuffed Chicken

Serves 4

INGREDIENTS

4 boneless chicken breasts, about150 g/5¹/² oz each, skinned
4 sprigs fresh tarragon
¹/² small orange (bell) pepper, deseeded and sliced
1¹/² small green (bell) pepper, deseeded and sliced

15 g/¹/² oz wholemeal breadcrumbs
1 tbsp sesame seeds
4 tbsp lemon juice
1 small red (bell) pepper, halved and deseeded
200 g/7 oz can chopped tomatoes

1 small red chilli, deseeded and chopped
¹/4 tsp celery salt
salt and pepper
fresh tarragon, to garnish

1 Preheat the oven to 200°C/400°F/Gas Mark 6. Slit the chicken breasts with a sharp knife to create a pocket in each. Season inside each pocket.

2 Place a sprig of tarragon and a few slices of orange and green (bell) peppers in each pocket. Place the chicken breasts on a baking sheet (cookie sheet) and sprinkle over the breadcrumbs and sesame seeds.

3 Spoon 1 tbsp lemon juice over each chicken breast and bake in the oven for 35–40 minutes until the chicken is cooked through.

4 Preheat the grill (broiler) to hot. Arrange the red (bell) pepper halves, skin side up, on the rack and cook for 5–6 minutes until the skin blisters. Cool for 10 minutes; peel off the skins.

5 Put the red (bell) pepper in a blender,

add the tomatoes, chilli and celery salt and process for a few seconds. Season to taste. Alternatively, finely chop the red (bell) pepper and press through a sieve with the tomatoes and chilli.

6 When the chicken is cooked, heat the sauce, spoon a little on to a warm plate and arrange a chicken breast in the centre. Garnish with tarragon and serve.

Chicken with a Curried Yogurt Crust

Serves 4

INGREDIENTS

1 garlic clove, crushed

2.5 cm/1 inch piece root (fresh) ginger, finely chopped

1 fresh green chilli, deseeded and finely chopped

6 tbsp low-fat natural (unsweetened) yogurt

1 tbsp tomato purée (paste)

1 tsp ground turmeric

1 tsp garam masala

1 tbsp lime juice

4 boneless, skinless chicken breasts, each 125 g/4¹/₂ oz

salt and pepper

wedges of lime or lemon, to serve

RELISH:

4 medium tomatoes

¹/₄ cucumber

1 small red onion

2 tbsp fresh coriander (cilantro), chopped

1 Preheat the oven to 190°C/375°F/Gas Mark 5. In a small bowl mix together the garlic, ginger, chilli, yogurt, tomato purée (paste), turmeric, garam masala, lime juice and seasoning.

2 Wash and pat dry the chicken breasts and place them on a baking sheet (cookie sheet). Brush or spread the spicy yogurt mix over the chicken and bake in the oven for 30–35 minutes until the meat is tender and cooked through.

3 Meanwhile, make the relish. Finely chop the tomatoes, cucumber and onion and mix together with the coriander (cilantro). Season, cover and chill until required.

4 Drain the cooked chicken on absorbent kitchen paper and serve hot with the relish. Or, allow to cool, chill for at least 1 hour and serve sliced as part of a salad.

VARIATION

The spicy yogurt coating would work just as well if spread on a chunky white fish, such as cod fillet. The cooking time should be reduced to 15–20 minutes.

Grilled Chicken with Lemon & Honey

Serves 4

INGREDIENTS

4 boneless chicken breasts, about
125 g/4$^1/_2$ oz each
2 tbsp clear honey
1 tbsp dark soy sauce
1 tsp lemon rind, finely grated
1 tbsp lemon juice

salt and pepper

TO GARNISH:
1 tbsp fresh chives, chopped
lemon rind, grated

NOODLES:
225 g/8 oz rice noodles
2 tsp sesame oil
1 tbsp sesame seeds
1 tsp lemon rind, finely grated

1 Preheat the grill (broiler) to medium. Skin and trim the chicken breasts to remove any excess fat, then wash and pat dry with absorbent kitchen paper. Using a sharp knife, score the chicken breasts with a criss-cross pattern on both sides (making sure that you do not cut all the way through the meat).

2 Mix together the honey, soy sauce, lemon rind and juice in a small bowl, and then season well with black pepper.

3 Arrange the chicken breasts on the grill (broiler) rack and brush with half of the honey mixture. Cook for 10 minutes, turn over and brush with the remaining mixture. Cook for a further 8–10 minutes or until cooked through.

4 Meanwhile, prepare the noodles according to the instructions on the packet. Drain well and

transfer to a warm serving bowl. Mix the noodles with the sesame oil, sesame seeds and the lemon rind. Season and keep warm.

5 Drain the chicken and serve with a small mound of noodles, garnished with freshly chopped chives and grated lemon rind.

Chicken & Plum Casserole

Serves 4

INGREDIENTS

2 rashers lean back bacon, rinds removed, trimmed and chopped
1 tbsp sunflower oil
450 g/1 lb skinless, boneless chicken thighs, cut into 4 equal strips

1 garlic clove, crushed
175 g/6 oz shallots, halved
225 g/8 oz plums, halved or quartered (if large) and stoned
1 tbsp light muscovado sugar
150 ml/5 fl oz/²⁄₃ cup dry sherry

2 tbsp plum sauce
450 ml/16 fl oz/2 cups fresh chicken stock
2 tsp cornflour (cornstarch) mixed with 4 tsp cold water
2 tbsp flat-leaf parsley, chopped, to garnish
crusty bread, to serve

1 In a large, non-stick frying pan (skillet), dry fry the bacon for 2–3 minutes until the juices run out. Remove the bacon from the pan with a slotted spoon, set aside and keep warm until required.

2 In the same frying pan (skillet), heat the oil and fry the chicken with the garlic and shallots for 4–5 minutes, stirring occasionally, until well browned all over.

3 Return the bacon to the frying pan (skillet) and stir in the plums, sugar, sherry, plum sauce and stock. Bring to the boil and simmer for 20 minutes until the plums have softened and the chicken is cooked through.

4 Add the cornflour (cornstarch) mixture to the frying pan (skillet) and cook, stirring, for a further 2–3 minutes until thickened.

5 Spoon the casserole on to warm serving plates and garnish with chopped parsley. Serve with chunks of bread to mop up the fruity gravy.

VARIATION

Chunks of lean turkey or pork would also go well with this combination of flavours. The cooking time will remain the same.

Oat Chicken Pieces

Serves 4

INGREDIENTS

25 g/1 oz/¹⁄₃ cup rolled oats
1 tbsp chopped fresh rosemary
4 skinless chicken quarters

1 egg white
150 g/5¹⁄₂ oz/¹⁄₂ cup natural low-fat
    fromage frais

2 tsp wholegrain mustard
salt and pepper
grated carrot salad, to serve

1 Mix together the rolled oats, fresh rosemary and salt and pepper.

2 Brush each piece of chicken evenly with egg white, then coat in the oat mixture. Place on a baking sheet and bake in a preheated oven, 200°C/400°F/Gas Mark 6, for about 40 minutes or until the juices run clear when the chicken is pierced.

3 In a bowl, mix together the fromage frais and wholegrain mustard, season with salt and pepper to taste then serve with the chicken, hot or cold, with a grated carrot salad.

VARIATION

To make oaty chicken nuggets, chop up 4 skinless, boneless chicken breasts into small pieces. Reduce the cooking time by about 10 minutes and test that they are done. These nuggets would be ideal at a picnic, buffet or children's party.

VARIATION

Add 1 tablespoon sesame or sunflower seeds to the oat mixture for an even crunchier texture. Experiment with different herbs, instead of the rosemary.

Solomongundy

Serves 4

INGREDIENTS

1 large lettuce	125 g/4^1/$_2$ oz/^{2}/$_3$ cup cooked ham, sliced	60 g/2 oz/^{1}/$_2$ cup flaked (slivered)
4 chicken breasts, cooked and sliced thinly	125 g/4^1/$_2$ oz/^{2}/$_3$ cup roast lamb, sliced	almonds
8 rollmop herrings and their marinade	150 g/5^1/$_2$ oz/1 cup mangetout (snow peas), cooked	60 g/2 oz/^{1}/$_3$ cup sultanas (golden raisins)
125 g/4^1/$_2$ oz/2^2/$_3$ cups roast beef, sliced	125 g/4^1/$_2$ oz/^{3}/$_4$ cup seedless black grapes	2 oranges
6 hard-boiled (hard-cooked) eggs, quartered	20 stuffed olives, sliced	sprig of mint
	12 shallots, boiled	salt and pepper
		fresh crusty bread, to serve

1 Spread out the lettuce leaves on a large oval platter.

2 Arrange the chicken in three sections on the platter.

3 Place the rollmops, eggs and meats in lines or sections over the remainder of the platter.

4 Use the mangetout (snow peas), grapes, olives, shallots, almonds and sultanas (golden raisins) to fill in the spaces between the sections.

5 Grate the rind from the oranges and sprinkle over the whole platter. Peel and slice the oranges and add the orange slices and mint sprig to the platter. Season well with salt and pepper. Sprinkle with the herring marinade and serve.

VARIATION

Should you wish, serve with cold, cooked vegetables, such as sliced beans, baby sweetcorn (baby corn) and cooked beetroot (beets).

Spiced Chicken Casserole

Serves 4–6

INGREDIENTS

3 tbsp olive oil	3 tsp ground cinnamon	1 tbsp chopped fresh thyme
900 g/2 lb chicken meat, sliced	300 ml/^{1}/$_2$ pint/1^1/$_4$ cups white wine	grated rind of 1 orange
10 shallots or pickling onions	300 ml/^{1}/$_2$ pint/1^1/$_4$ cups chicken	1 tbsp dark muscovado sugar
3 carrots, chopped	stock	125 g/4^1/$_2$ oz/^{3}/$_4$ cup seedless black
60 g/2 oz/^{1}/$_2$ cup chestnuts, sliced	175 ml/6 fl oz/^{3}/$_4$ cup white wine	grapes, halved
60 g/2 oz/^{1}/$_2$ cup flaked (slivered)	vinegar	sea salt and pepper
almonds, toasted	1 tbsp chopped fresh tarragon	fresh herbs, to garnish
1 tsp freshly grated nutmeg	1 tbsp chopped fresh flat leaf parsley	wild rice or puréed potato, to serve

1 Heat the olive oil in a large saucepan and fry the chicken, shallots or pickling onions, and carrots for about 6 minutes or until browned.

2 Add the remaining ingredients, except the grapes, and simmer over a low heat for 2 hours until the meat is very tender. Stir the casserole occasionally.

3 Add the grapes just before serving and serve with wild rice or puréed potato. Garnish with herbs.

VARIATION

Experiment with different types of nuts and fruits – try sunflower seeds instead of the almonds, and add 2 fresh apricots, chopped.

COOK'S TIP

This casserole would also be delicious served with thick slices of crusty wholemeal (whole wheat) bread to soak up the sauce.

Country Chicken Bake

Serves 4

INGREDIENTS

2 tbsp sunflower oil	400 g/14 oz can red kidney beans	1 tsp paprika
4 chicken quarters	4 medium tomatoes, quartered	60 g/2 oz/4 tbsp butter
16 small whole onions, peeled	200 ml/7 fl oz/ scant 1 cup dry cider	12 slices French bread
3 sticks (stalks) celery, sliced	or stock	salt and pepper
	4 tbsp chopped fresh parsley	

1 Heat the oil in a flameproof casserole and fry the chicken quarters two at a time until golden. Using a slotted spoon, remove the chicken from the pan and set aside until required.

2 Add the onions and fry, turning occasionally, until golden brown. Add the celery and fry for 2–3 minutes. Return the chicken to the pan, then stir in the beans, tomatoes, cider, half the parsley, salt and pepper. Sprinkle with the paprika.

3 Cover and cook in a preheated oven, 200°C/ 400°F/ Gas Mark 6, for 20–25 minutes, until the chicken juices run clear when pierced with a skewer.

4 Mix the remaining parsley with the butter and spread evenly over the French bread.

5 Uncover the casserole, arrange the bread slices overlapping on top and bake for a further 10–12 minutes, until golden and crisp.

VARIATION

For a more Italian-tasting dish, replace the garlic and parsley bread topping with Pesto Toasts

COOK'S TIP

Add a crushed garlic clove to the parsley butter for extra flavour.

Chicken in Exotic Mushroom and Ginger Sauce

Serves 6–8

INGREDIENTS

6 tbsp sesame oil	500 g/1 lb 2 oz/6 cups wild	2 tbsp grated fresh root ginger
900 g/1¾ lb chicken meat	mushrooms, roughly chopped	150 ml/¼ pint/⅔ cup yogurt
60 g/2 oz/½ cup flour, seasoned	300 ml/½ pint/1¼ cups chicken stock	salt and pepper
32 shallots, sliced	2 tbsp Worcestershire sauce	flat leaf parsley, to garnish
	1 tbsp honey	wild rice and white rice, to serve

1 Heat the oil in a large frying pan (skillet). Coat the chicken in the seasoned flour and cook for about 4 minutes, until browned all over. Transfer to a large deep casserole and keep warm until required.

2 Slowly fry the shallots and mushrooms in the juices.

3 Add the chicken stock, Worcestershire sauce, honey and fresh ginger, then season to taste with salt and pepper.

4 Pour the mixture over the chicken, and cover the casserole with a lid or cooking foil.

5 Cook in the centre of a preheated oven, 150°C/300°F/ Gas Mark 2, for about 1½ hours, until the meat is very tender. Add the yogurt and cook for a further 10 minutes. Serve the casserole with a mixture of wild rice and white rice, and garnish with fresh parsley.

COOK'S TIP

Mushrooms can be stored in the refrigerator for 24–36 hours. Keep them in paper bags as they 'sweat' in plastic. You do not need to peel mushrooms but wild mushrooms must be washed thoroughly.

Honey & Mustard-Baked Chicken

Serves 4–6

INGREDIENTS

8 chicken portions	4 tbsp clear honey	3 tbsp poppy seeds
60 g/2 oz/4 tbsp butter, melted	2 tbsp lemon juice	salt and pepper
4 tbsp mild mustard	1 tsp paprika	tomato and sweetcorn salad, to serve

1 Place the chicken pieces, skinless side down, on a large baking tray (cookie sheet).

2 Place all the ingredients except the poppy seeds into a large bowl and blend together thoroughly.

3 Brush the mixture over the chicken portions.

4 Bake in the centre of a preheated oven, 200°C/400°F/ Gas Mark 6, for 15 minutes.

5 Carefully turn over the chicken pieces and coat the top side of the chicken with the remaining honey and mustard mixture.

6 Sprinkle the chicken with poppy seeds and return to the oven for a further 15 minutes.

7 Arrange the chicken on a serving dish, pour over the cooking juices and serve with a tomato and sweetcorn salad, if desired.

COOK'S TIP

Mexican rice makes an excellent accompaniment to this dish: boil the rice for 10 minutes, drain, then fry for 5 minutes. Add chopped onions, garlic, tomatoes, carrots and chilli and cook for 1 minute before adding stock. Bring to the boil, cover and simmer for 20 minutes, adding more stock if necessary. Add peas 5 minutes before the end of the cooking time.

Cheddar-Baked Chicken

Serves 4

INGREDIENTS

1 tbsp milk	60 g/2 oz/1 cup grated mature	3 tbsp plain (all-purpose) flour
2 tbsp prepared English mustard	Cheddar cheese	2 tbsp chopped fresh chives
		4 skinless, boneless chicken breasts

1 Mix together the milk and mustard in a bowl. In another bowl, combine the cheese, flour and chives.

2 Dip the chicken into the milk and mustard mixture, brushing to coat evenly.

3 Dip the chicken breasts into the cheese mixture, pressing to coat evenly. Place on a baking tray (cookie sheet) and spoon any spare cheese coating over the top.

4 Bake in a preheated oven, 200°C/400°F/Gas Mark 6, for 30–35 minutes, or until golden brown and the juices run clear, not pink, when pierced with a skewer. Serve the chicken hot, with jacket potatoes and fresh vegetables, or serve cold, with a crisp salad.

COOK'S TIP

There are several varieties of mustard available. For a sharper flavour try French varieties – Meaux mustard has a grainy texture with a warm, spicy flavour while Dijon mustard is medium-hot and tangy.

COOK'S TIP

It is a good idea to freeze herbs as they retain their colour, flavour and nutrients very well. Chives are particularly suitable for freezing – store them in labelled plastic bags and shake them dry before use. Dried chives are not an adequate substitute for fresh.

Spicy Sesame Chicken

Serves 4

INGREDIENTS

4 chicken quarters	finely grated rind and juice of 1 small	1 tbsp sesame seeds
150 g/5¹/2 oz/¹/2 cup natural	lemon	lemon wedges, to serve
(unsweetened) yogurt	2 tsp medium-hot curry paste	

1 Remove the skin from the chicken and make cuts in the flesh at intervals with a sharp knife.

2 In a bowl, combine the natural (unsweetened) yogurt, lemon rind, lemon juice and curry paste to form a smooth mixture.

3 Spoon the mixture over the chicken and arrange on a foil-lined grill (broiler) pan or baking tray (cookie sheet).

4 Place the chicken quarters under a preheated moderately hot grill (broiler) and grill (broil) for 12–15 minutes, turning once. Grill (broil) until golden brown and thoroughly cooked. Just before the end of the cooking time, sprinkle the chicken with the sesame seeds.

5 Serve with a salad, naan bread and lemon wedges.

COOK'S TIP

If you have time, leave the chicken and the sauce in the refrigerator to marinate overnight so the flavours are fully absorbed.

VARIATION

Poppy seeds, fennel seeds or cumin seeds, or a mixture of all three, can also be used to sprinkle over the chicken.

Grilled Chicken
& Vegetable Salad

Serves 4

INGREDIENTS

1 small aubergine (eggplant), sliced	4 boneless chicken breasts	1 large red onion, sliced thickly
2 garlic cloves, crushed	2 medium courgettes (zucchini),	1 small ciabatta loaf or 1 French
finely grated rind of 1/2 lemon	sliced	baguette, sliced
1 tbsp chopped fresh mint	1 medium red (bell) pepper, quartered	extra olive oil
6 tbsp olive oil	1 small bulb fennel, sliced thickly	salt and pepper

1 Place the aubergine (eggplant) slices in a colander and sprinkle with salt. Leave over a bowl to drain for 30 minutes, then rinse and dry. This will get rid of the bitter juices.

2 Mix together the garlic, lemon rind, mint, and olive oil and season.

3 Slash the chicken breasts at intervals with a sharp knife. Spoon over about half of the oil mixture and stir to combine.

4 Combine the aubergines (eggplants) and the remaining vegetables, then toss in the remaining oil mixture. Marinate the chicken and vegetables for about 30 minutes.

5 Place the chicken breasts and vegetables on a preheated hot grill (broiler) or barbecue (grill), turning occasionally, until they are golden brown and tender, or cook on a ridged griddle pan on the hob.

6 Brush the bread slices with olive oil and grill (broil) until golden.

7 Drizzle a little olive oil over the chicken and grilled vegetables and serve hot or cold with the crusty bread toasts.

Tropical Chicken Skewers

Serves 6

INGREDIENTS

750 g/1 lb 10 oz boneless chicken breasts	3 mangoes	2 tbsp coarsely shredded coconut
2 tbsp medium sherry	bay leaves	pepper
	2 tbsp oil	

1 Remove the skin from the chicken and cut into 2.5 cm/1 inch cubes and toss in the sherry, with a little pepper.

2 Using a sharp knife, cut the mangoes into 2.5 cm/1 inch cubes, discarding the stone and skin.

3 Thread the chicken, mango cubes and bay leaves alternately on to long skewers, then brush lightly with oil.

4 Grill (broil) the skewers on a preheated moderately hot grill (broiler) for about 8–10 minutes, turning occasionally until golden.

5 Sprinkle the skewers with the coconut and grill (broil) for a further 30 seconds. Serve with a crisp salad.

COOK'S TIP

Use mangoes that are ripe but still firm so that they hold together on the skewers during cooking. Another firm fruit that would be suitable is pineapple.

COOK'S TIP

Remember that if you are using metal skewers, they will get very hot, so be sure to use gloves or tongs to turn them. Wooden skewers should be soaked in water for 30 minutes before use to prevent them from burning on the barbeue, and the exposed ends should be covered with pieces of kitchen foil.

Skewered Spicy Tomato Chicken

Serves 4

INGREDIENTS

500 g/1 lb 2 oz skinless, boneless chicken breasts	2 tbsp clear honey	250 g/9 oz cherry tomatoes
3 tbsp tomato purée (paste)	2 tbsp Worcestershire sauce	sprigs of rosemary, to garnish
	1 tbsp chopped fresh rosemary	couscous or rice, to serve

1 Using a sharp knife, cut the chicken into 2.5 cm/1 inch chunks and place in a bowl.

2 Mix together the tomato purée (paste), honey, Worcestershire sauce and rosemary. Add to the chicken, stirring to coat evenly.

3 Alternating the chicken pieces and tomatoes, thread them on to eight wooden skewers. Spoon over any remaining glaze.

4 Cook under a preheated hot grill (broiler) for 8–10 minutes, turning occasionally, until the chicken is thoroughly cooked. Serve on a bed of couscous or rice and garnish with sprigs of rosemary.

COOK'S TIP

Cherry tomatoes are ideal for barbecues as they can be threaded straight on to skewers. As they are kept whole, the skins keep in the natural juices.

COOK'S TIP

Couscous is made from semolina that has been made into separate grains. It is very easy to prepare – simply soak it in a bowl of boiling water and then fluff up the grains with a fork. Flavourings such as lemon or nutmeg can be added.

Minty Lime Chicken

Serves 6

INGREDIENTS

3 tbsp finely chopped mint

4 tbsp clear honey

4 tbsp lime juice

12 boneless chicken thighs

salad, to serve

SAUCE:

150 g/5¹/₂ oz/¹/₂ cup natural

(unsweetened) thick yogurt

1 tbsp finely chopped mint

2 tsp finely grated lime rind

1 Combine the mint, honey and lime juice in a bowl.

2 Use cocktail sticks to keep the chicken thighs in neat shapes and add the chicken to the marinade, turning to coat evenly.

3 Leave to marinate for at least 30 minutes, preferably overnight. Cook the chicken on a preheated moderately hot barbecue (grill) or grill (broiler), turning frequently and basting with the marinade.

The chicken is cooked if the juices run clear when the chicken is pierced in the thickest part with a skewer.

4 Meanwhile, mix together the sauce ingredients.

5 Remove the cocktail sticks and serve the chicken with a salad and the sauce.

COOK'S TIP

Mint can be grown very easily in a garden or window box. It is a useful herb for marinades and salad dressings. Other useful herbs to grow are parsley and basil.

VARIATION

Use this marinade for chicken kebabs, alternating the chicken with lime and red onion wedges.

Skewered Chicken with Blackberry Sauce

Serves 4

INGREDIENTS

4 chicken breasts or 8 thighs
4 tbsp dry white wine or cider
2 tbsp chopped fresh rosemary
pepper

rosemary sprigs and blackberries,
   to garnish
green salad, to serve

SAUCE:
200 g/7 oz/scant 2 cups blackberries
1 tbsp cider vinegar
2 tbsp redcurrant jelly
$^{1}/_{4}$ tsp grated nutmeg

1 Using a sharp knife, cut the chicken into 2.5cm/1 inch pieces and place in a bowl. Sprinkle over the white wine and rosemary, and season well with pepper. Cover and leave to marinate for at least an hour.

2 Drain the chicken, reserving the marinade, and thread the meat on to 8 metal or pre-soaked wooden skewers.

3 Cook on a preheated moderately hot grill (broiler) for 8–10 minutes, turning occasionally, until golden and evenly cooked.

4 Meanwhile, to make the sauce, place the marinade in a pan with the blackberries and simmer gently until soft. Press the mixture though a sieve (strainer) using the back of a spoon.

5 Return the blackberry purée to the pan with the cider vinegar and redcurrant jelly and bring to the boil. Boil uncovered until the sauce is reduced by about one-third.

6 Spoon a little blackberry sauce on to each plate and place a chicken skewer on top. Sprinkle with nutmeg and serve hot. Garnish with rosemary and blackberries and serve.

COOK'S TIP

If you use tinned fruit, omit the redcurrant jelly.

Grilled Rock Cornish Chicken with Lemon and Tarragon

Serves 2

INGREDIENTS

2 poussin	25 g/1 oz/2 tbsp butter	1 garlic clove, crushed
4 sprigs fresh tarragon	rind of ½ lemon	salt and pepper
1 tsp oil	1 tbsp lemon juice	tarragon and orange slices, to garnish

1 Prepare the baby poussin, turn them breast-side down on a chopping board and cut them through the backbone using kitchen scissors. Crush each bird gently to break the bones so that they lie flat while cooking. Season each with salt.

2 Turn them over and insert a sprig of tarragon under the skin over each side of the breast.

3 Brush the chickens with oil, using a pastry brush, and place under a preheated hot grill (broiler) about 13 cm/5 inches from the heat. Grill (broil) the chickens for about 15 minutes, turning half way, until they are lightly browned.

4 Meanwhile, to make the glaze, melt the butter in a small saucepan, add the lemon rind, lemon juice and garlic and season with salt and pepper.

5 Brush the poussin with the glaze and cook for a further 15 minutes, turning them once and brushing regularly so that they stay moist. Garnish the chickens with tarragon and orange slices. This is delicious served with new potatoes.

COOK'S TIP

Once the chickens are flattened, insert 2 metal skewers through them to keep them flat.

Barbecued Chicken Quarters with Warm Aioli

Serves 4

INGREDIENTS

4 chicken quarters
2 tbsp oil
2 tbsp lemon juice
2 tsp dried thyme
salt and pepper

green salad and lemon slices, to serve

AIOLI:
5 garlic cloves, crushed
2 egg yolks

120 ml/4 fl oz/$^1/_2$ cup each olive oil
    and sunflower oil
2 tsp lemon juice
2 tbsp boiling water

1 Using a skewer, prick the chicken quarters in several places then place them in a shallow dish.

2 Combine the oil, lemon juice, thyme and seasoning, then pour over the chicken, turning to coat the chicken evenly. Set aside for 2 hours.

3 To make the aioli, beat together the garlic and a pinch of salt to make a paste. Add the egg yolks and beat well. Gradually add the oils, drop by drop,

beating vigorously, until the mayonnaise becomes creamy and smooth. Add the oils in a thin steady trickle and continue beating until the aioli is thick. Stir in the lemon juice and season with pepper. Set aside in a warm place.

4 Place the chicken on a preheated barbecue (grill) and cook for 25–30 minutes. Brush with the marinade and turn the portions to cook evenly. Remove and arrange on a serving plate.

5 Beat the water into the aioli and turn into a warmed serving bowl. Serve the chicken with the aioli, a green salad and lemon slices.

COOK'S TIP

To make a quick aioli, add the garlic to 300 ml/ $^1/_2$ pint/$1^1/_4$ cups good quality mayonnaise then place in a bowl over a pan of warm water and beat together. Just before serving add 1–2 tbsp hot water.

Chicken with Peppers & Black Bean Sauce

Serves 4

INGREDIENTS

400 g/14 oz chicken breasts, sliced thinly

pinch of cornflour (cornstarch)

2 tbsp oil

1 garlic clove, crushed

1 tbsp black bean sauce

1 each small red and green (bell) pepper, cut into strips

1 red chilli, chopped finely

75 g/2³/₄ oz/1 cup mushrooms, sliced

1 onion, chopped

6 spring onions (scallions), chopped

salt and pepper

fresh noodles, to serve

SEASONING:

¹/₂ tsp salt

¹/₂ tsp sugar

3 tbsp chicken stock

1 tbsp dark soy sauce

2 tbsp beef stock

2 tbsp rice wine

1 tsp cornflour (cornstarch), blended with a little rice wine

1 Put the chicken strips in a bowl. Add a pinch of salt and a pinch of cornflour and cover with water. Leave for 30 minutes.

2 Heat 1 tbsp of the oil in a wok or deep-sided frying pan (skillet) and stir-fry the chicken for 4 minutes. Transfer the chicken to a warm serving dish and clean the wok or pan.

3 Add the remaining oil to the wok and add the garlic, black bean sauce, green and red (bell) peppers, chilli, mushrooms, onion and spring onions (scallions). Stir-fry the vegetables for 2 minutes then return the chicken strips to the wok.

4 Add the seasoning ingredients, fry for 3 minutes and thicken with a little of the cornflour (cornstarch) paste. Serve with fresh noodles.

COOK'S TIP

Black bean sauce can be found in specialist shops and in many supermarkets. Use dried noodles if you can't find fresh noodles.

Teppanyaki

Serves 4

INGREDIENTS

4 boneless chicken breasts	8 baby corn sweetcorn (baby corn)	4 tbsp soy sauce
1 red (bell) pepper	100g/3½ oz/½ cup bean sprouts	4 tbsp mirin
1 green (bell) pepper	1 tbsp sesame or sunflower oil	1 tbsp grated fresh ginger root
4 spring onions (scallions)		

1 Remove the skin from the chicken and slice at a slight angle, to a thickness of about 5 mm/¼ inch.

2 Deseed and thinly slice the (bell) peppers and trim and slice the spring onions (scallions) and baby sweetcorn (baby corn). Arrange the (bell) peppers, spring onions (scallions), corn cobs and bean sprouts on a plate with the sliced chicken.

3 Heat a large griddle or heavy frying pan (skillet) then lightly brush with oil. Add the vegetables and chicken slices in small batches, allowing space between them so that they cook thoroughly.

4 In a small bowl, mix together the soy sauce, mirin and ginger and serve as a dip with the chicken and vegetables.

VARIATION

If you cannot find mirin add one tablespoon of soft, light brown sugar to the sauce instead.

VARIATION

Instead of serving the sauce as a dip, you could use it as a marinade. However, do not leave it to marinate for more than 2 hours as the soy sauce will cause the chicken to dry out and become tough. Use other vegetables, such as mangetout (snow peas) or thinly sliced carrots, if you prefer.

Thai Stir-Fried Chicken with Vegetables

Serves 4

INGREDIENTS

3 tbsp sesame oil

350 g/12 oz chicken breast, sliced thinly

8 shallots, sliced

2 garlic cloves, finely chopped

1 green chilli, finely chopped

2.5 cm/1 inch piece fresh root ginger, grated

1 each red and green (bell) pepper, sliced thinly

3 courgettes (zucchini), thinly sliced

2 tbsp ground almonds

1 tsp ground cinnamon

1 tbsp oyster sauce

50 g/1¾ oz/¼ cup creamed coconut, grated

salt and pepper

1 Heat the sesame oil in a wok, add the chicken, season with salt and pepper, and stir fry for about 4 minutes.

2 Add the shallots, garlic, ginger and chilli and stir-fry for 2 minutes.

3 Add the (bell) peppers and courgettes (zucchini) and cook for about 1 minute.

4 Finally, add the remaining ingredients and seasoning. Stir-fry for 1 minute and serve.

COOK'S TIP

Creamed coconut is sold in blocks by supermarkets and oriental stores. It is a useful store-cupboard standby as it adds richness and depth of flavour.

COOK'S TIP

Since most of the heat of chillies comes from the seeds, remove them before cooking if you want a milder flavour. Be very careful when handling chillies – do not touch your face or eyes as the chilli juice can be very painful. Always wash your hands after preparing chillies.

Cumin-Spiced Apricot Chicken

Serves 4

INGREDIENTS

4 large, skinless chicken leg quarters
finely grated rind of 1 lemon
200 g/7 oz/1 cup ready-to-eat dried
    apricots
1 tbsp ground cumin
1 tsp ground turmeric

125 g/4$^1/_2$ oz/$^1/_2$ cup low-fat natural
    (unsweetened) yogurt
salt and pepper

TO SERVE:
250 g/9 oz/1$^1/_2$ cups brown rice

2 tbsp flaked (slivered) hazelnuts or
    almonds, toasted
2 tbsp sunflower seeds, toasted
lemon wedges and a fresh salad

1 Remove any excess fat from the chicken legs.

2 Use a small sharp knife to carefully cut the flesh away from the thigh bone.

3 Scrape the meat away down as far as the knuckle. Grasp the thigh bone firmly and twist it to break it away from the drumstick.

4 Open out the boned part of the chicken and sprinkle with lemon rind and pepper. Pack the dried apricots into each piece of chicken. Fold over to enclose, and secure with cocktail sticks.

5 Mix together the cumin, turmeric, yogurt and salt and pepper, then brush this mixture over the chicken to coat evenly. Place the chicken in an ovenproof dish or roasting tin (pan) and bake in a preheated oven, 190°C/375°F/ Gas Mark 5, for about 35–40 minutes, or until the juices run clear, not pink, when the chicken is pierced through the thickest part with a skewer.

6 Meanwhile, cook the rice in boiling, lightly salted water until just tender, then drain well. Stir the hazelnuts and sunflower seeds into the rice. Serve the chicken with the nutty rice, lemon wedges and a fresh salad.

Orange Turkey with Rice & Green Vegetables

Serves 4

INGREDIENTS

1 tbsp olive oil	225 g/8 oz small broccoli florets	in brine, drained and
1 medium onion, chopped	1 large courgette (zucchini),	quartered, to garnish
450 g/1 lb skinless lean turkey	diced	
(such as fillet), cut into thin	1 large orange	
strips	350 g/12 oz/6 cups cooked	
300 ml/^{1}/$_2$ pint/1^1/$_4$ cups	brown rice	
unsweetened orange juice	salt and pepper	
1 bay leaf	25 g/1 oz pitted black olives	

1 Heat the oil in a large frying pan (skillet) and fry the onion and turkey, stirring, for 4–5 minutes until lightly browned.

2 Pour in the orange juice and add the bay leaf and seasoning. Bring to the boil and simmer for 10 minutes.

3 Meanwhile, bring a large saucepan of water to the boil and cook the broccoli florets, covered, for 2 minutes. Add the diced courgette (zucchini), bring back to the boil, cover and cook for a further 3 minutes (do not overcook). Drain and set aside until required.

4 Using a sharp knife, peel off the skin and white pith from the orange. Slice down the orange to make thin, round slices, then cut each slice in half.

5 Stir the broccoli, courgette (zucchini), rice and orange slices into the turkey mixture. Gently mix together and heat through for 3–4 minutes until piping hot.

6 Transfer the turkey rice to serving plates and garnish with black olives.

Curried Turkey with Apricots & Sultanas

Serves 4

INGREDIENTS

1 tbsp vegetable oil	175 g/6 oz frozen peas	1 tsp ground coriander
1 large onion, chopped	400 g/14 oz can apricot halves in	4 tbsp fresh coriander (cilantro),
450 g/1 lb skinless turkey breast,	natural juice	chopped
cut into cubes	50 g/1³/4 oz/¹/₃ cup sultanas	1 green chilli, deseeded and
3 tbsp mild curry paste	(golden raisins)	sliced
300 ml/¹/2 pint/1¹/4 cups fresh	350 g/12 oz/6 cups basmati rice,	salt and pepper
chicken stock	freshly cooked	

1 Heat the oil in a large saucepan and fry the onion and turkey for 4–5 minutes until the onion has softened and the turkey is a light golden colour.

2 Stir in the curry paste. Pour in the stock, stirring, and bring to the boil. Cover and simmer for 15 minutes. Stir in the peas and bring back to the boil. Cover and simmer for about 5 minutes.

3 Drain the apricots, reserving the juice, and cut into thick slices. Add to the curry, stirring in a little of the juice if the mixture is becoming dry. Add the sultanas (golden raisins) and cook for 2 minutes.

4 Mix the rice with the ground coriander and fresh coriander (cilantro), stir in the chilli and season with salt and pepper to taste. Transfer the rice to warm plates and top with the turkey curry.

VARIATION

Peaches can be used instead of the apricots if you prefer. Cook in exactly the same way.

Turkey Loaf with Courgettes & Tomato

Serves 6

INGREDIENTS

1 medium onion, finely chopped
1 garlic clove, crushed
900 g/2 lb lean turkey, minced (ground)
1 tbsp fresh parsley, chopped

1 tbsp fresh chives, chopped
1 tbsp fresh tarragon, chopped
1 medium egg white, lightly beaten
1 medium, 1 large courgette (zucchini)

2 medium tomatoes
salt and pepper
tomato and herb sauce, to serve

1 Preheat the oven to 190°C/375°F/Gas Mark 5 and line a non-stick loaf tin (pan) with parchment. Place the onion, garlic and turkey in a bowl, add the herbs and season. Mix, then add the egg white to bind.

2 Press half of the mixture into the base of the tin (pan). Slice the medium courgette (zucchini) and the tomatoes and arrange over the meat. Top with the rest of the turkey; press down.

3 Cover with a layer of foil and place in a roasting tin (pan). Pour in enough boiling water to come half-way up the sides of the loaf tin (pan). Bake for 1–1¼ hours, removing the foil for the last 20 minutes of cooking time. Test the loaf is cooked by inserting a skewer into the centre – the juices should run clear. The loaf will also shrink away from the sides of the tin (pan) when it is cooked through.

4 Trim the large courgette (zucchini). Using a vegetable peeler or hand-held metal cheese slicer, cut the courgette (zucchini) into thin strips. Bring a saucepan of water to the boil and blanch the ribbons for 1–2 minutes until tender. Drain and keep warm. Transfer the turkey loaf to a warm platter. Drape over the courgette (zucchini) strips and serve with a tomato and herb sauce.

Duck with Kiwi Fruit & Raspberries

Serves 4

INGREDIENTS

450 g/1 lb boneless duck breasts, skin removed

2 tbsp raspberry vinegar

2 tbsp brandy

1 tbsp clear honey

1 tsp sunflower oil

2 kiwi fruit, peeled and sliced thinly

salt and pepper

SAUCE:

225 g/8 oz raspberries, thawed if frozen

300 ml/½ pint/1¼ cups rosé wine

2 tsp cornflour (cornstarch) blended with 4 tsp cold water

1 Preheat the grill (broiler) to medium. Skin and trim the duck breasts to remove any excess fat. Score the flesh in diagonal lines and pound it with a meat mallet or a covered rolling pin until it is 1.5 cm/¾ inch thick.

2 Place the duck breasts in a shallow dish. Mix together the vinegar, brandy and honey in a small bowl and spoon over the duck. Cover and leave to chill for about 1 hour.

3 Drain the duck, reserving the marinade, and place on the grill (broiler) rack. Season and brush with oil. Cook for 10 minutes, turn over, season and brush with oil again. Cook for 8–10 minutes until the meat is cooked through.

4 For the sauce, reserve 60 g/2 oz raspberries and place the rest in a pan. Add the reserved marinade and the wine. Bring to the boil and simmer for 5 minutes until slightly reduced.

5 Strain the sauce through a sieve, pressing the raspberries with the back of a spoon. Return the liquid to the pan and add the cornflour (cornstarch) paste. Heat through, stirring, until thickened. Add the reserved raspberries and season.

6 Slice the duck breast and arrange fanned out on warm serving plates, alternating with slices of kiwi fruit. Spoon over the sauce and serve.

Roast Duck with Apples & Apricots

Serves 4

INGREDIENTS

4 duckling portions,
350 g/12 oz each
4 tbsp dark soy sauce
2 tbsp light muscovado sugar
2 red-skinned apples
2 green-skinned apples

juice of 1 lemon
2 tbsp clear honey
few bay leaves
salt and pepper
assorted fresh vegetables, to
serve

SAUCE:
400 g/14 oz can apricots, in
natural juice
4 tbsp sweet sherry

1 Preheat the oven to
190°C/375°F/Gas
Mark 5. Wash the duck and
trim away any excess fat.
Place on a wire rack over a
roasting tin (pan) and prick
all over with a fork.

2 Brush the duck with
the soy sauce. Sprinkle
over the sugar and season
with pepper. Cook in the
oven, basting occasionally,
for 50–60 minutes until the
meat is cooked – the juices
should run clear when a
skewer is inserted into the
thickest part of the meat.

3 Core the apples and
cut each into 6 wedges.
Place in a bowl and mix
with the lemon juice and
honey. Transfer to a small
roasting tin (pan), add a
few bay leaves and season.
Cook alongside the duck,
basting occasionally, for
20–25 minutes until tender.
Discard the bay leaves.

4 To make the sauce,
place the apricots in a
blender or food processor
together with the juice
from the can and the
sherry. Process for a few

seconds until smooth.
Alternatively, mash the
apricots with a fork until
smooth and mix with the
juice and sherry.

5 Just before serving, heat
the apricot purée (paste)
in a pan. Remove the skin
from the duck (if wished)
and pat the flesh with kitchen
paper to absorb any fat.

6 Serve the duck with
the apple wedges
and the apricot sauce, and
accompanied with vegetables.

Moroccan Lamb Kebabs

Makes 4

INGREDIENTS

450 g/1 lb lean lamb
1 lemon
1 red onion
4 small courgettes (zucchini)
couscous, to serve (see
   Cook's Tip)

MARINADE:
grated rind and juice of
   1 lemon
2 tbsp olive oil
1 clove garlic, crushed
1 red chilli, sliced (optional)

1 tsp ground cinnamon
1 tsp ground ginger
$^1/_2$ tsp ground cumin
$^1/_2$ tsp ground coriander

---

1 Cut the lamb into large, evenly-sized chunks.

2 To make the marinade, combine the lemon rind and juice, oil, garlic, chilli (if using), ground cinnamon, ginger, cumin and coriander in a large non-metallic dish.

3 Add the meat to the marinade, tossing to coat the meat completely. Cover and leave to marinate in the refrigerator for at least 2 hours.

4 Cut the lemon into 8 pieces. Cut the onion into wedges, then separate each wedge into 2 pieces.

5 Using a canelle knife (or potato peeler), cut thin strips of peel from the courgettes (zucchini), then cut them into chunks.

6 Remove the meat from the marinade, reserving the liquid for basting. Thread the meat on to skewers alternating with the onion, lemon and courgette (zucchini).

7 Barbecue (grill) over hot coals for 8–10 minutes, basting with the reserved marinade.

COOK'S TIP

Serve these kebabs (kabobs) with couscous or tabouleh. Soak the couscous in cold water for about 20 minutes until the grains have softened. Then drain and steam them for 10 minutes or until piping hot.

Shish Kebabs

Makes 4

INGREDIENTS

50 g/1 lb lean lamb
1 red onion, cut into wedges
1 green (bell) pepper, deseeded

MARINADE:
1 onion

4 tbsp olive oil
grated rind and juice of
  $\frac{1}{2}$ lemon
1 clove garlic, crushed
$\frac{1}{2}$ tsp dried oregano
$\frac{1}{2}$ tsp dried thyme

TO SERVE:
4 pitta breads
2 tomatoes, sliced
few crisp lettuce leaves,
  shredded
chilli sauce (optional)

1 Cut the lamb into large, evenly-sized chunks.

2 To make the marinade, grate the onion or chop it very finely in a food processor. Remove the juice by squeezing the onion between two plates set over a small bowl.

3 Combine the onion juice with the remaining marinade ingredients in a non-metallic dish and add the meat. Toss the meat in the marinade, cover and leave to marinate in the refrigerator for at least 2 hours or overnight .

4 Divide the onion wedges into 2. Cut the (bell) peppers into chunks.

5 Remove the meat from the marinade, reserving the liquid for basting. Thread the meat on to skewers, alternating with the onion and (bell) peppers. Barbecue (grill) for 8–10 minutes, turning and basting frequently.

6 Split open the pitta breads and fill with a little lettuce, and the meat and vegetables. Top with tomatoes and chilli sauce.

VARIATION

These kebabs (kabobs) are delicious served with saffron-flavoured rice. For easy saffron rice, simply use saffron stock cubes when cooking the rice.

Lamb Cutlets with Rosemary

Serves 4

INGREDIENTS

8 lamb cutlets
5 tbsp olive oil
2 tbsp lemon juice
1 clove garlic, crushed
½ tsp lemon pepper
salt
8 sprigs rosemary

jacket potatoes, to serve

SALAD:
4 tomatoes, sliced
4 spring onions (scallion), sliced
   diagonally

DRESSING:
2 tbsp olive oil
1 tbsp lemon juice
1 clove garlic, chopped
¼ tsp fresh rosemary, chopped
   finely

1 Trim the lamb chops by cutting away the flesh with a sharp knife to expose the tips of the bones.

2 Place the oil, lemon juice garlic, lemon pepper and salt in a shallow, non-metallic dish and whisk with a fork to combine.

3 Lay the sprigs of rosemary in the dish and place the lamb on top. Leave to marinate for at least 1 hour, turning the lamb cutlets once.

4 Remove the chops from the marinade and wrap a little kitchen foil around the bones to stop them from burning.

5 Place the sprigs of rosemary on the rack and place the lamb on top. Barbecue (grill) for 10–15 minutes, turning once.

6 Meanwhile make the salad and dressing. Arrange the tomatoes on a serving dish and scatter the spring onions (scallions) on top. Place all the ingredients for the dressing in a screw-top jar, shake well and pour over the salad. Serve with the barbecued (grilled) lamb cutlets and jacket potatoes.

Lamb with Mango & Chilli

Serves 4

INGREDIENTS

4 chump lamb chops
4 tbsp mango chutney (relish)
2 tsp chilli sauce
grilled vegetables, to serve

SPICY MANGO RELISH:
1 ripe mango
2 tbsp cider vinegar
2 tbsp light muscovado sugar

$\frac{1}{2}$ tsp ground cinnamon
$\frac{1}{2}$ tsp ground ginger

1 To make the spicy mango relish, cut the mango lengthwise down both sides of the large, flat stone and discard the stone. Peel the mango and cut the flesh into evenly-sized chunks.

2 Place the cider vinegar, sugar, cinnamon and spices in a small pan and heat gently, stirring continuously, until the sugar dissolves.

3 Stir the mango into the mixture in the pan and cook gently at the side of the barbecue (grill) or on the stove for about 5 minutes or until the mango is soft.

4 Barbecue (grill) the chops on an oiled rack for about 4 minutes on each side.

5 Combine the mango chutney (relish) and chilli sauce in a small bowl and brush the glaze over the chops.

6 Continue to barbecue (grill) for a few more minutes on each side until the lamb is cooked, turning and basting frequently with the mango chutney (relish) and chilli glaze.

7 Serve with grilled vegetables and the spicy mango relish.

VARIATION

The relish can also be served cold. Simmer the combined ingredients for 5 minutes, then remove from the heat and allow to cool. Leave to chill in the refrigerator until required. You can also use the mango chutney (relish) and chilli glaze on other cuts of lamb or on pork chops.

Indian Kofta

Makes 8

INGREDIENTS

1 small onion	TOMATO SAMBAL:	TO SERVE:
450 g/1 lb minced lamb	3 tomatoes, deseeded and diced	poppadoms
2 tbsp curry paste	pinch of ground coriander	chutney (relish)
2 tbsp natural yogurt	pinch of ground cumin	
oil, to baste	2 tsp chopped, fresh coriander	
sprigs of fresh coriander	(cilantro)	
(cilantro), to garnish	salt and pepper	

1 Put the onion in a food processor and chop finely. Add the lamb and process briefly to chop the mince further. Chopping the mince again will help the meat mixture to hold together during cooking. If you do not have a food processor, grate the onion finely before mixing it with the lamb.

2 Add the curry paste and yogurt and mix well. Divide the mixture into 8 equal portions.

3 Press and shape the mixture into 8 sausage shapes and push each one on to a skewer, pressing the mixture together firmly so that it holds its shape. Leave to hill in the refrigerator for at least 30 minutes or until required.

4 To make the tomato sambal, mix together the tomatoes, spices, chopped coriander (cilantro) and salt and pepper to taste in a bowl. Leave to stand for at least 30 minutes for the flavours to combine.

5 Barbecue (grill) the kebabs (kabobs) on an oiled rack over hot coals for 10–15 minutes, turning frequently. Baste with a little oil if required.

6 Transfer to serving plates and garnish with fresh coriander (cilantro). Serve accompanied with poppadoms, chutney (relish) and the tomato sambal.

Pork & Apple Skewers with Mustard

Makes 4

INGREDIENTS

450 g/1 lb pork fillet
2 (dessert) eating apples
a little lemon juice
1 lemon

2 tsp wholegrain mustard
2 tsp Dijon mustard
2 tbsp apple or orange juice
2 tbsp sunflower oil
crusty brown bread, to serve

MUSTARD SAUCE:
1 tbsp wholegrain mustard
1 tsp Dijon mustard
6 tbsp single (light) cream

1 To make the mustard sauce, combine the mustards in a small bowl and slowly blend in the cream. Leave to stand while you prepare the pork and apple skewers.

2 Cut the pork fillet into bite-size pieces and set aside until required.

3 Core the apples, then cut them into thick wedges. Toss the apple wedges in a little lemon juice – this will prevent any discoloration. Cut the lemon into slices.

4 Thread the pork, apple and lemon slices alternately on to 4 skewers.

5 Mix together the mustards, fruit juice and oil. Brush the mixture over the kebabs (kabobs) and barbecue (grill) over hot coals for 10–15 minutes, turning and basting with the marinade.

6 Transfer the kebabs (kabobs) to warm serving plates and spoon over a little of the mustard sauce. Serve with fresh, crusty brown bread.

COOK'S TIP

There are many varieties of mustard available, including English, which is very hot, Dijon, which is milder, and wholegrain, which contains whole mustard seeds. Mustards flavoured with other ingredients, such as honey or chilli, are also available.

Fruity Pork Skewers

Makes 4

INGREDIENTS

4 boneless pork loin steaks
8 ready-to-eat prunes

8 ready-to-eat dried apricots
4 bay leaves
slices of orange and lemon, to
garnish

MARINADE:
4 tbsp orange juice
2 tbsp olive oil
1 tsp ground bay leaves
salt and pepper

1 Trim the visible fat from the pork and cut the meat into evenly-sized chunks.

2 Place the pork in a shallow, non-metallic dish and add the prunes and apricots.

3 To make the marinade, mix together the orange juice, oil, bay leaves and salt and pepper to taste in a bowl.

4 Pour the marinade over the pork and fruit and toss until well coated.

Leave to marinate in the refrigerator for at least 1 hour or preferably overnight.

5 Soak 4 wooden skewers in cold water to prevent them from catching alight on the barbecue (grill).

6 Remove the pork and fruit from the marinade, using a perforated spoon, reserving the marinade for basting. Thread the pork and fruit on to the skewers, alternating with the bay leaves.

7 Barbecue (grill) the skewers on an oiled rack over medium hot coals for 10–15 minutes, turning and frequently basting with the reserved marinade, or until the pork is cooked through.

8 Transfer the pork and fruit skewers to warm serving plates. Garnish with slices of orange and lemon and serve hot.

Honey-Glazed Pork Chops

Serves 4

INGREDIENTS

4 lean pork loin chops

4 tbsp clear honey

1 tbsp dry sherry

4 tbsp orange juice

2 tbsp olive oil

2.5 cm/1 inch piece root (fresh)

ginger, grated

salt and pepper

1 Season the pork chops with salt and pepper to taste. Set aside while you make the glaze.

2 To make the glaze, place the honey, sherry, orange juice, oil and ginger in a small pan and heat gently, stirring continuously, until all of the ingredients are well blended.

3 Barbecue (grill) the chops on an oiled rack over hot coals for about 5 minutes on each side.

4 Brush the chops with the glaze and barbecue (grill) for a further 2–4 minutes on each side, basting frequently with the glaze.

5 Transfer the chops to warm serving plates and serve hot.

COOK'S TIP

To give the recipe a little more punch, stir ½ teaspoon of chilli sauce or 1 tablespoon of wholegrain mustard into the basting glaze.

VARIATION

This recipe works equally well with lamb chops and with chicken portions, such as thighs or drumsticks. Barbecue (grill) the meat in exactly the same way as in this recipe, basting frequently with the honey glaze – the result will be just as delicious!

Fish & Seafood

Naturally low in fat yet rich in minerals and proteins, white fish and seafood will be regular and important ingredients in any low-fat diet. There are so many flavours and textures available that the possible combinations are endless.

White fish, such as monkfish, haddock, cod and turbot, are widely available and easy to cook. Shellfish, too, are low in fat and rich in flavour, and they can be cooked in a variety of ways to produce mouthwatering, low-fat dishes. Some fish – salmon, tuna, trout and mackerel, for example – are oily and should be eaten in moderation. They are rich in the fat-soluble vitamins A and D, however, and it is also believed that the oil in these fish is beneficial in breaking down cholesterol in the bloodstream.

Prawn & Tuna Pasta Bake

Serves 4

INGREDIENTS

225 g/8 oz tricolour pasta shapes
1 tbsp vegetable oil
1 bunch spring onions (scallions),
   trimmed and chopped
175 g/6 oz button mushrooms,
   sliced

400 g/14 oz can tuna in brine,
   drained and flaked
175 g/6 oz peeled prawns
   (shrimp), thawed if frozen
2 tbsp cornflour (cornstarch)
425 ml/15 fl oz/1¾ cups
   skimmed milk

4 medium tomatoes, sliced thinly
25 g/1 oz fresh breadcrumbs
25 g/1 oz reduced-fat Cheddar
   cheese, grated
salt and pepper

1 Preheat the oven to 190°C/375°F/Gas Mark 5. Bring a large pan of water to the boil and cook the pasta according to the instructions on the packet. Drain well.

2 Heat the oil in a frying pan (skillet) and fry all but a handful of the spring onions (scallions) and all of the mushrooms, stirring, for 4–5 minutes until softened.

3 Place the cooked pasta in a bowl and mix in the spring onions (scallions), mushrooms, tuna and prawns (shrimp). Set aside until required.

4 Blend the cornflour (cornstarch) with a little milk to make a paste. Pour the remaining milk into a saucepan and stir in the paste. Heat, stirring, until the sauce begins to thicken. Season well.

5 Pour the sauce over the pasta mixture and stir until well combined. Transfer to the base of an ovenproof gratin dish and place on a baking sheet (cookie sheet).

6 Arrange the tomato slices over the pasta and sprinkle with the breadcrumbs and cheese. Bake for 25–30 minutes. Sprinkle with the reserved spring onions (scallions).

Fish Cakes with Piquant Tomato Sauce

Serves 4

INGREDIENTS

450 g/1 lb potatoes, diced
225 g/8 oz haddock fillet
225 g/8 oz trout fillet
1 bay leaf
425 ml/15 fl oz/1³/4 cups fresh
   fish stock
2 tbsp low-fat natural fromage
   frais (unsweetened yogurt)

4 tbsp fresh snipped chives
75 g/2³/4 oz dry white
   breadcrumbs
1 tbsp sunflower oil
salt and pepper
freshly snipped chives, to garnish
lemon wedges and salad leaves,
   to serve

piquant tomato sauce:
200 ml/7 fl oz/³/4 cup passata
   (sieved tomatoes)
4 tbsp dry white wine
4 tbsp low-fat natural
   (unsweetened) yogurt
chilli powder

1 Place the potatoes in a pan and cover with water. Bring to the boil and cook for 10 minutes until tender. Drain and mash.

2 Place the fish in a pan with the bay leaf and stock. Bring to the boil and simmer for 7–8 minutes. Remove the fish and flake the flesh away from the skin.

3 Mix the fish with the potato, fromage frais (yogurt), chives and seasoning. Cool, then cover and chill for 1 hour.

4 Sprinkle the breadcrumbs on to a plate. Divide the fish mixture into 8 and form each portion into a patty, about 7.5 cm/3 inches in diameter. Press each fish cake into the breadcrumbs.

5 Brush a frying pan (skillet) with oil and fry the fish cakes for 6 minutes. Turn the fish cakes over and cook for a further 5–6 minutes until golden. Drain on kitchen paper and keep warm.

6 To make the sauce, heat the passata (sieved tomatoes) and wine. Season, remove from the heat and stir in the yogurt. Return to the heat, sprinkle with chilli powder and serve with the fish cakes.

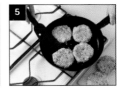

Provençal-Style Mussels

Serves 4

INGREDIENTS

1 tbsp olive oil
1 large onion, finely chopped
1 garlic clove, finely chopped
1 small red (bell) pepper,
    deseeded and finely chopped
sprig of rosemary
2 bay leaves
400 g/14 oz can chopped
    tomatoes

150 ml/5 fl oz/²⁄₃ cup white wine
1 courgette (zucchini), diced
    finely
2 tbsp tomato purée (paste)
1 tsp caster (superfine) sugar
50 g/1¾ oz pitted black olives in
    brine, drained and chopped

675 g/1½ lb cooked New
    Zealand mussels in their
    shells
1 tsp orange rind
salt and pepper
2 tbsp chopped, fresh parsley, to
    garnish
crusty bread, to serve

1 Heat the oil in a large saucepan and gently fry the onion, garlic and (bell) pepper for 3–4 minutes until just softened.

2 Add the sprig of rosemary and the bay leaves to the saucepan with the tomatoes and 100 ml/3½ fl oz/⅓ cup wine. Season to taste, then bring to the boil and simmer for 15 minutes.

3 Stir in the courgette (zucchini), tomato purée (paste), sugar and olives. Simmer for about 10 minutes.

4 Meanwhile, bring a pan of water to the boil. Arrange the mussels in a steamer or a large sieve (strainer) and place over the water. Sprinkle with the remaining wine and the orange rind. Cover and steam until the mussels open (discard any that remain closed).

5 Remove the mussels with a slotted spoon and arrange on a warm serving plate. Discard the herbs and spoon the sauce over the mussels. Garnish with chopped fresh parsley and serve with fresh, crusty bread.

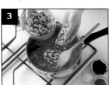

Fish & Rice with Dark Rum

Serves 4

INGREDIENTS

450 g/1 lb firm white fish fillets (such as cod or monkfish), skinned and cut into 2.5 cm/ 1 inch cubes
2 tsp ground cumin
2 tsp dried oregano
2 tbsp lime juice
150 ml/5 fl oz/²/₃ cup dark rum
1 tbsp dark muscovado sugar
3 garlic cloves, chopped finely

1 large onion, chopped
1 medium red (bell) pepper, deseeded and sliced into rings
1 medium green (bell) pepper, deseeded and sliced into rings
1 medium yellow (bell) pepper, deseeded and sliced into rings

1.2 litres/2 pints/5 cups fish stock
350 g/12 oz/2 cups long-grain rice
salt and pepper
crusty bread, to serve

TO GARNISH:
fresh oregano leaves
lime wedges

1 Place the cubes of fish in a bowl and add the cumin, oregano, salt and pepper, lime juice, rum and sugar. Mix well, cover and leave to chill for 2 hours.

2 Place the garlic, onion and (bell) peppers in a large pan. Pour over the stock and stir in the rice. Bring to the boil, cover and cook for 15 minutes.

3 Gently add the fish and the marinade juices to the pan. Bring back to the boil and simmer, uncovered, stirring occasionally but taking care not to break up the fish, for 10 minutes until the fish is cooked and the rice is just tender.

4 Season with salt and pepper to taste and

transfer to a warm serving plate. Garnish with fresh oregano and lime wedges and serve with crusty bread.

VARIATION

If you prefer, use unsweetened orange juice in the marinade instead of the rum.

Seafood Stir-Fry

Serves 4

INGREDIENTS

100 g/3¹/₂ oz small, thin
    asparagus spears, trimmed
1 tbsp sunflower oil
2.5 cm/1 inch piece root (fresh)
    ginger, cut into thin strips
1 medium leek, shredded
2 medium carrots, julienned

100 g/3¹/₂ oz baby sweetcorn
    cobs, quartered lengthwise
2 tbsp light soy sauce
1 tbsp oyster sauce
1 tsp clear honey
450 g/1 lb cooked, assorted
    shellfish, thawed if frozen

freshly cooked egg noodles, to
    serve

TO GARNISH:
4 large cooked prawns
small bunch fresh chives, freshly
    snipped

1 Bring a small pan of water to the boil and blanch the asparagus for 1–2 minutes. Drain, set aside and keep warm.

2 Heat the oil in a wok or large frying pan (skillet) and stir-fry the ginger, leek, carrot and sweetcorn for 3 minutes.

3 Add the soy sauce, oyster sauce and honey to the wok or frying pan (skillet). Stir in the shellfish and stir-fry for 2–3 minutes until the vegetables are just tender and the shellfish are heated through. Add the blanched asparagus and stir-fry for about 2 minutes.

4 To serve, pile the cooked noodles on to 4 warm serving plates and spoon over the seafood and vegetable stir fry. Serve garnished with a large prawn and freshly snipped chives.

COOK'S TIP

When you are preparing dense vegetables, such as carrots and other root vegetables, for stir frying, slice them into thin, evenly sized pieces so that they cook quickly and at the same rate. Delicate vegetables, such as (bell) peppers, leeks and spring onions (scallions), do not need to be cut as thinly.

Smoky Fish Pie

Serves 4

INGREDIENTS

900 g/2 lb smoked haddock or
 cod fillets
600 ml/1 pint/2½ cups
 skimmed milk
2 bay leaves
115 g/4 oz button mushrooms,
 quartered

115 g/4 oz frozen peas
115 g/4 oz frozen sweetcorn
 kernels
675 g/1½ lb potatoes, diced
5 tbsp low-fat natural
 (unsweetened) yogurt
4 tbsp chopped fresh parsley

60 g/2 oz smoked salmon, sliced
 into thin strips
3 tbsp cornflour (cornstarch)
25 g/1 oz smoked cheese, grated
salt and pepper

1 Preheat the oven to
200°C/400°F/Gas
Mark 6. Place the fish in a
pan and add the milk and
bay leaves. Bring to the
boil, cover and then
simmer for 5 minutes.

2 Add the mushrooms,
peas and sweetcorn to
the pan, bring back to a
simmer, cover and cook for
5–7 minutes. Leave to cool.

3 Place the potatoes in a
pan, cover with water,
boil and cook for 8 minutes.

Drain and mash with a fork
or a potato masher. Stir in
the yogurt, parsley and
seasoning. Set aside.

4 Using a slotted spoon,
remove the fish from
the pan. Flake the cooked
fish away from the skin and
place in an ovenproof
gratin dish. Reserve the
cooking liquid.

5 Drain the vegetables,
reserving the cooking
liquid, and stir into the fish
with the salmon strips.

6 Blend a little cooking
liquid into the
cornflour (cornstarch) to
make a paste. Transfer the
rest of the liquid to a pan
and add the paste. Heat
through, stirring, until
thickened. Discard the bay
leaves and season to taste.

7 Pour the sauce over
the fish and vegetables.
Spoon over the mashed
potato so that the fish is
covered, sprinkle with
cheese and bake for
25–30 minutes. Serve.

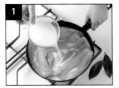

Seafood Spaghetti

Serves 4

INGREDIENTS

2 tsp olive oil
1 small red onion, chopped finely
1 tbsp lemon juice
1 garlic clove, crushed
2 sticks celery, chopped finely
150 ml/5 fl oz/$^2/_3$ cup fresh
    fish stock

150 ml/5 fl oz/$^2/_3$ cup dry white
    wine
small bunch fresh tarragon
450 g/1 lb fresh mussels,
    prepared
225 g/8 oz fresh prawns
    (shrimp), peeled and
    deveined

225 g/8 oz baby squid, cleaned,
    trimmed and sliced into rings
8 small cooked crab claws,
    cracked and peeled
225 g/8 oz spaghetti
salt and pepper
2 tbsp chopped fresh tarragon,
    to garnish

1 Heat the oil in a large pan and fry the onion with the lemon juice, garlic and celery for 3–4 minutes until just softened.

2 Pour in the stock and wine. Bring to the boil and add the tarragon and mussels. Cover and simmer for 5 minutes. Add the prawns (shrimp), squid and crab claws to the pan, mix and cook for 3–4 minutes until the mussels

have opened, the prawns (shrimp) are pink and the squid is opaque. Discard any mussels that have not opened and the tarragon.

3 Meanwhile, cook the spaghetti in a saucepan of boiling water according to the instructions on the packet. Drain well.

4 Add the spaghetti to the shellfish mixture and toss together. Season.

5 Transfer to warm serving plates and spoon over the cooking juices. Serve garnished with freshly chopped tarragon.

COOK'S TIP

Crab claws contain lean crab meat. Ask your fishmonger to crack the claws for you, leaving the pincers intact, because the shell is very tough.

Chilli & Crab-Stuffed Red Snapper

Serves 4

INGREDIENTS

4 red snappers, cleaned and
  scaled, 175 g/6 oz each
2 tbsp dry sherry
salt and pepper
stir-fried shredded vegetables, to
  serve

STUFFING:
1 small red chilli
1 garlic clove
1 spring onion (scallion)
$\frac{1}{2}$ tsp finely grated lime rind
1 tbsp lime juice

100 g/3$\frac{1}{2}$ oz white crab meat,
  flaked

TO GARNISH:
wedges of lime
red chilli strips

1 Rinse the fish and pat dry on absorbent kitchen paper. Season inside and out and place in a shallow dish. Spoon over the sherry and set aside.

2 Meanwhile, make the stuffing. Carefully halve, deseed and finely chop the chilli. Place in a small bowl.

3 Peel and finely chop the garlic. Trim and finely chop the spring onion (scallion). Add to the chilli together with the grated lime rind, lime juice and the flaked crab meat. Season with salt and pepper to taste and combine. Spoon some of the stuffing into the cavity of each fish.

4 Bring a large pan of water to the boil. Arrange the fish in a steamer lined with baking parchment or in a large sieve (strainer) and place over the boiling water. Cover and steam for 10 minutes. Turn the fish over and steam for 10 minutes or until the fish is cooked.

5 Drain the fish and transfer to serving plates. Garnish with wedges of lime and serve with stir-fried vegetables.

COOK'S TIP

Always wash your hands thoroughly after handling chillies as they can irritate your skin and eyes.

Citrus Fish Skewers

Serves 4

INGREDIENTS

450 g/1 lb firm white fish fillets (such as cod or monkfish)	1 bunch fresh bay leaves	salt and pepper
450 g/1 lb thick salmon fillet	1 tsp finely grated lemon rind	
2 large oranges	3 tbsp lemon juice	TO SERVE:
1 pink grapefruit	2 tsp clear honey	crusty bread
	2 garlic cloves, crushed	mixed salad

1 Skin the white fish and the salmon, rinse and pat dry on absorbent kitchen paper. Cut each fillet into 16 pieces.

2 Using a sharp knife, remove the skin and pith from the oranges and grapefruit. Cut out the segments of flesh, removing all remaining traces of the pith and dividing membrane.

3 Thread the pieces of fish alternately with the orange and grapefruit segments and the bay leaves on to 8 skewers. Place the kebabs (kabobs) in a shallow dish.

4 Mix together the lemon rind and juice, the honey and garlic. Pour over the fish kebabs (kabobs) and season well. Cover and chill for 2 hours, turning occasionally.

5 Preheat the grill (broiler) to medium. Remove the skewers from the marinade and place on the rack. Cook for 7–8 minutes, turning once, until cooked through.

6 Drain, transfer to serving plates and serve with crusty bread and a fresh salad.

VARIATION

This dish makes an unusual starter. Try it with any firm fish – swordfish or shark, for example – or with tuna for a meatier texture.

Seafood Pizza

Serves 4

INGREDIENTS

145 g/5 oz standard pizza
    base mix
4 tbsp chopped fresh dill or
    2 tbsp dried dill
fresh dill, to garnish

SAUCE:
1 large red (bell) pepper

400 g/14 oz can chopped
    tomatoes with onion and
    herbs
3 tbsp tomato purée (paste)
salt and pepper

TOPPING:
350 g/12 oz assorted cooked
    seafood, thawed if frozen

1 tbsp capers in brine, drained
25 g/1 oz pitted black olives in
    brine, drained
25 g/1 oz low-fat Mozzarella
    cheese, grated
1 tbsp grated, fresh Parmesan
    cheese

1 Preheat the oven to 200°C/400°F/Gas Mark 6. Place the pizza base mix in a bowl and stir in the dill. Make the dough according to the instructions on the packet.

2 Press the dough into a round measuring 25.5 cm/10 inches across on a baking sheet (cookie sheet) lined with baking parchment. Set aside to prove (rise).

3 Preheat the grill (broiler) to hot. To make the sauce, halve and deseed the (bell) pepper and arrange on a grill (broiler) rack. Cook for 8–10 minutes until softened and charred. Leave to cool slightly, peel off the skin and chop the flesh.

4 Place the tomatoes and (bell) pepper in a saucepan. Bring to the boil and simmer for 10 minutes.

Stir in the tomato purée (paste) and season to taste.

5 Spread the sauce over the pizza base and top with the seafood. Sprinkle over the capers and olives, top with the grated cheeses and bake for 25–30 minutes. Garnish with sprigs of dill and serve hot.

Pan-Seared Halibut with Red Onion Relish

Serves 4

INGREDIENTS

1 tsp olive oil	2 tbsp fresh chives, snipped, to garnish	1 tbsp lemon juice
4 halibut steaks, skinned, 175 g/6 oz each		2 tsp olive oil
½ tsp cornflour (cornstarch) mixed with 2 tsp cold water	RED ONION RELISH:	2 tbsp red wine vinegar
	2 medium red onions	2 tsp caster (superfine) sugar
salt and pepper	6 shallots	150 ml/5 fl oz/²⁄₃ cup fresh fish stock

1 To make the relish, peel and thinly shred the onions and shallots. Place in a small bowl and toss in the lemon juice.

2 Heat the oil in a pan and fry the onions and shallots for 3–4 minutes until just softened.

3 Add the vinegar and sugar and continue to cook for a further 2 minutes over a high heat. Pour in the stock and season well. Bring to the boil and simmer gently for a further 8–9 minutes until the sauce has thickened and is slightly reduced.

4 Brush a non-stick, ridged frying pan (skillet) with oil and heat until hot. Press the fish steaks into the pan to seal, lower the heat and cook for 4 minutes. Turn the fish over and cook for 4–5 minutes until cooked through. Drain on kitchen paper and keep warm.

5 Stir the cornflour (cornstarch) paste into the onion sauce and heat through, stirring, until thickened. Season to taste.

6 Pile the relish on to 4 warm serving plates and place a halibut steak on top of each. Garnish with chives and pepper.

Five-Spice Salmon with Ginger Stir-Fry

Serves 4

INGREDIENTS

4 salmon fillets, skinned,
115 g/4 oz each
2 tsp five-spice powder
1 large leek
1 large carrot
115 g/4 oz mangetout
(snow peas)

2.5 cm/1 inch piece root (fresh)
ginger
2 tbsp ginger wine
2 tbsp light soy sauce
1 tbsp vegetable oil
salt and pepper
freshly boiled noodles, to serve

TO GARNISH:
shredded leek
shredded root (fresh) ginger
shredded carrot

1 Wash the salmon and pat dry on absorbent kitchen paper. Rub the five-spice powder into both sides of the fish and season with salt and pepper. Set aside until required.

2 Trim the leek, slice it down the centre and rinse under cold water to remove any dirt. Finely shred the leek. Peel the carrot and cut it into very thin strips. Top and tail the mangetout (snow peas) and

cut them into shreds. Peel the ginger and slice thinly into strips.

3 Place all of the vegetables into a large bowl and toss in the ginger wine and 1 tablespoon of soy sauce. Set aside.

4 Preheat the grill (broiler) to medium. Place the salmon fillets on the rack and brush with the remaining soy sauce. Cook for 2–3 minutes on each side until cooked through.

5 While the salmon is cooking, heat the oil in a non-stick wok or large frying pan (skillet) and stir-fry the vegetables for 5 minutes until just tender. Take care that you do not overcook the vegetables – they should still have bite. Transfer to serving plates.

6 Drain the salmon on kitchen paper and serve on a bed of stir-fried vegetables. Garnish with shredded leek, ginger and carrot and serve.

Skewered Oriental Shellfish

Makes 12

INGREDIENTS

350 g/12 oz raw tiger prawns
    (jumbo shrimp), peeled
    leaving tails intact
350 g/12 oz scallops, cleaned,
    trimmed and halved
1 bunch spring onions (scallions),
    sliced into 2.5 cm/1 inch pieces
1 red (bell) pepper, deseeded and
    cubed

100 g/3½ oz baby corn, trimmed
    and sliced into 1 cm/½ inch
    pieces
3 tbsp dark soy sauce
1½ tsp hot chilli powder
½ tsp ground ginger
1 tbsp sunflower oil
1 red chilli, deseeded and sliced

DIP:
4 tbsp dark soy sauce
4 tbsp dry sherry
2 tsp clear honey
2.5 cm/1 inch piece root (fresh)
    ginger, peeled and grated
1 spring onion (scallion),
    trimmed and very finely sliced

1 Soak 12 wooden skewers in cold water for 10 minutes to prevent them from burning.

2 Divide the prawns (shrimp), scallops, spring onions (scallions), (bell) pepper and baby corn cobs into 12 portions and thread on to the skewers. Cover the ends with foil so that they do not burn and place in a shallow dish.

3 Mix the soy sauce, chilli powder and ground ginger and coat the shellfish and vegetable kebabs (kabobs). Cover and leave to chill for about 2 hours.

4 Preheat the grill (broiler) to hot. Place the kebabs (kabobs) on the rack, brush the shellfish and vegetables with oil and cook for 2–3 minutes on each side until the prawns (shrimp) turn pink, the scallops become opaque and the vegetables are soft.

5 Mix together the dip ingredients.

6 Remove the foil and transfer the kebabs (kabobs) to a warm serving platter. Garnish with sliced chilli and serve with the dip.

Tuna Steaks with Fragrant Spices & Lime

Serves 4

INGREDIENTS

4 tuna steaks, 175 g/6 oz each
$\frac{1}{2}$ tsp finely grated lime rind
1 garlic clove, crushed
2 tsp olive oil
1 tsp ground cumin

1 tsp ground coriander
pepper
1 tbsp lime juice
fresh coriander (cilantro), to
    garnish

TO SERVE:
avocado relish (see Cook's Tip,
    below)
lime wedges
tomato wedges

1 Trim the skin from the tuna steaks, rinse and pat dry on absorbent kitchen paper.

2 In a small bowl, mix together the lime rind, garlic, olive oil, cumin, ground coriander and pepper to make a paste.

3 Spread the paste thinly on both sides of the tuna. Heat a non-stick, ridged frying pan (skillet) until hot and press the tuna steaks into the pan to seal

them. Lower the heat and cook for 5 minutes. Turn the fish over and cook for a further 4–5 minutes until the fish is cooked through. Drain on absorbent kitchen paper and transfer to a serving plate.

4 Sprinkle the lime juice and chopped coriander (cilantro) over the fish.

5 Serve with freshly made avocado relish (see Cook's Tip, right), lime wedges and tomatoes.

COOK'S TIP

For low-fat avocado relish to serve with tuna, peel and remove the stone from one small ripe avocado. Toss in 1 tbsp lime juice. Mix in 1 tbsp freshly chopped coriander (cilantro) and 1 small finely chopped red onion. Stir in some chopped fresh mango or a chopped medium tomato and season well.

Baked Trout Mexican-Style

Serves 4

INGREDIENTS

4 trout, 225 g/8 oz each
1 small bunch fresh coriander (cilantro)
4 shallots, shredded finely
1 small yellow (bell) pepper, deseeded and very finely chopped

1 small red (bell) pepper, deseeded and very finely chopped
2 green chillies, deseeded and finely chopped
1–2 red chillies, deseeded and finely chopped

1 tbsp lemon juice
1 tbsp white wine vinegar
2 tsp caster (superfine) sugar
salt and pepper
fresh coriander (cilantro), to garnish
salad leaves, to serve

1 Preheat the oven to 180°C/350°F/Gas Mark 4. Wash the trout and pat dry with absorbent kitchen paper. Season the cavities with salt and pepper and fill with a few coriander (cilantro) leaves.

2 Place the fish side by side in a shallow ovenproof dish. Sprinkle over the shallots, (bell) peppers and chillies.

3 Mix together the lemon juice, vinegar and sugar in a bowl. Spoon over the trout and season to taste. Cover the dish and bake for 30 minutes or until the fish is tender and the flesh is opaque.

4 Remove the the fish with a fish slice and drain. Transfer to warm serving plates and spoon the cooking juices over the fish. Garnish with fresh coriander (cilantro) and serve immediately with chilli bean rice, if you wish (see Cook's Tip, right).

COOK'S TIP

To make chilli bean rice to serve with this recipe, cook 225 g/8 oz/1¼ cup long-grain white rice in boiling water. Drain and return to the pan. Drain and rinse a 400 g/14 oz can kidney beans and stir into the rice along with 1 tsp each of ground cumin and ground coriander. Stir in 4 tbsp freshly chopped coriander (cilantro) and season well.

Blackened Fish

Serves 4

INGREDIENTS

4 white fish steaks
1 tbsp paprika
1 tsp dried thyme
1 tsp cayenne pepper

1 tsp freshly ground black
  pepper
$^1/_2$ tsp freshly ground white
  pepper

$^1/_2$ tsp salt
$^1/_4$ tsp ground allspice
50 g/1$^3/_4$ oz unsalted butter
3 tbsp sunflower oil

1 Rinse the fish steaks and pat them dry with absorbent kitchen paper.

2 Mix together the paprika, thyme, cayenne peppers, black and white peppers, salt and allspice in a shallow dish.

3 Place the butter and oil in a small saucepan and heat, stirring occasionally, until the butter melts.

4 Brush the butter mixture liberally all over the fish steaks, on both sides.

5 Dip the fish into the spicy mix until well coated on both sides.

6 Barbecue (grill) the fish over hot coals for about 10 minutes on each side, turning once. Continue to baste the blackened fish with the remaining butter mixture during the cooking time.

COOK'S TIP

Basting the fish with the butter mixture will ensure that the fish remains moist during cooking.

VARIATION

A whole fish - red mullet, for example - rather than steaks is also delicious cooked this way. The spicy seasoning can also be used to coat chicken portions, if you prefer.

Monkfish Skewers with Courgette & Lemon

Serves 4

INGREDIENTS

450 g/1 lb monkfish tail	SAUCE:	salt
2 courgettes (zucchini)	4 tbsp olive oil	
1 lemon	2 tbsp lemon juice	TO SERVE:
12 cherry tomatoes	1 tsp chopped, fresh thyme	green salad leaves
8 bay leaves	$\frac{1}{2}$ tsp lemon pepper	fresh, crusty bread

1 Using a sharp knife, cut the monkfish into 5 cm/2 inch chunks. Cut the courgettes (zucchini) into thick slices and the lemon into wedges.

2 Thread the monkfish, courgettes (zucchini), lemon, tomatoes and bay leaves on to 4 skewers.

3 To make the basting sauce, combine the oil, lemon juice, thyme, lemon pepper and salt to taste in a small bowl.

4 Brush the basting sauce liberally all over the fish, lemon, tomatoes and bay leaves on the skewers.

5 Cook the skewers on the barbecue (grill) for about 15 minutes, basting frequently with the sauce, until the fish is cooked through.

6 Serve the kebabs with green salad leaves and warm, fresh crusty bread.

VARIATION

Use plaice (flounder) fillets instead of the monkfish, if you prefer. Allow two fillets per person, and skin and cut each fillet lengthwise into two. Roll up each piece and thread them on to the skewers.

Monkfish Skewers with Coconut & Coriander

Serves 4

INGREDIENTS

450 g/1 lb monkfish tails
225 g/8 oz uncooked peeled
    prawns (shrimp)
desiccated (shredded) coconut,
    toasted, to garnish (optional)

MARINADE:
1 tsp sunflower oil
$\frac{1}{2}$ small onion, finely grated
1 tsp root (fresh) ginger, grated

150 ml/5 fl oz/$\frac{2}{3}$ cup canned
    coconut milk
2 tbsp chopped, fresh coriander
    (cilantro)

1 To make the marinade, heat the oil in a wok or saucepan and fry the onion and ginger for 5 minutes until just softened but not browned.

2 Add the coconut milk to the pan and bring to the boil. Boil rapidly for about 5 minutes or until reduced to the consistency of single (light) cream.

3 Remove the pan from the heat and allow to cool completely. Once cooled, stir in the coriander (cilantro) and pour into a shallow dish.

4 Cut the fish into bite-sized chunks and stir gently into the coconut mixture with the prawns (shrimp). Chill in the refrigerator for 1–4 hours.

5 Thread the fish and prawns (shrimp) on to skewers and discard any remaining marinade.

Barbecue (grill) over hot coals for 10–15 minutes, turning often. Garnish with toasted coconut.

VARIATION

Look out for uncooked prawns (shrimp) in the freezer cabinet in large supermarkets. If you cannot find them, use cooked prawns (shrimp), but they only need heating through.

Charred Tuna Steaks

Serves 4

INGREDIENTS

4 tuna steaks
3 tbsp soy sauce
1 tbsp Worcestershire sauce
1 tsp wholegrain mustard

1 tsp caster (superfine) sugar
1 tbsp sunflower oil
green salad, to serve

TO GARNISH:
flat-leaf parsley
lemon wedges

1 Place the tuna steaks in a shallow dish.

2 Mix together the soy sauce, Worcestershire sauce, mustard, sugar and oil in a small bowl. Pour the marinade over the tuna steaks.

3 Gently turn over the tuna steaks, using your fingers or a fork, so that they are well coated with the marinade.

4 Cover and place the tuna steaks in the refrigerator and leave to chill for up to 2 hours.

5 Barbecue (grill) the marinated fish over hot coals for 10–15 minutes, turning once. Baste frequently the marinade.

6 Garnish with flat-leaf parsley and lemon wedges, and serve with a fresh green salad.

COOK'S TIP

Tuna has a dark red flesh, which turns paler on cooking. Tuna has a good meaty texture, but if you are unable to obtain it, use swordfish steaks instead.

COOK'S TIP

If a marinade contains soy sauce, the marinating time should be limited, usually to 2 hours. If allowed to marinate for too long, the fish will dry out and become tough.

Chargrilled Bream

Serves 2

INGREDIENTS

2 small sea bream, scaled, gutted, trimmed and cleaned	BASTE:	TO GARNISH:
2 slices lemon	4 tbsp olive oil	fresh bay leaves
2 bay leaves	2 tbsp lemon juice	fresh thyme sprig
salt and pepper	1/2 tsp chopped, fresh oregano	lemon wedges
	1/2 tsp chopped, fresh thyme	

1 Using a sharp knife, cut 2–3 deep slashes into the bodies of both fish in order to help them fully absorb the flavour of the basting sauce.

2 Place a slice of lemon and a bay leaf inside the cavity of each fish. Season inside the cavity with salt and pepper.

3 In a small bowl, mix together the ingredients for the baste using a fork. Alternatively, place the basting ingredients in a small screw-top jar and shake well to combine.

4 Brush some of the baste liberally over the fish and place them on a rack over hot coals. Barbecue (grill) over hot coals for 20-30 minutes, turning and basting frequently.

5 Transfer the fish to a serving plate, garnish with fresh bay leaves, thyme and lemon wedges and serve.

VARIATION

If you prefer, use brill or a fish like gurnand instead of the sea bream.

COOK'S TIP

The flavour of the dish will be enhanced if you use good fresh ingredients in the sauce. Dried herbs can be used, but remember that the flavour is much more intense, so only use half the quantity of the fresh herbs listed above.

Salmon Yakitori

Serves 4

INGREDIENTS

350 g/12 oz chunky salmon fillet	YAKITORI SAUCE:	5 tbsp dry white wine
8 baby leeks	5 tbsp light soy sauce	3 tbsp sweet sherry
	5 tbsp fish stock	1 clove garlic, crushed
	2 tbsp caster (superfine) sugar	

1 Skin the salmon and cut the flesh into 5 cm/2 inch chunks. Trim the leeks and cut them into 5 cm/2 inch lengths.

2 Thread the salmon and leeks alternately on to 8 pre-soaked wooden skewers. Leave to chill in the refrigerator until required.

3 To make the sauce, place all of the ingredients in a small pan and heat gently, stirring, until the sugar dissolves. Bring to the boil, then reduce the heat and simmer for 2 minutes. Strain the sauce and leave to cool.

4 Pour about one-third of the sauce into a small dish and set aside to serve with the kebabs (kabobs).

5 Brush plenty of the remaining sauce over the skewers and cook directly on the rack or, if preferred, place a sheet of oiled kitchen foil on the rack and cook the salmon on that. Barbecue (grill) the skewers over hot coals for about 10 minutes, turning once. Baste frequently during cooking with the remaining sauce to prevent the fish and vegetables from drying out. Serve the kebebs (kabobs) with the reserved sauce for dipping.

COOK'S TIP

Soak the wooden skewers in cold water for at least 30 minutes to prevent them from burning during cooking. You can make the kebabs (kabobs) and sauce several hours before required and refrigerate.

Salmon Brochettes

Serves 4

INGREDIENTS

450 g/1 lb salmon, skinned and
    cut into large chunks
1 tbsp cornflour (cornstarch)
½ tsp salt
½ tsp pepper
1 small egg white, beaten
1 red (bell) pepper, deseeded and
    cut into chunks

1 green (bell) pepper, deseeded
    and cut into chunks
4 tbsp olive oil
ciabatta bread, to serve

TOMATO SAUCE:
4 tomatoes, deseeded and
    quartered

¼ cucumber, peeled, deseeded
    and chopped
8 basil leaves
6 tbsp olive oil
2 tbsp lemon juice
salt and pepper

1 Place the salmon in a
shallow dish and
sprinkle over the cornflour
(cornstarch), and salt and
pepper to taste. Add the
beaten egg white and toss
well to coat. Leave to chill
for 15 minutes.

2 Thread the pieces
of salmon on to 4
skewers, alternating the
fish pieces with the chunks
of red and green (bell)
peppers. Set the skewers
aside until required.

3 To make the sauce,
place all of the
ingredients in a food
processor and chop
coarsely. Alternatively, chop
the tomatoes, cucumber
and basil leaves by hand
and mix with the oil, lemon
juice and seasoning. Leave
to chill.

4 To serve, barbecue
(grill) the salmon
brochettes over hot coals
for 10 minutes, brushing
frequently with olive oil to

prevent them from drying
during cooking.

5 Slice the ciabatta bread
at an angle to produce
4 long slices. Lightly toast
on the barbecue (grill).

6 Spread the sauce over
each slice of bread and
top with a brochette. You
can serve the brochettes on
toasted French sticks.

Japanese-Style Chargrilled Flounder

Serves 4

INGREDIENTS

4 small plaice (flounders)	2 tbsp light muscovado sugar	TO GARNISH:
6 tbsp soy sauce	1 tsp root (fresh) ginger, grated	1 small carrot
2 tbsp sake or dry white wine	1 clove garlic, crushed	4 spring onions (scallion)
2 tbsp sesame oil		
1 tbsp lemon juice		

1 Rinse the fish and pat them dry on absorbent kitchen paper. Cut a few slashes into both sides of each fish.

2 Mix together the soy sauce, sake or wine, oil, lemon juice, sugar, ginger and garlic in a large, shallow dish.

3 Place the fish in the marinade and turn so that they are coated on both sides. Chill in the refrigerator for 1–6 hours.

4 Meanwhile, prepare the garnish. Cut the carrot into evenly-sized thin sticks and clean and shred the spring onions (scallions).

5 Barbecue (grill) the fish over hot coals for about 10 minutes, turning the fish once.

6 Scatter the spring onions (scallions) and carrot over the fish and transfer the fish to a serving dish. Serve immediately.

VARIATION

Use sole instead of the plaice (flounders) and scatter over some toasted sesame seeds instead of the carrot and spring onions (scallions), if you prefer.

Smoky Fish Skewers

Serves 4

INGREDIENTS

350 g/12 oz smoked cod fillet
350 g/12 oz cod fillet
8 large raw prawns (shrimp)
8 bay leaves
fresh dill, to garnish (optional)

MARINADE:
4 tbsp sunflower oil
2 tbsp lemon or lime juice
rind of $\frac{1}{2}$ lemon or lime, grated
$\frac{1}{4}$ tsp dried dill

salt and pepper

1 Skin both types of cod and cut the flesh into bite-size pieces. Peel the prawns (shrimp), leaving just the tail.

2 To make the marinade, combine the sunflower oil, lemon or lime juice, grated lemon or lime rind, dried dill and salt and pepper to taste in a shallow, non-metallic dish.

3 Place the fish in the marinade and stir until the fish is well coated on all sides. Leave to marinate for 1–4 hours.

4 Thread the fish on to 4 skewers, alternating the 2 types of cod with the prawns (shrimp) and bay leaves.

5 Cover the rack with lightly buttered kitchen foil and place the fish skewers on top of the foil.

6 Barbecue (grill) the fish skewers over hot coals for 5-10 minutes, basting with any remaining marinade, turning once.

7 Garnish with fresh dill and serve.

COOK'S TIP

Cod fillet can be rather flaky, so choose the thicker end which is easier to cut into chunky pieces. Line the rack with kitchen foil rather than cooking the fish directly on the rack so that, even if the fish does break away from the skewer, it is not wasted.

Apricot Chargrilled Mackerel

Serves 4

INGREDIENTS

4 mackerel

400 g/14 oz can apricots
   in natural juice

3 tbsp dark muscovado sugar

3 tbsp Worcestershire sauce

3 tbsp soy sauce

2 tbsp tomato purée (paste)

1 tsp ground ginger

dash Tabasco sauce

1 clove garlic, crushed (optional)

salt and pepper

1 Clean and gut the mackerel, removing the heads if preferred. Place the fish in a large, shallow dish.

2 Drain the apricots, reserving the juice. Roughly chop half of the apricots and set aside until required.

3 Place the remaining apricots in a food processor with the sugar, Worcestershire sauce, soy sauce, tomato purée (paste), ginger, Tabasco sauce and garlic (if using) and process until smooth. Alternatively, chop the apricots and mix with the other ingredients.

4 Pour the sauce over the fish, turning them so that they are well coated on both sides. Leave to chill in the refrigerator.

5 Transfer the mackerel to the barbecue (grill) either directly on the rack or on a piece of greased kitchen foil. Barbecue (grill) the mackerel over hot coals for 5–7 minutes, turning once.

6 Spoon any remaining marinade into a saucepan. Add the reserved chopped apricots and about half of the reserved apricot juice and bring to the boil. Reduce the heat and simmer for 2 minutes.

7 Transfer the mackerel to a serving plate and serve with the sauce.

COOK'S TIP

Use a hinged rack if you have one as it will make it much easier to turn the fish during barbecueing (grilling).

Mackerel with Lime & Coriander

Serves 4

INGREDIENTS

4 small mackerel, trout or sardines	3 tbsp chopped, fresh coriander (cilantro)	2 tbsp sunflower oil
¼ tsp ground coriander	1 red chilli, deseeded and chopped	salt and pepper
¼ tsp ground cumin	grated rind and juice of 1 lime	1 lime, sliced, to garnish
4 sprigs fresh coriander (cilantro)		chilli flowers, to garnish (optional)
		salad leaves, to serve

1 To make the chilli flowers (if using), cut the tip of a small chilli lengthwise into thin strips, leaving the chilli intact at the stem end. Remove the seeds and place in iced water until curled.

2 Clean and gut the mackerel, removing the heads if preferred. Place on a chopping board.

3 Sprinkle the fish with the ground spices and salt and pepper to taste. Place a sprig of coriander (cilantro) inside the cavity of each fish.

4 Mix together the chopped coriander (cilantro), chilli, lime rind and juice and the oil in a small bowl. Brush the mixture liberally over the fish.

5 Place the fish in a hinged rack if you have one. Barbecue (grill) the fish over hot coals for 3–4 minutes on each side, turning once. Brush frequently with the remaining basting mixture.

6 Garnish with lime slices and chilli flowers, if using, and serve with salad leaves.

Mediterranean-Style Sardines

Serves 4

INGREDIENTS

8–12 fresh sardines
8–12 sprigs of fresh thyme
3 tbsp lemon juice

4 tbsp olive oil
salt and pepper

TO GARNISH:
lemon wedges
tomato slices
fresh herbs

1 Clean and gut the fish if this has not already been done.

2 Remove the scales by rubbing the back of a knife from head to tail along the body. Wash and pat the sardines dry on absorbent kitchen paper.

3 Tuck a sprig of fresh thyme into the body of each sardine. Transfer the sardines to a large, non-metallic dish and season with salt and pepper.

4 Beat together the lemon juice and oil in a bowl and pour the mixture over the sardines. Leave the sardines to marinate in the refrigerator for about 30 minutes.

5 Remove the sardines from the marinade and place them in a hinged basket, if you have one, or on a rack. Barbecue (grill) the sardines over hot coals for 3–4 minutes on each side, basting frequently with any of the remaining marinade.

6 Serve garnished with lemon wedges, tomato slices and fresh herbs.

COOK'S TIP

Look out for small sardines or sprats. Prepare them as above and use the same marinade. Place a piece of greased kitchen foil on the rack and cook over hot coals for 2–3 minutes on each side.

VARIATION

For a slightly different flavour and texture, toss the fish in dried breadcrumbs, then baste with a little olive oil for a crispy coating.

Barbecued Herrings with Lemon

Serves 4

INGREDIENTS

4 herrings, cleaned
4 bay leaves
salt

1 lemon, sliced
50 g/1¾ oz unsalted butter
2 tbsp chopped, fresh parsley

½ tsp lemon pepper
fresh crusty bread, to serve

1 Season the prepared herrings inside and out with freshly ground salt to taste.

2 Place a bay leaf inside the cavity of each fish.

3 Place 4 squares of kitchen foil on the work surface and divide the lemon slices evenly among them. Place a fish on top of the lemon slices.

4 Beat the butter until softened, then mix in the parsley and lemon pepper. Dot the flavoured butter liberally all over the fish.

5 Wrap the fish tightly in the kitchen foil and barbecue (grill) over medium hot coals for 15-20 minutes or until the fish is cooked through – the flesh should be white in colour and firm to the touch (unwrap the foil to check, then wrap up the fish again).

6 Transfer the wrapped fish parcels to individual, warm serving plates.

7 Unwrap the foil parcels just before serving and serve the fish with fresh, crusty bread to mop up the deliciously flavoured cooking juices.

VARIATION

For a main course use trout instead of herring. Cook for 20–30 minutes until the flesh is firm to the touch and opaque in colour.

Teriyaki Stir-Fried Salmon with Crispy Leeks

Serves 4

INGREDIENTS

450 g/1 lb salmon fillet, skinned	1 tsp rice wine vinegar	4 tbsp corn oil
2 tbsp sweet soy sauce	1 tbsp demerara sugar	450 g/1 lb leeks, thinly shredded
2 tbsp tomato ketchup	1 clove garlic, crushed	finely chopped red chillies, to garnish

1 Using a sharp knife, cut the salmon into slices. Place the slices of salmon in a shallow non-metallic dish.

2 Mix together the soy sauce, tomato ketchup, rice wine vinegar, sugar and garlic.

3 Pour the mixture over the salmon, toss well and leave to marinate for about 30 minutes.

4 Meanwhile, heat 3 tablespoons of the corn oil in a large preheated wok.

5 Add the leeks to the wok and stir-fry over a medium high heat for about 10 minutes, or until the leeks become crispy and tender.

6 Using a slotted spoon, carefully remove the leeks from the wok and transfer to warmed serving plates.

7 Add the remaining oil to the wok. Add the salmon and the marinade to the wok and cook for 2 minutes. Spoon over the leeks, garnish and serve immediately.

VARIATION

You can use a fillet of beef instead of the salmon, if you prefer.

Stir-Fried Salmon with Pineapple

Serves 4

INGREDIENTS

100 g/3¾ oz/1 cup baby corn cobs, halved

2 tbsp sunflower oil

1 red onion, sliced

1 orange (bell) pepper, deseeded and sliced

1 green (bell) pepper, deseeded and sliced

450 g/1 lb salmon fillet, skin removed

1 tbsp paprika

225 g/8 oz can cubed pineapple, drained

100 g/3½ oz/1 cup beansprouts

2 tbsp tomato ketchup

2 tbsp soy sauce

2 tbsp medium sherry

1 tsp cornflour (cornstarch)

1 Using a sharp knife, cut the baby corn cobs in half.

2 Heat the sunflower oil in a large preheated wok. Add the onion, (bell) peppers and baby corn cobs to the wok and stir-fry for 5 minutes.

3 Rinse the salmon fillet under cold running water and pat dry with absorbent kitchen paper.

4 Cut the salmon flesh into thin strips and place in a large bowl.

Sprinkle with the paprika and toss until well coated.

5 Add the salmon to the wok together with the pineapple and stir-fry for a further 2–3 minutes or until the fish is tender.

6 Add the beansprouts to the wok and toss well.

7 Mix together the tomato ketchup, soy sauce, sherry and cornflour (cornstarch). Add the mixture to the wok and cook until the juices start to thicken. Transfer to warm

serving plates and serve immediately.

VARIATION

You can use trout fillets instead of the salmon as an alternative, if you prefer.

Tuna & Vegetable Stir-Fry

Serves 4

INGREDIENTS

225 g/8 oz carrots
2 tbsp corn oil
1 onion, sliced
175 g/6 oz/2½ cups mangetout
(snow peas)

175 g/6 oz/1¾ cups baby corn cobs,
halved
450 g/1 lb fresh tuna
2 tbsp fish sauce
15 g/½ oz/1 tbsp palm sugar

finely grated zest and juice of 1
orange
2 tbsp sherry
1 tsp cornflour (cornstarch)
rice or noodles, to serve

1 Using a sharp knife, cut the carrots into thin sticks.

2 Heat the corn oil in a large preheated wok.

3 Add the onion, carrots, mangetout (snow peas) and baby corn cobs to the wok and stir-fry for 5 minutes.

4 Using a sharp knife, thinly slice the tuna.

5 Add the tuna to the wok and stir-fry for 2–3 minutes, or until the tuna turns opaque.

6 Mix together the fish sauce, palm sugar, orange zest and juice, sherry and cornflour (cornstarch).

7 Pour the mixture over the tuna and vegetables and cook for 2 minutes, or until the juices thicken. Serve with rice or noodles.

VARIATION

Try using swordfish steaks instead of the tuna. Swordfish steaks are now widely available and are similar in texture to tuna.

COOK'S TIP

Palm sugar is a thick, coarse brown sugar that has a slightly caramel taste. It is sold in round cakes or in small, round, flat containers.

Stir-Fried Cod with Mango

Serves 4

INGREDIENTS

175 g/6 oz carrots	1 green (bell) pepper, deseeded	1 tbsp soy sauce
2 tbsp vegetable oil	and sliced	100 ml/3 1/2 fl oz/1 1/3 cup tropical fruit
1 red onion, sliced	450 g/1 lb skinless cod fillet	juice
1 red (bell) pepper, deseeded and	1 ripe mango	1 tbsp lime juice
sliced	1 tsp cornflour (cornstarch)	1 tbsp chopped coriander (cilantro)

1 Using a sharp knife, slice the carrots into thin sticks.

2 Heat the vegetable oil in a preheated wok.

3 Add the onions, carrots and (bell) peppers to the wok and stir-fry for 5 minutes.

4 Using a sharp knife, cut the cod into small cubes.

5 Peel the mango, then carefully remove the flesh from the centre stone. Cut the flesh into thin slices.

6 Add the cod and mango to the wok and stir-fry for a further 4–5 minutes, or until the fish is cooked through. Do not stir the mixture too much or you may break the fish up.

7 Mix the cornflour (cornstarch), soy sauce, fruit juice and lime juice in a small bowl.

8 Pour the cornflour (cornstarch) mixture over the stir-fry and allow the mixture to bubble and the juices to thicken. Scatter with coriander (cilantro) and serve immediately.

VARIATION

You can use paw-paw (papaya) as an alternative to the mango, if you prefer.

Stir-Fried Gingered Monkfish

Serves 4

INGREDIENTS

450 g/1 lb monkfish
1 tbsp freshly grated root ginger
2 tbsp sweet chilli sauce

1 tbsp corn oil
100 g/3½ oz/1 cup fine asparagus

3 spring onions (scallions), sliced
1 tsp sesame oil

1 Using a sharp knife, slice the monkfish into thin flat rounds.

2 Mix the ginger with the chilli sauce in a small bowl.

3 Brush the ginger and chilli sauce mixture over the monkfish pieces.

4 Heat the corn oil in a large preheated wok.

5 Add the monkfish, asparagus and spring onions (scallions) to the wok and stir-fry for about 5 minutes.

6 Remove the wok from the heat, drizzle the sesame oil over the stir-fry and toss well to combine.

7 Transfer to warm serving plates and serve immediately.

VARIATION

Monkfish is quite expensive, but it is well worth using it as it has a wonderful flavour and texture. At a push you could use cubes of chunky cod fillet instead.

COOK'S TIP

Some recipes specify to grate ginger before it is cooked with other ingredients. To do this, just peel the flesh and rub it at a 45° angle up and down on the fine section of a metal grater, or use a special wooden or ceramic ginger grater.

Braised Fish Fillets

Serves 4

INGREDIENTS

3–4 small Chinese dried mushrooms
300–350 g/10^1/$_2$–12 oz fish fillets
1 tsp salt
^{1}/$_2$ egg white, lightly beaten
1 tsp cornflour (cornstarch) paste
600 ml/1 pint/2^1/$_2$ cups vegetable oil
1 tsp finely chopped ginger root

2 spring onions (scallions), finely
    chopped
1 garlic clove, finely chopped
^{1}/$_2$ small green (bell) pepper,
    deseeded and cut into small cubes
^{1}/$_2$ small carrot, thinly sliced
60 g/2 oz/^{1}/$_2$ cup canned sliced bamboo
    shoots, rinsed and drained

^{1}/$_2$ tsp sugar
1 tbsp light soy sauce
1 tsp rice wine or dry sherry
1 tbsp chilli bean sauce
2–3 tbsp Chinese stock or water
a few drops of sesame oil

1 Soak the dried mushrooms in a bowl of warm water for 30 minutes. Drain the mushrooms thoroughly on paper towels, reserving the soaking water for stock or soup. Squeeze the mushrooms to extract all of the moisture, cut off and discard any hard stems and slice thinly.

2 Cut the fish into bite-sized pieces, then place in a shallow dish and mix with a pinch of salt, the egg white and cornflour (cornstarch) paste, turning the fish to coat well.

3 Heat the oil in a preheated wok. Add the fish pieces to the wok and deep-fry for about 1 minute. Remove the fish pieces with a slotted spoon and leave to drain on paper towels.

4 Pour off the excess oil, leaving about 1 tablespoon in the wok. Add the ginger, spring onions (scallions) and garlic to flavour the oil for a few seconds, then add the (bell) pepper, carrots and bamboo shoots and stir-fry for about 1 minute.

5 Add the sugar, soy sauce, wine, chilli bean sauce, stock or water, and the remaining salt and bring to the boil. Add the fish pieces, stir to coat well with the sauce, and braise for 1 minute.

6 Sprinkle with sesame oil and serve immediately.

Chinese Leaves with Shiitake Mushrooms & Crab Meat

Serves 4

INGREDIENTS

225 g/8 oz shiitake mushrooms
2 tbsp vegetable oil
2 cloves garlic, crushed
6 spring onions (scallions), sliced

1 head Chinese leaves, shredded
1 tbsp mild curry paste
6 tbsp coconut milk

200 g/7 oz can white crab meat,
    drained
1 tsp chilli flakes

1 Using a sharp knife, cut the the mushrooms into slices.

2 Heat the vegetable oil in a large preheated wok.

3 Add the mushrooms and garlic to the wok and stir-fry for 3 minutes or until the mushrooms have softened.

4 Add the spring onions (scallions) and shredded Chinese leaves to the wok and stir-fry until the leaves have wilted.

5 Mix together the mild curry paste and coconut milk in a small bowl.

6 Add the curry paste and coconut milk mixture to the wok together with the crab meat and chilli flakes. Mix together until well combined and heat through until the juices start to bubble.

7 Transfer to warm serving bowls and then serve immediately.

COOK'S TIP

Shiitake mushrooms are now readily available in the fresh vegetable section of most large supermarkets.

Stir-Fried Lettuce with Mussels & Lemon Grass

Serves 4

INGREDIENTS

1 kg/2 lb 4oz mussels in their shells, scrubbed	2 tbsp lemon juice	1 Iceberg lettuce
	100 ml/3 1/2 fl oz/ 1/3 cup water	finely grated zest of 1 lemon
2 stalks lemon grass, thinly sliced	25 g/1 oz/2 tbsp butter	2 tbsp oyster sauce

1 Place the mussels in a large saucepan.

2 Add the lemon grass, lemon juice and water to the pan of mussels, cover with a tight-fitting lid and cook for 5 minutes or until the mussels have opened. Discard any mussels that do not open.

3 Carefully remove the cooked mussels from their shells, using a fork.

4 Heat the butter in a large preheated wok.

5 Add the lettuce and lemon zest to the wok and stir-fry for 2 minutes, or until the lettuce begins to wilt.

6 Add the oyster sauce to the mixture in the wok, stir and heat through. Serve immediately.

COOK'S TIP

Lemon grass with its citrus fragrance and lemon flavour looks like a fibrous spring onion (scallion) and is often used in Thai cooking.

COOK'S TIP

When using fresh mussels, be sure to discard any opened mussels before scrubbing and any unopened mussels after cooking.

Mussels in Black Bean Sauce with Spinach

Serves 4

INGREDIENTS

350 g/12 oz leeks

350 g/12 oz cooked green-lipped
  mussels (shelled)

1 tsp cumin seeds

2 tbsp vegetable oil

2 cloves garlic, crushed

1 red (bell) pepper, deseeded and
  sliced

50 g/1³/₄ oz/³/₄ cup canned bamboo
  shoots, drained

175 g/6 oz baby spinach

160 g/5³/₄ oz jar black bean sauce

1 Using a sharp knife, trim the leeks and shred them.

2 Place the mussels in a large bowl, sprinkle with the cumin seeds and toss well to coat all over.

3 Heat the vegetable oil in a large preheated wok.

4 Add the leeks, garlic and red (bell) pepper to the wok and stir-fry for 5 minutes, or until the vegetables are tender.

5 Add the bamboo shoots, baby spinach leaves and cooked green-lipped mussels to the wok and stir-fry for about 2 minutes.

6 Pour the black bean sauce over the ingredients in the wok, toss well to coat all over and leave to simmer for a few seconds, stirring occasionally.

7 Transfer the stir-fry to warm serving bowls and serve immediately.

COOK'S TIP

If the green-lipped mussels are not available they can be bought shelled in cans and jars from most large supermarkets.

Prawns with Peppers

Serves 4

INGREDIENTS

450 g/1 lb frozen prawns
   (shrimp)
$\frac{1}{2}$ bunch fresh coriander
   (cilantro) leaves

1 tsp fresh garlic, crushed
1 tsp salt
1 medium green (bell) pepper,
   sliced

1 medium red (bell) pepper
75 g/2$\frac{3}{4}$ oz/5$\frac{1}{2}$ tbsp unsalted
   butter

1 Defrost the prawns (shrimp). Once they are completely thawed, rinse them under cold running water twice. Drain the prawns (shrimp) thoroughly and place in a large mixing bowl.

2 Using a sharp knife, finely chop the bunch of fresh coriander (cilantro) leaves.

3 Add the garlic, salt and fresh, chopped coriander (cilantro) leaves to the prawns (shrimp), then set the bowl aside until required.

4 Deseed the (bell) peppers and cut into thin slices, using a sharp knife.

5 Melt the butter in a large frying pan (skillet). Add the prawns (shrimp) to the pan and stir-fry, stirring and tossing the prawns (shrimp) gently, for 10-12 minutes.

6 Add the (bell) peppers to the pan and fry for a further 3-5 minutes, stirring occasionally.

7 Transfer the prawns (shrimp) and (bell) pepper to a serving dish and serve hot.

VARIATION

You could use large tiger prawns (shrimp) in this dish, if you prefer.

Prawns with Spinach

Serves 4-6

INGREDIENTS

225 g/8 oz frozen prawns (shrimp)	2 tomatoes	1 tsp fresh ginger root, finely chopped
350 g/12 oz canned spinach purée or frozen spinach, thawed and chopped	150 ml/¹/₄ pint/²/₃ cup oil ¹/₂ tsp mustard seeds ¹/₂ tsp onion seeds	1 tsp fresh garlic, crushed 1 tsp chilli powder 1 tsp salt

1 Place the prawns (shrimp) in a bowl of cold water and set aside to defrost thoroughly.

2 Drain the can of spinach purée, if using.

3 Using a sharp knife, cut the tomatoes into slices and set aside.

4 Heat the oil in a large frying pan (skillet). Add the mustard and onion seeds to the pan.

5 Reduce the heat and add the tomatoes,

spinach, ginger, garlic, chilli powder and salt to the pan and stir-fry for about 5-7 minutes.

6 Drain the prawns (shrimp) thoroughly.

7 Add the prawns (shrimp) to the spinach mixture in the pan. Gently stir the prawn (shrimp) and spinach mixture until well combined, cover and leave to simmer over a low heat for about 7-10 minutes.

8 Transfer the cooked prawns (shrimp) and

spinach to a serving dish and serve hot.

COOK'S TIP

If using frozen spinach, it should be thawed and squeezed dry before using. You could use fresh spinach, if you prefer.

Tandoori-Style Prawns

Serves 4

INGREDIENTS

10-12 king prawns (shrimp)
100 g/3^1/$_2$ oz/8 tbsp unsalted
    butter
1 tsp fresh ginger root, finely
    chopped
1 tsp fresh garlic, crushed
1 tsp chilli powder

^{1}/$_2$ tsp salt
1 tsp ground coriander
1 tsp ground cumin
fresh coriander (cilantro) leaves,
    finely chopped
a few drops of red food
    colouring

TO GARNISH:
8 lettuce leaves
1-2 green chillies, finely chopped
1 lemon, cut into wedges

1 Carefully remove the shells from the king prawns (shrimp).

2 Transfer the shelled prawns (shrimp) to a heatproof dish.

3 Melt the butter in a large saucepan.

4 Add the ginger, garlic, chilli powder, salt, ground coriander, ground cumin, fresh coriander (cilantro) leaves and the red food colouring to the butter and mix together until well combined.

5 Brush the melted butter and spice mixture over the prawns (shrimp).

6 Cook the prawns (shrimp) under a very hot pre-heated grill (broiler) for 10-12 minutes, turning once.

7 Serve the prawns (shrimp) on a bed of lettuce and garnish with finely chopped green chillies and lemon wedges.

COOK'S TIP

Though not essential, it is best to shell the prawns (shrimp) before cooking them as some people find it a bit awkward to shell them at the table.

Dried Prawns

Serves 4

INGREDIENTS

200 g/7 oz dried prawns (shrimp)
2 medium onions, sliced
3 green chillies, finely chopped
fresh coriander (cilantro) leaves,
     finely chopped

150 ml/¼ pint/½ cup oil
1½ tsp fresh ginger root, finely
     chopped
1½ tsp fresh garlic, crushed
pinch of turmeric

1 tsp salt
1 tsp chilli powder, plus extra
     to garnish
2 tbsp lemon juice

1 Soak the prawns (shrimp) in a bowl of cold water for about 2 hours. Drain the prawns (shrimp) thoroughly and rinse under cold running water twice. Drain the prawns (shrimp) again thoroughly.

2 Heat 150 ml/¼ pint/⅔ cup of the oil in a large saucepan. Add the onions, 2 of the green chillies and half of the fresh coriander (cilantro) to the pan and stir-fry until the onions are golden.

3 Add the ginger, garlic, turmeric, salt and chilli powder to the pan and stir-fry for a further 2 minutes over a low heat. Set aside until required.

4 Heat the remaining oil in a separate saucepan. Add the prawns (shrimp) and fry, stirring occasionally, until the prawns (shrimp) are crisp.

5 Add the fried prawns (shrimp) to the onions and blend together. Return the prawn (shrimp) and

onion mixture to the heat, sprinkle with the lemon juice and stir-fry for 3-5 minutes.

6 Transfer to a serving dish, garnish with a pinch of chilli powder and serve with Chapatis.

VARIATION

You could use 450 g/1 lb fresh prawns (shrimp) instead of the dried prawns (shrimp), if you prefer.

Vegetables & Salads

Too frequently, leaf vegetables are overcooked
and limp, with all the goodness and flavour boiled
out, while salads are often nothing more than a
dismal leaf or two of pale green lettuce with a slice
of tomato and a dry ring of onion. Make the most of
the wonderful range of fresh produce that is
available in our shops and markets.

Steam broccoli and cabbage so that they
are colourful and crunchy. Enjoy the wonderfully
appetizing shades of orange and yellow (bell)
peppers and the purple-brown of aubergine
(eggplant). Try grating root vegetables to add
flavour and texture to garnishes and casseroles.
Look out for red and curly lettuces to bring
excitement to an enticing summer salad. Use
sweet baby tomatoes in salads and on skewers,
and raid your garden for sprigs of fresh mint
and basil leaves.

Nuts and seeds are high in fat, so both should
be used in moderation. However, they are a
valuable source of protein and minerals, and
vegetarians and vegans in particular need to ensure
that their diets contain these valuable ingredients.

Vegetable Spaghetti with Lemon Dressing

Serves 4

INGREDIENTS

225 g/8 oz celeriac	1 tbsp lemon juice	1 tbsp lemon juice
2 medium carrots	300 g/10½ oz spaghetti	4 tbsp low-fat natural fromage
2 medium leeks	celery leaves, chopped, to	frais (unsweetened yogurt)
1 small red (bell) pepper	garnish	salt and pepper
1 small yellow (bell) pepper		2 tbsp snipped fresh chives
2 garlic cloves	LEMON DRESSING:	
1 tsp celery seeds	1 tsp finely grated lemon rind	

1 Peel the celeriac and carrots, cut into thin matchsticks and place in a bowl. Slice the leeks, rinse to flush out any trapped dirt, then shred finely. Halve, deseed and slice the (bell) peppers. Peel and thinly slice the garlic. Add these vegetables to the celeriac and the carrots.

2 Toss the vegetables with the celery seeds and lemon juice.

3 Bring a large pan of water to the boil and cook the spaghetti according to the instructions on the packet. Drain well and keep warm.

4 Bring another large saucepan of water to the boil, put the vegetables in a steamer or sieve (strainer) and place over the boiling water. Cover and steam for 6–7 minutes or until just tender.

5 When the spaghetti and vegetables are cooked, mix the ingredients for the lemon dressing together.

6 Transfer the spaghetti and vegetables to a warm serving bowl and mix with the dressing. Garnish with chopped celery leaves and serve.

Pesto Pasta

Serves 4

INGREDIENTS

225 g/8 oz chestnut mushrooms,
    sliced
150 ml/5 fl oz/³/₄ cup fresh
    vegetable stock
175 g/6 oz asparagus, trimmed
    and cut into
    5 cm/2 inch lengths

300 g/10¹/₂ oz green and white
    tagliatelle
400 g/14 oz canned artichoke
    hearts, drained and halved
Grissini (bread sticks), to serve

TO GARNISH:
basil leaves, shredded
Parmesan shavings

PESTO:
2 large garlic cloves, crushed
15 g/¹/₂ oz fresh basil leaves,
    washed
6 tbsp low-fat natural fromage
    frais (unsweetened yogurt)
2 tbsp freshly grated Parmesan
    cheese
salt and pepper

1 Place the mushrooms in a pan with the stock. Bring to the boil, cover and simmer for 3–4 minutes until tender. Drain; set aside.

2 Bring a small pan of water to the boil and cook the asparagus for 3–4 minutes until tender. Drain and set aside.

3 Bring a large pan of lightly salted water to the boil and cook the tagliatelle according to the instructions on the packet. Drain, return to the pan and keep warm.

4 Make the pesto. Place all of the ingredients in a blender or food processor and process for a few seconds until smooth. Alternatively, finely chop the basil and mix all the ingredients together.

5 Add the mushrooms, asparagus and artichoke hearts to the pasta and cook, stirring, over a low heat for 2–3 minutes. Remove from the heat, mix with the pesto and transfer to a warm bowl. Garnish with shredded basil leaves and Parmesan shavings and serve with Grissini (bread sticks), if wished.

Rice-Stuffed Mushrooms

Serves 4

INGREDIENTS

4 large flat mushrooms
100 g/3¹/₂ oz assorted wild
　mushrooms, sliced
4 dry-pack, sun-dried tomatoes,
　shredded
150 ml/5 fl oz/²/₃ cup dry red
　wine

4 spring onions (scallions),
　trimmed and finely chopped
75 g/23/4 oz/1¹/₂ cups cooked
　red rice
2 tbsp freshly grated Parmesan
　cheese
4 thick slices granary bread

salt and pepper
spring onion (scallion), shredded,
　to garnish

1 Preheat the oven to
190°C/375°F/Gas
Mark 5. Peel the flat
mushrooms, pull out the
stalks and set aside. Finely
chop the stalks and place in
a saucepan.

2 Add the wild
mushrooms to the pan
with the tomatoes and red
wine. Bring to the boil,
cover and simmer gently
for 2–3 minutes until just
tender. Drain, reserving the
cooking liquid, and place in
a small bowl.

3 Stir in the spring
onions (scallions) and
cooked rice. Season well
and spoon into the flat
mushrooms, pressing the
mixture down gently.
Sprinkle with the grated
Parmesan cheese.

4 Arrange the
mushrooms in an
ovenproof baking dish and
pour the reserved cooking
juices around them. Bake
in the oven for 20–25
minutes until they are
just cooked.

5 Meanwhile, preheat
the grill (broiler) to
hot. Trim the crusts from
the bread and toast on each
side until lightly browned.

6 Drain the mushrooms
and place each one on
to a piece of toasted bread.
Garnish with spring onions
(scallions) and serve.

Biryani with Caramelised Onions

Serves 4

INGREDIENTS
---

175 g/6 oz/1 cup Basmati rice, rinsed

60 g/2 oz/⅓ cup red lentils, rinsed

1 bay leaf

6 cardamom pods, split

1 tsp ground turmeric

6 cloves

1 tsp cumin seeds

1 cinnamon stick, broken

1 onion, chopped

225 g/8 oz cauliflower, broken into small florets

1 large carrot, diced

100 g/3½ oz frozen peas

60 g/2 oz sultanas (golden raisins)

600 ml/1 pint/2½ cups fresh vegetable stock

salt and pepper

naan bread, to serve

CARAMELIZED ONIONS:

2 tsp vegetable oil

1 medium red onion, shredded

1 medium onion, shredded

2 tsp caster (superfine) sugar

---

1 Place the rice, lentils, bay leaf, spices, onion, cauliflower, carrot, peas and sultanas (golden raisins) in a large saucepan. Season with salt and pepper and mix well.

2 Pour in the stock, bring to the boil, cover and simmer for 15 minutes, stirring occasionally, until the rice is tender. Remove from the heat and leave

to stand, covered, for 10 minutes to allow the stock to be absorbed. Discard the bay leaf, cardamom pods, cloves and cinnamon stick.

3 Meanwhile, make the caramelized onions. Heat the oil in a frying pan (skillet) and fry the onions over a medium heat for 3–4 minutes until just softened. Add the caster (superfine) sugar, raise the heat and

cook, stirring, for a further 2–3 minutes until the onions are golden.

4 Gently mix the rice and vegetables and transfer to warm serving plates. Spoon over the caramelized onions and serve with plain, warmed naan bread.

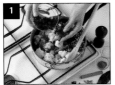

Soft Pancakes with Stir-Fried Vegetables & Tofu

Serves 4

INGREDIENTS

1 tbsp vegetable oil
1 garlic clove, crushed
2.5 cm/1 inch piece root (fresh) ginger, grated
1 bunch spring onions (scallions), trimmed and shredded lengthwise
100 g/3½ oz mangetout (snow peas), topped, tailed and shredded

225 g/8 oz tofu (bean curd), drained and cut into 1 cm/½ inch pieces
2 tbsp dark soy sauce, plus extra to serve
2 tbsp hoi-sin sauce, plus extra to serve
60 g/2 oz canned bamboo shoots, drained
60 g/2 oz canned water chestnuts, drained and sliced

100 g/3½ oz bean sprouts
1 small red chilli, deseeded and sliced thinly
1 small bunch fresh chives
12 soft Chinese pancakes

TO SERVE:
shredded Chinese leaves
1 cucumber, sliced
strips of red chilli

1 Heat the oil in a non-stick wok or a large frying pan (skillet) and stir-fry the garlic and ginger for 1 minute. Add the spring onions (scallions), mangetout (snow peas), tofu (bean curd), soy and hoi-sin sauces. Stir-fry for 2 minutes.

2 Add the bamboo shoots, water chestnuts, bean sprouts and red chilli to the pan. Stir-fry for 2 minutes until the vegetables are tender but still have bite. Snip the chives into 2.5 cm/1 inch lengths and stir them into the mixture in the pan.

3 Heat the pancakes according to the instructions on the packet and keep warm.

4 Divide the vegetables and tofu (bean curd) among the pancakes. Roll up the pancakes and serve with the Chinese leaves.

Chargrilled Mediterranean Vegetable Skewers

Makes 8

INGREDIENTS

1 large red (bell) pepper	2 tbsp lemon juice	TO SERVE:
1 large green (bell) pepper	1 tbsp olive oil	cracked wheat, cooked
1 large orange (bell) pepper	1 garlic clove, crushed	tomato and olive relish
1 large courgette (zucchini)	1 tbsp chopped, fresh rosemary	
4 baby aubergines (eggplant)	or 1 tsp dried rosemary	
2 medium red onions	salt and pepper	

1 Halve and deseed the (bell) peppers and cut into even sized pieces, about 2.5 cm/1 inch wide. Trim the courgettes (zucchini), cut in half lengthwise and slice into 2.5 cm/1 inch pieces. Place the (bell) peppers and courgettes (zucchini) into a large bowl and set aside.

2 Trim the aubergines (eggplant) and quarter them lengthwise. Peel the onions, then cut each one into 8 even-sized wedges. Add the aubergines and onions to the bowl containing the (bell) peppers and courgettes (zucchini).

3 In a small bowl, mix together the lemon juice, olive oil, garlic, rosemary and seasoning. Pour the mixture over the vegetables and stir to coat.

4 Preheat the grill (broiler) to medium.

Thread the vegetables on to 8 skewers. Arrange the kebabs (kabobs) on the rack and cook for 10–12 minutes, turning frequently until the vegetables are lightly charred and just softened.

5 Drain the vegetable kebabs (kabobs) and serve on a bed of cracked wheat accompanied with a tomato and olive relish, if wished.

Stuffed Vegetables Middle-Eastern Style

Serves 4

INGREDIENTS

4 large beefsteak tomatoes

4 medium courgettes (zucchini)

2 orange (bell) peppers

salt and pepper

warm pitta bread and low-fat
   hummus, to serve

FILLING:

225 g/8 oz/1 1/4 cups cracked
   wheat

1/4 cucumber

1 medium red onion

2 tbsp lemon juice

2 tbsp chopped fresh coriander
   (cilantro)

2 tbsp chopped fresh mint

1 tbsp olive oil

2 tsp cumin seeds

1 Preheat the oven to 200°C/400°F/Gas Mark 6. Cut off the tops of the tomatoes and reserve. Scoop out the tomato pulp, chop and place in a bowl. Season the tomato shells, then turn them upside down on kitchen paper.

2 Trim the courgettes (zucchini) and cut a V-shaped groove lengthwise down each one. Finely chop the cut-out courgette (zucchini) flesh and add to the tomato pulp. Season

the courgettes (zucchini) shells and set aside.

3 Halve the (bell) peppers. Leaving the stalks intact, cut out the seeds and discard. Season the (bell) pepper shells.

4 To make the filling, soak the cracked wheat according to the instructions on the packet. Finely chop the cucumber and add to the reserved tomato pulp and courgette (zucchini) mixture.

5 Finely chop the red onion, and add to the vegetable mixture with the lemon juice, herbs, olive oil, cumin and seasoning and mix together well.

6 Mix the wheat with the vegetables and stuff into the tomato, courgette (zucchini) and (bell) pepper shells. Place the tops on the tomatoes, transfer to a roasting tin (pan) and bake for 20–25 minutes until cooked through. Drain and serve.

Fragrant Asparagus & Orange Risotto

Serves 4-6

INGREDIENTS

115 g/4 oz fine asparagus
   spears, trimmed
1.2 litres/2 pints/5 cups
   vegetable stock
2 bulbs fennel
25 g/1 oz low-fat spread

1 tsp olive oil
2 sticks celery, trimmed and
   chopped
2 medium leeks, trimmed
   and shredded

350 g/12 oz/2 cups arborio
   rice
3 medium oranges
salt and pepper

1 Bring a small saucepan of water to the boil and cook the asparagus for 1 minute. Drain and set aside until required.

2 Pour the stock into a saucepan and bring to the boil. Reduce the heat to maintain a gentle simmer.

3 Meanwhile, trim the fennel, reserving the fronds, and cut into thin slices. Carefully melt the low-fat spread with the oil in a large saucepan, taking care that the water in the low-fat spread does not evaporate, and gently fry the fennel, celery and leeks for 3–4 minutes until just softened. Add the rice and cook, stirring, for a further 2 minutes until mixed.

4 Add a ladleful of stock to the pan and cook gently, stirring, until absorbed. Continue ladling the stock into the rice until the rice becomes creamy, thick and tender. This process will take about 25 minutes and shouldn't be hurried.

5 Finely grate the rind and extract the juice from 1 orange and mix in to the rice. Carefully remove the peel and pith from the remaining oranges. Holding the fruit over the saucepan, cut out the orange segments and add to the rice, along with any juice that falls.

6 Stir the orange into the rice along with the asparagus spears. Season with salt and pepper, garnish with the reserved fennel fronds, and serve.

Spicy Black Eye Beans

Serves 4

INGREDIENTS

350 g/12 oz/2 cups black-eyed
   beans, soaked overnight in
   cold water
1 tbsp vegetable oil
2 medium onions, chopped
1 tbsp clear honey
2 tbsp treacle (molasses)
4 tbsp dark soy sauce

1 tsp dry mustard powder
4 tbsp tomato purée (paste)
450 ml/16 fl oz/2 cups fresh
   vegetable stock
1 bay leaf
1 sprig each of rosemary,
   thyme and sage
1 small orange

1 tbsp cornflour (cornstarch)
2 medium red (bell) peppers,
   deseeded and diced
pepper
2 tbsp chopped fresh flat-leaf
   parsley, to garnish
crusty bread, to serve

1 Preheat the oven to 150°C/300°F/Gas Mark 2. Rinse the beans and place in a saucepan. Cover with water, bring to the boil and boil rapidly for 10 minutes. Drain and place in an ovenproof casserole dish.

2 Meanwhile, heat the oil in a frying pan (skillet) and fry the onions for 5 minutes. Stir in the honey, treacle (molasses), soy sauce, mustard and tomato purée (paste). Pour in the stock, bring to the boil and pour the mixture over the beans.

3 Tie the bay leaf, rosemary, thyme and sage together with a clean piece of string and add to the pan containing the beans. Using a vegetable peeler, pare off 3 pieces of orange rind and mix into the beans, along with plenty of pepper. Cover and bake for 1 hour.

4 Extract the juice from the orange and blend with the cornflour (cornstarch) to form a paste. Stir into the beans along with the red (bell) peppers. Cover and cook for 1 hour, until the sauce is rich and thick and the beans are tender. Discard the herbs and orange rind.

5 Garnish with chopped fresh flat-leaf parsley and serve with fresh crusty bread.

Mexican-Style Pizzas

Serves 4

INGREDIENTS

4 x ready-made individual
    pizza bases
1 tbsp olive oil
200 g/7 oz can chopped
    tomatoes with garlic and
    herbs

2 tbsp tomato purée (paste)
200 g/7 oz can kidney beans,
    drained and rinsed
115 g/4 oz sweetcorn kernels,
    thawed if frozen
1–2 tsp chilli sauce

1 large red onion, shredded
100 g/3½ oz reduced-fat
    Cheddar cheese, grated
1 large green chilli, sliced into
    rings
salt and pepper

1 Preheat the oven to 220°C/425°F/Gas Mark 7. Arrange the pizza bases on a baking sheet (cookie sheet) and brush them lightly with the oil.

2 In a bowl, mix together the chopped tomatoes, tomato purée (paste), kidney beans and sweetcorn, and add chilli sauce to taste. Season with salt and pepper.

3 Spread the tomato and kidney bean mixture evenly over each pizza base to cover. Top each pizza with shredded onion and sprinkle with some grated cheese and a few slices of green chilli to taste. Bake in the oven for about 20 minutes until the vegetables are tender, the cheese has melted and the base is crisp and golden.

4 Remove the pizzas from the baking sheet (cookie sheet) and transfer to serving plates. Serve immediately.

COOK'S TIP

For a low-fat Mexican-style salad to serve with this pizza, arrange sliced tomatoes, fresh coriander (cilantro) leaves and a few slices of a small, ripe avocado. Sprinkle with fresh lime juice and coarse sea salt. Avocados have quite a high oil content, so eat in moderation.

Aubergine Pasta Cake

Serves 6-8

INGREDIENTS

1 medium aubergine (eggplant)
300 g/10½ oz tricolour pasta
shapes

115 g/4 oz low-fat soft cheese
with garlic and herbs
350ml/12 fl oz/1⅓ cups passata
(sieved tomatoes)

4 tbsp grated Parmesan cheese
1½ tsp dried oregano
2 tbsp dry white breadcrumbs
salt and pepper

1 Preheat the oven to 190°C/375°F/Gas Mark 5. Grease and line a 20.5 cm/8 inch round spring-form cake tin (pan).

2 Trim the aubergine (eggplant) and cut lengthwise into slices about 5 mm/¼ inch thick. Place in a bowl, sprinkle with salt, and set aside for 30 minutes to remove any bitter juices. Rinse well and drain.

3 Bring a saucepan of water to the boil and blanch the aubergine (eggplant) slices for 1 minute. Drain and pat dry using absorbent kitchen paper. Set aside.

4 Cook the pasta shapes according to the instructions on the packet; for best results, the pasta should be slightly undercooked. Drain well and return to the pan. Add the soft cheese and allow it to melt over the pasta.

5 Stir in the passata (sieved tomatoes), Parmesan cheese, oregano and seasoning. Set aside.

6 Arrange the aubergine (eggplant) over the base and sides of the tin (pan), overlapping the slices so that there are no gaps.

7 Pile the pasta mixture into the tin (pan), packing down well, and sprinkle with breadcrumbs. Bake for 20 minutes and let stand for 15 minutes.

8 Loosen the cake round the edge with a palette knife (spatula) and release from the tin. Turn out aubergine (eggplant) side uppermost and serve hot.

Mushroom Cannelloni

Serves 4

INGREDIENTS

350 g/12 oz chestnut
   mushrooms, chopped finely
1 medium onion, chopped finely
1 garlic clove, crushed
1 tbsp chopped fresh thyme
1/2 tsp ground nutmeg

4 tbsp dry white wine
4 tbsp fresh white breadcrumbs
12 dried 'quick-cook' cannelloni
salt and pepper
Parmesan cheese shavings, to
   garnish (optional)

TOMATO SAUCE:
1 large red (bell) pepper
200 ml/7 fl oz/3/4 cup dry white
   wine
450 ml/16 fl oz/2 cups passata
   (sieved tomatoes)
2 tbsp tomato purée (paste)
2 bay leaves
1 tsp caster (superfine) sugar

1 Preheat the oven to 200°C/400°F/Gas Mark 6. Place the mushrooms, onion and garlic in a pan. Stir in the thyme, nutmeg and 4 tbsp wine. Bring to the boil, cover and simmer for 10 minutes. Stir in the breadcrumbs to bind the mixture together and season. Cool for 10 minutes.

2 Preheat the grill (broiler) to hot. To make the sauce, halve and

deseed the (bell) pepper, place on the grill (broiler) rack and cook for 8–10 minutes until charred. Let cool for 10 minutes.

3 Once the (bell) pepper has cooled, peel off the skin. Chop the flesh and place in a food processor with the wine. Blend until smooth; pour into a pan.

4 Mix the remaining sauce ingredients with

the (bell) pepper and wine and season. Bring to the boil and simmer for 10 minutes. Discard the bay leaves.

5 Cover the base of an ovenproof dish with a thin layer of sauce. Fill the cannelloni with the mushroom mixture and place in the dish. Spoon over the remaining sauce, cover with foil and bake for 35–40 minutes. Serve hot.

Tofu & Chickpea Burgers

Serves 4

INGREDIENTS

---

1 small red onion, chopped finely
1 garlic clove, crushed
1 tsp ground cumin
1 tsp ground coriander
2 tbsp lemon juice
425 g/15 oz can chick-peas
  (garbanzo beans), drained
  and rinsed
75 g/3 oz soft silken tofu (bean
  curd), drained

115 g/4 oz cooked potato, diced
4 tbsp freshly chopped coriander
  (cilantro)
75 g/2³/₄ oz dry brown
  breadcrumbs
1 tbsp vegetable oil
4 burger buns, split in half
2 medium tomatoes, sliced
1 large carrot, grated
salt and pepper

RELISH:

1 tsp tahini (sesame seed) paste
4 tbsp low-fat natural fromage
  frais (unsweetened yogurt)
2.5 cm/1 inch piece cucumber,
  finely chopped
1 tbsp chopped, fresh coriander
  (cilantro)
garlic salt, to season

---

1 Place the onion, garlic, spices and lemon juice in a pan, bring to the boil, cover and simmer for 5 minutes until softened.

2 Place the chick-peas (garbanzo beans), tofu (bean curd) and potato in a bowl and mash well. Stir in the onion mixture, coriander (cilantro) and seasoning, and mix. Divide into 4 equal portions and form into patties 10 cm/ 4 inch across.

3 Sprinkle the breadcrumbs on to a plate and press the burgers into the crumbs to coat.

4 Heat the oil in a non-stick frying pan (skillet) and fry the burgers for 5 minutes on each side until cooked and golden. Drain on kitchen paper.

5 Mix all of the relish ingredients together in a bowl and leave to chill.

6 Line the bottom half of the buns with tomato and carrot and top each with a burger. Spoon the relish over the burger and place the top half of the bun on top.

Sweet Potato & Leek Patties

Serves 4

INGREDIENTS

900 g/2 lb sweet potato
4 tsp sunflower oil
2 medium leeks, chopped
1 garlic clove, crushed
2.5 cm/1 inch piece root ginger,
  finely chopped
200 g/7 oz can sweetcorn,
  drained
2 tbsp low-fat natural fromage
  frais (unsweetened yogurt)

60 g/2 oz wholemeal flour
salt and pepper

GINGER SAUCE:
2 tbsp white wine vinegar
2 tsp caster (superfine) sugar
1 red chilli, deseeded and
  chopped
2.5 cm/1 inch piece root (fresh)
  ginger, cut into thin strips

2 tbsp ginger wine
4 tbsp fresh vegetable stock
1 tsp cornflour (cornstarch)

TO SERVE:
lettuce leaves
spring onions (scallions),
  shredded

1 Peel the potatoes and cut into 2 cm/³/₄ inch thick pieces. Place in a pan, cover with water and boil for 10–15 minutes. Drain and mash. Leave to cool.

2 Heat 2 tsp of oil and fry the leeks, garlic and ginger for 2–3 minutes. Stir the leek mixture into the potato with the sweetcorn, seasoning and fromage frais (yogurt). Form into 8 patties and toss in flour to coat. Chill for 30 minutes.

3 Preheat the grill (broiler) to medium. Place the patties on a grill (broiler) rack and brush with oil. Grill (broil) for 5 minutes, then turn, oil and grill (broil) for another 5 minutes, or until golden. Drain on kitchen paper.

4 For the sauce, place the vinegar, sugar, chilli and ginger in a pan. Bring to the boil and simmer for 5 minutes. Stir in the ginger wine. Blend the stock and cornflour (cornstarch) to form a paste and stir into the sauce. Heat through, stirring, until thickened. Transfer the patties to serving plates, spoon over the sauce and serve.

Ratatouille Vegetable Grill

Serves 4

INGREDIENTS

2 medium onions	2 medium courgettes (zucchini)	900 g/2 lb potatoes
1 garlic clove	2 x 400 g/14 oz cans chopped	75 g/2³/₄ oz reduced-fat Cheddar
1 medium red (bell) pepper	tomatoes	cheese, grated
1 medium green (bell) pepper	1 bouquet garni	salt and pepper
1 medium aubergine (eggplant)	2 tbsp tomato purée (paste)	2 tbsp snipped fresh chives, to
		garnish

1 Peel and finely chop the onions and garlic. Rinse, deseed and slice the (bell) peppers. Rinse, trim and cut the aubergine (eggplant) into small dice. Rinse, trim and thinly slice the courgettes (zucchini).

2 Place the onion, garlic and (bell) peppers into a pan. Add the tomatoes, and stir in the bouquet garni, tomato purée (paste) and salt and pepper to taste. Bring to the boil, cover and simmer for 10 minutes, stirring half-way through.

3 Stir in the aubergine (eggplant) and courgettes (zucchini) and cook, uncovered, for 10 minutes, stirring.

4 Peel the potatoes and cut into 2.5 cm/1 inch cubes. Place the potatoes into another saucepan and cover with water. Bring to the boil and cook for 10–12 minutes until tender. Drain thoroughly and set aside until required.

5 Transfer the vegetables to a heatproof gratin

dish. Arrange the cooked potato cubes evenly over the vegetables.

6 Preheat the grill (broiler) to medium. Sprinkle grated cheese over the potatoes and place under the grill (broiler) for 5 minutes until golden, bubbling and hot. Serve garnished with freshly snipped chives.

Cauliflower & Broccoli with Herb Sauce

Serves 4

INGREDIENTS

2 baby cauliflowers	SAUCE:	5 tbsp chopped coriander
225 g/8 oz broccoli	8 tbsp olive oil	(cilantro)
salt and pepper	4 tbsp butter or vegetarian	5 tbsp grated Cheddar
	margarine	
	2 tsp grated root ginger	
	juice and rind of 2 lemons	

1 Using a sharp knife, cut the cauliflowers in half and the broccoli into very large florets.

2 Cook the cauliflower and broccoli in a saucepan of boiling salted water for 10 minutes. Drain well, transfer to a shallow ovenproof dish and keep warm until required.

3 To make the sauce, put the oil and butter or vegetarian margarine in a pan and heat gently until the butter melts. Add the grated root ginger, lemon juice, lemon rind and coriander (cilantro) and simmer for 2–3 minutes, stirring occasionally.

4 Season the sauce with salt and pepper to taste, then pour over the vegetables in the dish and sprinkle the cheese on top.

5 Cook under a preheated hot grill (broiler) for 2–3 minutes or until the cheese is bubbling and golden. Leave to cool for 1–2 minutes and then serve.

VARIATION

Lime or orange could be used instead of the lemon for a fruity and refreshing sauce.

Steamed Vegetables with Vermouth

Serves 4

INGREDIENTS

1 carrot, cut into batons	1 red (bell) pepper, sliced	zest of 1 lime
1 fennel bulb, sliced	4 small onions, halved	pinch of paprika
100 g/3½ oz courgettes (zucchini), sliced	8 tbsp vermouth	4 sprigs tarragon
	4 tbsp lime juice	salt and pepper
		fresh tarragon sprigs, to garnish

1 Place all of the vegetables in a large bowl and mix well.

2 Cut 4 large squares of baking parchment and place a quarter of the vegetables in the centre of each. Bring the sides of the paper up and pinch together to make an open parcel.

3 Mix together the vermouth, lime juice, lime zest and paprika and pour a quarter of the mixture into each parcel. Season with salt and pepper and add a tarragon

sprig to each. Pinch the tops of the parcels together to seal.

4 Place the parcels in a steamer, cover and cook for 15–20 minutes or until the vegetables are tender. Garnish and serve.

COOK'S TIP

Seal the parcels well to prevent them opening during cooking and causing the juices to evaporate.

COOKS TIP

Vermouth is a fortified white wine flavoured with various herbs and spices. It its available in both sweet and dry forms.

Spicy Peas & Spinach

Serves 4

INGREDIENTS

225 g/8 oz/1 ¼ cups green
    split peas
900 g/2 lb spinach
4 tbsp vegetable oil
1 onion, halved and sliced

1 tsp grated root ginger
1 tsp ground cumin
½ tsp chilli powder
½ tsp ground coriander
2 garlic cloves, crushed

300 ml/½ pint/1¼ cups
    vegetable stock
salt and pepper
fresh coriander (cilantro) sprigs
    and lime wedges, to garnish

1 Rinse the peas under
cold running water.
Transfer to a mixing bowl,
cover with cold water and
leave to soak for 2 hours.
Drain well.

2 Meanwhile, cook the
spinach in a large
saucepan for 5 minutes
until wilted. Drain well
and roughly chop.

3 Heat the oil in a large
saucepan and sauté the
onion, spices and garlic.
Sauté for 2–3 minutes,
stirring well.

4 Add the peas and
spinach and stir in the
stock. Cover and simmer
for 10–15 minutes or until
the peas are cooked and the
liquid has been absorbed.
Season with salt and pepper
to taste, garnish and serve.

VARIATION
*If you do not have time to
soak the green peas, canned
lentils are a good substitute
but remember to drain and
rinse them first.*

COOK'S TIP

*Once the peas have been
added, stir occasionally to
prevent them from sticking
to the pan.*

Curried Cauliflower & Spinach

Serves 4

INGREDIENTS

1 medium cauliflower
6 tbsp vegetable oil
1 tsp mustard seeds
1 tsp ground cumin
1 tsp garam masala

1 tsp turmeric
2 garlic cloves, crushed
1 onion, halved and sliced
1 green chilli, sliced
450 g/1 lb spinach

85 ml/3 fl oz/6 tbsp
    vegetable stock
1 tbsp chopped coriander (cilantro)
salt and pepper
coriander (cilantro) sprigs,
    to garnish

1 Break the cauliflower into small florets.

2 Heat the oil in a deep flameproof casserole dish. Add the mustard seeds and cook until they begin to pop.

3 Stir in the remaining spices, the garlic, onion and chilli and cook for 2–3 minutes, stirring.

4 Add the cauliflower, spinach, vegetable stock, coriander (cilantro) and seasoning and cook over a gentle heat for 15 minutes or until the cauliflower is tender. Uncover the dish and boil for 1 minute to thicken the juices. Garnish and serve.

COOK'S TIP

Mustard seeds are used throughout India and are particularly popular in southern vegetarian cooking. They are fried in oil first to bring out their flavour before the other ingredients are added.

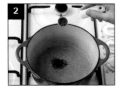

Marinated Tofu Skewers

Serves 4

INGREDIENTS

350 g/12 oz tofu (bean curd)
1 red (bell) pepper
1 yellow (bell) pepper
2 courgettes (zucchini)
8 button mushrooms

slices of lemon, to garnish

MARINADE:
grated rind and juice of
   ½ lemon

1 clove garlic, crushed
½ tsp fresh rosemary, chopped
½ tsp chopped, fresh thyme
1 tbsp walnut oil

1 To make the marinade, combine the lemon rind and juice, garlic, rosemary, thyme and oil in a shallow dish.

2 Drain the tofu (bean curd), pat it dry on kitchen paper and cut it into squares. Add to the marinade and toss to coat. Leave to marinate for 20–30 minutes.

3 Meanwhile, deseed and cut the (bell) peppers into 2.5 cm/1 inch pieces. Blanch in boiling water for 4 minutes,

refresh in cold water and drain well.

4 Using a canelle knife (or potato peeler), remove strips of peel from the courgettes (zucchini). Cut the courgette (zucchini) into 2.5 cm/1 inch chunks.

5 Remove the tofu (bean curd) from the marinade, reserving the liquid for basting. Thread the tofu (bean curd) on to 8 skewers, alternating with the (bell) peppers, courgette (zucchini) and button mushrooms.

6 Barbecue (grill) the skewers over medium hot coals for about 6 minutes, turning and basting with the marinade.

7 Transfer the skewers to warm serving plates, garnish with slices of lemon and serve.

VARIATION

For a spicy kebab (kabob), make a marinade from 1 tablespoon of curry paste, 2 tablespoons of oil and the juice of ½ lemon.

Crispy Potato Skins

Serves 4-6

INGREDIENTS

8 small baking potatoes,
   scrubbed
50 g/1¾ oz butter, melted
salt and pepper

OPTIONAL TOPPING:
6 spring onions (scallions), sliced
50 g/1¾ oz salami, cut into thin
   strips

50 g/1¾ oz grated gruyère
   cheese

1 Preheat the oven to
200°C/400°F/Gas
Mark 6. Prick the potatoes
with a fork and bake for
1 hour or until tender.
Alternatively, cook in a
microwave on High for
12–15 minutes.

2 Cut the potatoes in
half and scoop out the
flesh, leaving about
5 mm/¼ inch potato flesh
lining the skin.

3 Brush inside the potato
with melted butter.

4 Place the skins, cut-side
down, over medium

hot coals and barbecue
(grill) for 10–15 minutes.
Turn the potato skins over
and barbecue (grill) for a
further 5 minutes or until
they are crispy. Take care
that they do not burn.

5 Season the potato skins
with salt and pepper to
taste and serve while they
are still warm.

6 If wished, the skins can
filled with a variety of
toppings. Barbecue (grill)
the potato skins as above
for about 10 minutes, then
turn cut-side up and
sprinkle with slices of

spring onion (scallion),
grated cheese and chopped
salami. Barbecue (grill) for
a further 5 minutes until
the cheese begins to melt.
Serve hot.

COOK'S TIP

*Potato skins can be served
on their own but they are
delicious served with a dip.
Try a spicy tomato or
hummus dip.*

Barbecued Garlic Potato Wedges

Serves 4

INGREDIENTS

3 large baking potatoes, scrubbed	25 g/1 oz butter	1 tbsp chopped, fresh parsley
4 tbsp olive oil	2 garlic cloves, chopped	1 tbsp chopped, fresh thyme
	1 tbsp chopped, fresh rosemary	salt and pepper

1 Bring a large pan of water to the boil, add the potatoes and par-boil them for 10 minutes. Drain the potatoes, refresh under cold water and drain them again thoroughly.

2 Transfer the potatoes to a chopping board. When the potatoes are cold enough to handle, cut them into thick wedges, but do not remove the skins.

3 Heat the oil and butter in a small pan together with the garlic. Cook gently until the garlic begins to brown, then remove the pan from the heat.

4 Stir the herbs and salt and pepper to taste into the mixture in the pan.

5 Brush the herb mixture over the potatoes.

6 Barbecue (grill) the potatoes over hot coals for 10–15 minutes, brushing liberally with any of the remaining herb and butter mixture, or until the potatoes are just tender.

7 Transfer the barbecued garlic potatoes to a warm serving plate and serve as a starter or as a side dish.

COOK'S TIP

You may find it easier to barbecue (grill) these potatoes in a hinged rack or in a specially designed barbecue (grill) roasting tray.

Vegetarian Sausages

Makes 8

INGREDIENTS

1 tbsp sunflower oil
1 small onion, chopped finely
50 g/1¾ oz mushrooms,
    chopped finely
½ red (bell) pepper, deseeded
    and chopped finely

400 g/14 oz can cannolini beans,
    rinsed and drained
100 g/3½ oz fresh breadcrumbs
100 g/3½ oz Cheddar cheese,
    grated
1 tsp dried mixed herbs

1 egg yolk
seasoned plain (all-purpose)
    flour
oil, to baste
bread rolls and slices of fried
    onion, to serve

1 Heat the oil in a saucepan and fry the prepared onion, mushrooms and (bell) peppers until softened.

2 Mash the cannolini beans in a large mixing bowl. Add the onion, mushroom and (bell) pepper mixture, the breadcrumbs, cheese, herbs and egg yolk, and mix together well.

3 Press the mixture together with your fingers and shape into 8 sausages.

4 Roll each sausage in the seasoned flour. Leave to chill in the refrigerator for at least 30 minutes.

5 Barbecue (grill) the sausages on a sheet of oiled foil set over medium coals for 15–20 minutes, turning and basting frequently with oil, until golden.

6 Split a bread roll down the middle and insert a layer of fried onions. Place the sausage in the roll and serve.

COOK'S TIP

Take care not to break the sausages when you turning them over. If you have a hinged rack, oil this and place the sausages inside, turning and oiling frequently.

Aubergine & Mozzarella Sandwiches

Serves 2

INGREDIENTS

1 large aubergine (eggplant)
1 tbsp lemon juice
3 tbsp olive oil

125 g/4 ½ oz grated Mozzarella cheese
2 sun-dried tomatoes, chopped
salt and pepper

TO SERVE:
Italian bread
mixed salad leaves
slices of tomato

1 Slice the aubergine (eggplant) into thin rounds.

2 Combine the lemon juice and oil in a bowl and season the mixture with salt and pepper.

3 Brush the aubergine (eggplant) slices with the oil and lemon juice mixture and barbecue (grill) over medium hot coals for 2–3 minutes, without turning, until they are golden on the under side.

4 Turn half of the aubergine (eggplant) slices over and sprinkle with cheese and chopped sun-dried tomatoes.

5 Place the remaining aubergine (eggplant) slices on top of the cheese and tomatoes, turning them so that the pale side is uppermost.

6 Barbecue (grill) for 1–2 minutes, then carefully turn the sand - wich over and barbecue

(grill) for 1–2 minutes. Baste with the oil mixture.

7 Serve with Italian bread, mixed salad leaves and tomato.

VARIATION

Try Feta cheese instead of Mozzarella but omit the salt from the basting oil. A creamy goat's cheese would be equally delicious.

Chargrilled Aubergine

Serves 4

INGREDIENTS

1 large aubergine (eggplant)	PESTO:	CUCUMBER SAUCE:
3 tbsp olive oil	1 clove garlic	150 g/5½ oz natural yogurt
1 tsp sesame oil	25 g/1 oz pine nuts	5 cm/2 inch cucumber
salt and pepper	15 g/½ oz fresh basil leaves	½ tsp mint sauce
	2 tbsp Parmesan cheese	
	6 tbsp olive oil	
	salt and pepper	

1 Remove the stalk from the aubergine (eggplant), then cut it lengthwise into 8 thin slices.

2 Lay the slices on a plate or board and sprinkle them liberally with salt to remove the bitter juices. Leave to stand.

3 Meanwhile, prepare the baste. Combine the olive and sesame oils, season with pepper and set aside.

4 To make the pesto, put the garlic, pine nuts, basil and cheese in a food processor until finely chopped. With the machine running, gradually add the oil in a thin stream. Season to taste.

5 To make the minty cucumber sauce, place the yogurt in a mixing bowl. Remove the seeds from the cucumber and dice the flesh finely. Stir into the yogurt with the mint sauce.

6 Rinse the aubergine (eggplant) slices and pat them dry on absorbent kitchen paper. Baste with the oil mixture and barbecue (grill) over hot coals for about 10 minutes, turning once. The aubergine (eggplant) should be golden and tender.

7 Transfer the aubergine (eggplant) slices to serving plates and serve with either the cucumber sauce or the pesto.

Colourful Vegetable Kebabs

Serves 4

INGREDIENTS

1 red (bell) pepper, deseeded	1 small onion	SEASONED OIL:
1 yellow (bell) pepper, deseeded	8 cherry tomatoes	6 tbsp olive oil
1 green (bell) pepper, deseeded	100 g/3 ½ oz wild mushrooms	1 clove garlic, crushed
		1/2 tsp mixed dried herbs or
		herbes de Provence

1 Cut the (bell) peppers into 2.5 cm/1 inch pieces.

2 Peel the onion and cut it into wedges, leaving the root end just intact to help keep the wedges together.

3 Thread the (bell) peppers, onion wedges, tomatoes and mushrooms on to skewers, alternating the colours of the (bell) peppers.

4 To make the seasoned oil, mix together the oil, garlic and herbs in a small bowl. Brush the mixture liberally over the kebabs (kabobs).

5 Barbecue (grill) the kebabs (kabobs) over medium hot coals for 10–15 minutes, brushing with more of the seasoned oil and turning the skewers frequently.

6 Transfer the vegetable kebabs (kabobs) to warm serving plates. Serve the kebabs (kabobs) with walnut sauce (see Cook's Tip, right), if you wish.

COOK'S TIP

These kebabs (kabobs) are delicious when accompanied with a walnut sauce. To make the sauce, process 125 g/4 ½ oz walnuts in a food processor until they form a smooth paste. With the machine running, add 150 ml/5 fl oz/²⁄₃ cup double (heavy) cream and 1 tablespoon of olive oil. Season to taste. Alternatively, finely chop the walnuts then pound them in a pestle and mortar to form a paste. Mix with the cream and oil, and season.

Chargrilled Mixed Vegetables

Serves 4-6

INGREDIENTS

8 baby aubergines (eggplant)	4 tomatoes	BASTE:
4 courgettes (zucchini)	salt and pepper	75 g/2¾ oz butter
2 red onions	1 tsp balsamic vinegar, to serve	2 tsp walnut oil
		2 cloves garlic, chopped
		4 tbsp dry white wine or cider

1 Cut the aubergines (eggplant) in half. Trim and cut the courgettes (zucchini) in half lengthwise. Thickly slice the onion and halve the tomatoes.

2 Season all of the vegetables with salt and pepper to taste.

3 To make the baste, melt the butter with the oil in a saucepan. Add the garlic and cook gently for 1–2 minutes. Remove the pan from the heat and stir in the wine or cider.

4 Add the vegetables to the pan and toss them in the baste mixture. You may need to do this in several batches to ensure that all of the vegetables are coated evenly with the baste mixture.

5 Remove the vegetables from the baste mixture, reserving any excess baste. Place the vegetables on an oiled rack over medium hot coals. Barbecue (grill) them for 15–20 minutes, basting with the reserved baste mixture and turning once or twice during cooking.

6 Transfer the vegetables to warm serving plates and serve sprinkled with balsamic vinegar.

COOK'S TIP

Use a long-handled brush for basting food on the barbecue (grill).

Stuffed Mushrooms

Makes 12

INGREDIENTS

12 open-cap mushrooms	4 tsp olive oil	1 tsp fresh oregano, chopped
4 spring onions (scallions), chopped	100 g/3¹/₂ oz fresh brown breadcrumbs	100 g/3¹/₂ oz Feta cheese or chorizo sausage

1 Remove the stalks from the mushrooms and chop the stalks finely.

2 Sauté the mushroom stalks and spring onions (scallions) in half of the oil.

3 In a bowl, mix the mushroom stalks and spring onions (scallions). Add the breadcrumbs and oregano to the mushrooms and spring onions (scallions), mix and set aside.

4 If using Feta, crumble the cheese into small pieces in a small bowl.

5 If you are using chorizo sausage, remove the skin and chop the flesh finely.

6 Add the cheese or chorizo to the breadcrumb mixture and mix well.

7 Spoon the stuffing mixture into the mushroom caps. Drizzle the oil over the mushrooms. Barbecue (grill) on an oiled rack over medium hot coals for 8–10 minutes. Transfer the mushrooms to serving plates and serve hot.

COOK'S TIP

If using small mushrooms, place a sheet of oiled kitchen foil on top of the barbecue (grill) rack and cook the mushrooms on this. This will stop the mushrooms from cooking too quickly and burning, and will prevent any excess stuffing from dropping on the coals.

Corn on the Cob

Serves 4

INGREDIENTS

4 cobs of sweetcorn, with husks
butter to taste
1 tbsp chopped, fresh parsley

1 tsp chopped, fresh chives
1 tsp chopped, fresh thyme

rind of 1 lemon, grated
salt and pepper

1 To prepare the cobs of sweetcorn, peel back the husks and remove the silken hairs.

2 Fold back the husks and secure them in place with string if necessary.

3 Blanch the cobs of sweetcorn in a large pan of boiling water for about 5 minutes. Remove the cobs with a perforated spoon and drain.

4 Barbecue (grill) the cobs over medium hot coals for 20–30 minutes, turning frequently.

5 Meanwhile, soften the butter and beat in the parsley, chives, thyme, lemon rind and salt and pepper to taste.

6 Transfer the cobs of sweetcorn to serving plates, remove the string and pull back the husks. Serve with a generous portion of herb butter.

COOK'S TIP

When you are buying fresh sweetcorn, look for plump, tightly packed kernels. If you are unable to get fresh cobs, cook frozen sweetcorn cobs on the barbecue (grill). Spread some of the herb butter on to a sheet of double thickness kitchen foil. Wrap the cobs in the foil and barbecue (grill) among the coals for 20–30 minutes.

Pumpkin Parcels with Chilli & Lime

Serves 4

INGREDIENTS

700 g/1 lb 9oz pumpkin or squash	25 g/1 oz butter	rind of 1 lime, grated
2 tbsp sunflower oil	½ tsp chilli sauce	2 tsp lime juice

1 Halve the pumpkin or squash and scoop out the seeds. Rinse the seeds and reserve. Cut the pumpkin into thin wedges and peel.

2 Heat the oil and butter together in a large saucepan, stirring continuously until melted. Stir in the chilli sauce, lime rind and juice.

3 Add the pumpkin or squash and seeds to the pan and toss to coat in the flavoured butter.

4 Divide the mixture among 4 double thickness sheets of kitchen foil. Fold over the kitchen foil to enclose the pumpkin or squash mixture.

5 Barbecue (grill) the foil parcels for 15–25 minutes or until the pumpkin or squash is tender.

6 Transfer the foil parcels to warm serving plates. Open the parcels at the table and serve at once.

VARIATION

Add 2 teaspoons of curry paste to the oil instead of the lime and chilli.

COOK'S TIP

It is a good idea to wear disposable gloves when slicing and deseeding chillies. Alternatively, rub a little oil over your fingers before you begin – the oil will help to prevent your skin absorbing the chilli juice. Wash your hands thoroughly afterwards.

Tofu with Soy Sauce, Green Peppers & Crispy Onions

Serves 4

INGREDIENTS

350 g/12 oz tofu (bean curd)
2 cloves garlic, crushed
4 tbsp soy sauce

1 tbsp sweet chilli sauce
6 tbsp sunflower oil
1 onion, sliced

1 green (bell) pepper, deseeded and
    diced
1 tbsp sesame oil

1 Using a sharp knife, cut the tofu (bean curd) into bite-sized pieces. Place the tofu (bean curd) pieces in a shallow non-metallic dish.

2 Mix together the garlic, soy sauce and sweet chilli sauce and drizzle over the tofu (bean curd). Toss well to coat each piece and leave to marinate for about 20 minutes.

3 Meanwhile, heat the sunflower oil in a large preheated wok.

4 Add the onion slices to the wok and stir-fry over a high heat until they brown and become crispy. Remove the onion slices with a slotted spoon and leave to drain on absorbent kitchen paper.

5 Add the tofu (bean curd) to the hot oil and stir-fry for about 5 minutes.

6 Remove all but 1 tablespoon of the oil from the wok. Add the (bell) pepper to the wok and stir-fry for 2–3 minutes, or until softened.

7 Return the tofu (bean curd) and onions to the wok and heat through, stirring occasionally. Drizzle with the sesame oil.

8 Transfer to serving plates and serve immediately.

COOK'S TIP

If you are in a real hurry, buy ready-marinated tofu (bean curd) from your supermarket.

Stir-Fried Green Beans with Lettuce & Black Bean Sauce

Serves 4

INGREDIENTS

1 tsp chilli oil
25 g/1 oz/2 tbsp butter
225 g/8 oz fine green beans, sliced
4 shallots, sliced

1 clove garlic, crushed
100 g/3½ oz shiitake mushrooms,
    thinly sliced
1 Iceberg lettuce, shredded

4 tbsp black bean sauce

1 Heat the chilli oil and butter in a large preheated wok.

2 Add the green beans, shallots, garlic and mushrooms to the wok and stir-fry for 2–3 minutes.

3 Add the shredded lettuce to the wok and stir-fry until the leaves have wilted.

4 Stir the black bean sauce into the mixture in the wok and heat through, tossing to mix, until the sauce is bubbling.

COOK'S TIP

To make your own black bean sauce, soak 60 g/2 oz/ ⅓ cup of dried black beans overnight in cold water. Drain and place in a pan of cold water, boil for 10 minutes, then drain. Return the beans to the pan with 450 ml/¾ pint/ 2 cups vegetable stock and boil. Blend 1 tbsp each of malt vinegar, soy sauce, sugar, 1½ tsp cornflour (cornstarch), 1 chopped red chilli and ½ inch ginger root. Add to the pan and simmer for 40 minutes.

COOK'S TIP

If possible, use Chinese green beans which are tender and can be eaten whole. They are available from specialist Chinese stores.

Aspagarus & Red Pepper Parcels

Serves 4

INGREDIENTS

100 g/3¹/₂ oz fine tip asparagus
1 red (bell) pepper, deseeded and
    thinly sliced

50 g/1³/₄ oz/¹/₂ cup beansprouts
2 tbsp plum sauce
8 sheets filo pastry

1 egg yolk, beaten
oil, for deep-frying

1 Place the asparagus, (bell) pepper and beansprouts in a large mixing bowl.

2 Add the plum sauce to the vegetables and mix until well combined.

3 Lay the sheets of filo pastry out on to a clean work surface (counter).

4 Place a little of the asparagus and red (bell) pepper filling at the top end of each filo pastry sheet. Brush the edges of the filo pastry with a little of the beaten egg yolk.

5 Roll up the filo pastry, tucking in the ends and enclosing the filling like a spring roll.

6 Heat the oil for deep-frying in a large preheated wok.

7 Carefully cook the parcels, 2 at a time, in the hot oil for 4–5 minutes or until crispy.

8 Remove the parcels with a slotted spoon and leave to drain on absorbent kitchen paper.

9 Transfer the parcels to warm serving plates and serve immediately.

COOK'S TIP

Be sure to use fine-tipped asparagus as it is more tender than the larger stems.

Carrot & Orange Stir-Fry

Serves 4

INGREDIENTS

2 tbsp sunflower oil	2 oranges, peeled and segmented	2 tbsp light soy
450 g/1 lb carrots, grated	2 tbsp tomato ketchup	100 g/3½ oz/½ cup chopped peanuts
225 g/8 oz leeks, shredded	1 tbsp demerara sugar	

1 Heat the sunflower oil in a large preheated wok.

2 Add the grated carrot and leeks to the wok and stir-fry for 2–3 minutes, or until the vegetables have just softened.

3 Add the orange segments to the wok and heat through gently, ensuring that you do not break up the orange segments as you stir the mixture.

4 Mix the tomato ketchup, demerara sugar and soy sauce together in a small bowl.

5 Add the tomato and sugar mixture to the wok and stir-fry for a further 2 minutes.

6 Transfer the stir-fry to warm serving bowls and scatter with the chopped peanuts. Serve immediately.

VARIATION

Scatter with toasted sesame seeds instead of the peanuts, if you prefer.

VARIATION

You could use pineapple instead of orange. If using canned pineapple, make sure that it is in natural juice not syrup as it will spoil the fresh taste of this dish.

Spinach Stir-Fry with Shiitake & Honey

Serves 4

INGREDIENTS

3 tbsp groundnut oil	2 cloves garlic, crushed	2 tbsp clear honey
350 g/12 oz shiitake mushrooms, sliced	350 g/12 oz baby leaf spinach	4 spring onions (scallions), sliced
	2 tbsp dry sherry	

1 Heat the groundnut oil in a large preheated wok.

2 Add the shiitake mushrooms to the wok and stir-fry for about 5 minutes, or until the mushrooms have softened.

3 Add the crushed garlic and baby leaf spinach to the mushrooms in the wok and stir-fry for a further 2–3 minutes, or until the spinach leaves have just wilted.

4 Mix together the dry sherry and clear honey in a small bowl until well combined.

5 Drizzle the sherry and honey mixture over the spinach and heat through.

6 Transfer the stir-fry to warm serving dishes and scatter with spring onions (scallion) slices. Serve immediately.

COOK'S TIP

Nutmeg complements the flavour of spinach and it is a classic combination. Add a pinch of nutmeg to the dish in step 3, if you wish.

COOK'S TIP

A good quality, dry pale sherry should be used in this recipe. Cream or sweet sherry should not be substituted. Rice wine is often used in Oriental cooking, but sherry can be used instead.

Chinese Vegetable Rice

Serves 4

INGREDIENTS

350 g/12 oz/1¾ cups long-grain white rice
1 tsp turmeric
2 tbsp sunflower oil
225 g/8 oz courgettes (zucchini), sliced

1 red (bell) pepper, deseeded and sliced
1 green (bell) pepper, deseeded and sliced
1 green chilli, deseeded and finely chopped

1 medium carrot, coarsley grated
150 g/5½ oz/1½ cups beansprouts
6 spring onions (scallions), sliced, plus extra to garnish
2 tbsp soy sauce

1 Place the rice and turmeric in a saucepan of lightly salted water and bring to the boil. Reduce the heat and leave to simmer until the rice is just tender. Drain the rice thoroughly and press out any excess water with a sheet of double thickness kitchen paper.

2 Heat the sunflower oil in a large preheated wok.

3 Add the courgettes (zucchini) to the wok and stir-fry for about 2 minutes.

4 Add the (bell) peppers and chilli to the wok and stir-fry for 2–3 minutes.

5 Add the cooked rice to the mixture in the wok, a little at a time, tossing well after each addition.

6 Add the carrots, beansprouts and spring onions (scallions) to the wok and stir-fry for a further 2 minutes. Drizzle with soy sauce and serve at once, garnished with extra spring onions (scallions), if desired.

VARIATION

For real luxury, add a few saffron strands infused in boiling water instead of the turmeric.

Vegetable Stir-Fry with Hoisin Sauce

Serves 4

INGREDIENTS

2 tbsp sunflower oil
1 red onion, sliced
100 g/3½ oz carrots, sliced

1 yellow (bell) pepper, deseeded and diced
50 g/1¾ oz/1 cup cooked brown rice
175 g/6 oz mangetout (snow peas)

175 g/6 oz/1½ cups beansprouts
4 tbsp hoisin sauce
1 tbsp snipped fresh chives

1 Heat the sunflower oil in a large preheated wok.

2 Add the red onion slices, carrots and yellow (bell) pepper to the wok and stir-fry for about 3 minutes.

3 Add the cooked brown rice, mangetout (snow peas) and beansprouts to the mixture in the wok and stir-fry for a further 2 minutes.

4 Stir the hoisin sauce into the vegetables and mix until well combined and completely heated through.

5 Transfer to warm serving dishes and scatter with the snipped fresh chives. Serve immediately.

COOK'S TIP

Hoisin sauce is a dark brown, reddish sauce made from soy beans, garlic, chilli and various other spices, and is commonly used in Chinese cookery. It may also be used as a dipping sauce.

VARIATION

Almost any vegetables could be used in this dish: other good choices would be broccoli florets, baby corn cobs, green peas, Chinese leaves and young spinach leaves. Either white or black (oyster) mushrooms can also be used to give a greater diversity of textures. In addition, make sure that there is a good variety of colour in this dish.

Sweet & Sour Cauliflower & Coriander Stir-Fry

Serves 4

INGREDIENTS

450 g/1 lb cauliflower florets	100 g/3½ oz mangetout (snow peas)	3 tbsp fresh lime juice
2 tbsp sunflower oil	1 ripe mango, sliced	1 tbsp clear honey
1 onion, sliced	100 g/3½ oz/1 cup beansprouts	6 tbsp coconut milk
225 g/8 oz carrots, sliced	3 tbsp chopped fresh coriander (cilantro)	

1 Bring a large saucepan of water to the boil. Add the cauliflower to the pan and cook for 2 minutes. Drain the cauliflower thoroughly.

2 Heat the sunflower oil in a large preheated wok.

3 Add the onion and carrots to the wok and stir-fry for about 5 minutes.

4 Add the drained cauliflower and mangetout (snow peas) to the wok and stir-fry for 2–3 minutes.

5 Add the mango and bean-sprouts to the wok and stir-fry for about 2 minutes.

6 Mix together the coriander (cilantro), lime juice, honey and coconut milk in a bowl.

7 Add the coriander (cilantro) mixture to the wok and stir-fry for about 2 minutes or until the juices are bubbling.

VARIATION

Use broccoli instead of the cauliflower as an alternative, if you prefer.

Broccoli & Chinese Leaves with Black Bean Sauce

Serves 4

INGREDIENTS

450 g/1 lb broccoli florets

2 tbsp sunflower oil

1 onion, sliced

2 cloves garlic, thinly sliced

25 g/1 oz/¼ cup flaked (slivered) almonds

1 head Chinese leaves, shredded

4 tbsp black bean sauce

1 Bring a large saucepan of water to the boil. Add the broccoli florets to the pan and cook for 1 minute. Drain the broccoli thoroughly.

2 Meanwhile, heat the sunflower oil in a large preheated wok.

3 Add the onion and garlic to the wok and stir-fry until just beginning to brown.

4 Add the drained broccoli florets and the flaked almonds to the mixture in the wok and stir-fry for a further 2–3 minutes.

5 Add the Chinese leaves to the wok and stir-fry for a further 2 minutes.

6 Stir the black bean sauce into the vegetables in the wok, tossing to mix, and cook until the juices are just beginning to bubble.

7 Transfer the vegetables to warm serving bowls and serve immediately.

VARIATION

Use unsalted cashew nuts instead of the almonds, if preferred.

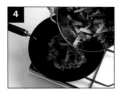

Quorn with Ginger & Mixed Vegetables

Serves 4

INGREDIENTS

1 tbsp grated fresh root ginger	1 clove garlic, crushed	100 g/3¹⁄₂ oz green beans, sliced
1 tsp ground ginger	2 tbsp soy sauce	4 stalks celery, sliced
1 tbsp tomato purée	350 g/12 oz Quorn or soya cubes	1 red (bell) pepper, deseeded and sliced
2 tbsp sunflower oil	225 g/8 oz carrots, sliced	boiled rice, to serve

1 Place the grated fresh ginger, ground ginger, tomato purée, 1 tablespoon of the sunflower oil, garlic, soy sauce and Quorn or soya cubes in a large bowl. Mix well to combine, stirring carefully so that you don't break up the Quorn or soya cubes. Cover and leave to marinate for 20 minutes.

2 Heat the remaining sunflower oil in a large preheated wok.

3 Add the marinated Quorn mixture to the wok and stir-fry for about 2 minutes.

4 Add the carrots, green beans, celery and red (bell) pepper to the wok and stir-fry for a further 5 minutes.

5 Transfer the stir-fry to warm serving dishes and serve immediately with freshly cooked boiled rice.

COOK'S TIP

Ginger root will keep for several weeks in a cool, dry place. Ginger root can also be kept frozen – break off lumps as needed.

VARIATION

Use tofu (bean curd) instead of the Quorn, if you prefer.

Leeks with Baby Corn
& Yellow Bean Sauce

Serves 4

INGREDIENTS

3 tbsp groundnut oil	225 g/8 oz Chinese leaves, shredded	6 spring onions (scallions), sliced
450 g/1 lb leeks, sliced	175 g/6 oz baby corn cobs, halved	4 tbsp yellow bean sauce

1 Heat the groundnut oil in a large preheated wok.

2 Add the leeks, shredded Chinese leaves and baby corn cobs to the wok and stir-fry over a high heat for about 5 minutes or until the edges of the vegetables are slightly brown.

3 Add the spring onions (scallions) to the wok, stirring to combine.

4 Add the yellow bean sauce to the mixture in the wok and stir-fry for a further 2 minutes, or until heated through.

5 Transfer to warm serving dishes and serve immediately.

COOK'S TIP

Yellow bean sauce adds an authentic Chinese flavour to stir-fries. It is made from crushed salted soya beans mixed with flour and spices to make a thick paste. It is mild in flavour and is excellent with a range of vegetables.

COOK'S TIP

Baby corn cobs are sweeter and have a more delicate flavour than the larger corn cobs and are therefore perfect for stir-frying.

Vegetable Stir-Fry

Serves 4

INGREDIENTS

3 tbsp olive oil

8 baby onions, halved

1 aubergine (eggplant), cubed

225 g/8 oz courgettes (zucchini), sliced

225 g/8 oz open-cap mushrooms, halved

2 cloves garlic, crushed

400 g/14 oz can chopped tomatoes

2 tbsp sundried tomato purée

freshly ground black pepper

fresh basil leaves, to garnish

1 Heat the olive oil in a large preheated wok.

2 Add the baby onions and aubergine (eggplant) to the wok and stir-fry for 5 minutes, or until the vegetables are golden and just beginning to soften.

3 Add the courgettes (zucchini), mushrooms, garlic, tomatoes and tomato purée to the wok and stir-fry for about 5 minutes. Reduce the heat and leave to simmer for 10 minutes, or until the vegetables are tender.

4 Season with freshly ground black pepper and scatter with fresh basil leaves. Serve immediately.

VARIATION

If you want to serve this as a vegetarian main meal, add cubed tofu (bean curd) in step 3.

COOK'S TIP

Wok cooking is an excellent means of cooking for vegetarians as it is a quick and easy way of serving up delicious dishes of crisp, tasty vegetables. All ingredients should be cut into uniform sizes with as many cut surfaces exposed as possible for quick cooking.

Spiced Aubergine Stir-Fry

Serves 4

INGREDIENTS

3 tbsp groundnut oil
2 onions, sliced
2 cloves garlic, chopped
2 aubergines (eggplants), diced

2 red chillies, deseeded and very
   finely chopped
2 tbsp demerara sugar
6 spring onions (scallions), sliced

3 tbsp mango chutney
oil, for deep-frying
2 cloves garlic, sliced, to garnish

1 Heat the groundnut oil in a large preheated wok.

2 Add the onions and chopped garlic to the wok, stirring well.

3 Add the aubergine (eggplant) and chillies to the wok and stir-fry for 5 minutes.

4 Add the sugar, spring onions (scallions) and mango chutney to the wok, stirring well. Reduce the heat, cover and leave to simmer, stirring from time to time, for 15 minutes or until the aubergine (eggplant) is tender.

5 Transfer the stir-fry to serving bowls and keep warm. Heat the oil for deep-frying in the wok and quickly stir-fry the slices of garlic. Garnish the stir-fry with the deep-fried garlic and serve immediately.

COOK'S TIP

Keep the vegetables moving around the wok as the aubergines (eggplant) will soak up the oil very quickly and may begin to burn if left unattended.

COOK'S TIP

The 'hotness' of chillies varies enormously so always use with caution, but as a general guide the smaller they are the hotter they will be. The seeds are the hottest part and so are usually discarded.

Vegetable Kebabs

Makes 10–12

INGREDIENTS

2 large potatoes, sliced
1 medium onion, sliced
¹/₂ medium cauliflower, cut into small florets
50 g/1³/₄ oz peas

1 tbsp spinach purée (paste)
2-3 green chillies
fresh coriander (cilantro) leaves
1 tsp fresh ginger root, finely chopped
1 tsp fresh garlic, crushed

1 tsp ground coriander
1 pinch turmeric
1 tsp salt
50 g/1³/₄ oz/1 cup breadcrumbs
300 ml/¹/₂ pint/1¹/₄ cups oil
fresh chilli strips, to garnish

1 Place the potatoes, onion and cauliflower florets in a pan of water and bring to the boil. Reduce the heat and leave to simmer until the potatoes are cooked through. Remove the vegetables from the pan with a perforated spoon and drain them thoroughly.

2 Add the peas and spinach to the vegetables and mix together, mashing down with a fork.

3 Using a sharp knife, finely chop the green chillies and fresh coriander (cilantro) leaves.

4 Mix the chillies and coriander (cilantro) with the ginger, garlic, ground coriander, turmeric and salt. Then blend the spice mixture into the vegetables, mixing with a fork to make a paste.

5 Scatter the breadcrumbs on to a large plate.

6 Break off 10-12 small balls from the spice paste. Flatten them with the palm of your hand to make flat, round shapes.

7 Dip each kebab (kabob) in the breadcrumbs, coating well.

8 Heat the oil in a heavy frying-pan (skillet) and fry the kebabs (kabobs) in batches until golden brown. Transfer to serving plates and garnish with fresh chilli strips.

Okra Curry

Serves 4

INGREDIENTS

450 g/1 lb okra (lady's fingers)
150 ml/¼ pint/⅔ cup oil
2 medium onions, sliced

3 green chillies, finely chopped
2 curry leaves
1 tsp salt

1 tomato, sliced
2 tbsp lemon juice
fresh coriander (cilantro) leaves

1 Rinse the okra (lady's fingers) and drain thoroughly. Using a sharp knife, chop and discard the ends of the okra (lady's fingers). Cut the okra (lady's fingers) into 2.5 cm/ 1 inch long pieces.

2 Heat the oil in a large, heavy frying-pan (skillet). Add the onions, green chillies, curry leaves and salt and mix together. Stir-fry the vegetables for 5 minutes.

3 Gradually add the okra (lady's fingers), mixing in gently with a perforated spoon. Stir-fry the vegetable mixture over a medium heat for 12-15 minutes.

4 Add the sliced tomato to the mixture and sprinkle over the lemon juice sparingly.

5 Garnish with coriander (cilantro) leaves, cover and leave to simmer for 3-5 minutes.

6 Transfer to serving plates and serve hot.

COOK'S TIP

Okra (lady's fingers) have a remarkable glutinous quality which naturally thickens curries and casseroles.

COOK'S TIP

When you buy fresh okra (lady's fingers), make sure they are not shriveled and that they do not have any brown spots. Fresh okra (lady's fingers) will keep, tightly wrapped, for up to 3 days in the refrigerator.

Vegetable Curry

Serves 4

INGREDIENTS

250 g/8 oz turnips or swede,
    peeled
1 aubergine (eggplant), leaf end
    trimmed
350 g/12 oz new potatoes,
    scrubbed
250 g/8 oz cauliflower
250 g/8 oz button mushrooms
1 large onion
250 g/8 oz carrots, peeled
6 tbsp vegetable ghee or oil

2 garlic cloves, crushed
5 cm/2 inch ginger root, chopped
    finely
1-2 fresh green chillies, seeded
    and chopped
1 tbsp paprika
2 tsp ground coriander
1 tbsp mild or medium curry
    powder or paste
450 ml/³/₄ pint/1³/₄ cups
    vegetable stock

400 g/14 oz can chopped
    tomatoes
1 green (bell) pepper, seeded and
    sliced
1 tbsp cornflour (cornstarch)
150 ml/¹/₄ pint/²/₃ cup coconut
    milk
2-3 tbsp ground almonds
salt
fresh coriander (cilantro) sprigs,
    to garnish

1 Cut the turnips or swede, aubergine (eggplant) and potatoes into 1 cm/¹/₂ inch cubes. Divide the cauliflower into small florets. Leave the mushrooms whole and slice the onion and carrots.

2 Heat the ghee or oil in a large saucepan, add the onion, turnip, potato and cauliflower and cook

gently for 3 minutes, stirring frequently. Add the garlic, ginger, chillies, paprika, ground coriander and curry powder or paste and cook for 1 minute.

3 Add the stock, tomatoes, aubergine (eggplant) and mushrooms and season with salt. Cover and simmer for 30 minutes or until tender. Add the (bell)

pepper and carrots, cover and cook for a further 5 minutes.

4 Blend the cornflour (cornstarch) with the coconut milk and stir into the mixture. Add ground almonds and simmer for 2 minutes, stirring all the time. Transfer to serving plates and garnish with fresh coriander (cilantro).

Courgettes & Fenugreek Seeds

Serves 4

INGREDIENTS

6 tbsp oil
1 medium onion, finely chopped
3 green chillies, finely chopped
1 tsp fresh ginger root, chopped
    finely

1 tsp fresh garlic, crushed
1 tsp chilli powder
450 g/1 lb courgettes (zucchini),
    sliced
2 tomatoes, sliced

fresh coriander (cilantro) leaves,
    plus extra to garnish
2 tsp fenugreek seeds

1 Heat the oil in a large frying pan (skillet).

2 Add the onion, green chillies, ginger, garlic and chilli powder to the pan, stirring well to combine.

3 Add the sliced courgettes (zucchini) and the sliced tomatoes to the pan and stir-fry for 5-7 minutes.

4 Add the coriander (cilantro) and fenugreek seeds to the courgette (zucchini) mixture in the pan and stir-fry for 5 minutes.

5 Remove the pan from the heat and transfer the courgette (zucchini) and fenugreek seed mixture to serving dishes. Garnish and serve hot with Chapatis

COOK'S TIP

Both the leaves and seeds of fenugreek are used, but the stalks and root should be discarded, as they have a bitter taste. Fresh fenugreek is sold in bunches. Fenugreek seeds are flat and yellowish brown in colour. You could use coriander seeds instead of the fenugreek seeds, if you prefer.

Mixed Vegetables

Serves 4

INGREDIENTS

300 ml/^{1}/$_2$ pint/1^1/$_4$ cups oil
1 tsp mustard seeds
1 tsp onion seeds
^{1}/$_2$ tsp white cumin seeds
3-4 curry leaves, chopped
450 g/1 lb onions, finely chopped
3 medium tomatoes, chopped
^{1}/$_2$ red, ^{1}/$_2$ green (bell) pepper, sliced

1 tsp fresh ginger root, finely chopped
1 tsp fresh garlic, crushed
1 tsp chilli powder
^{1}/$_4$ tsp turmeric
1 tsp salt
425 ml/^{3}/$_4$ pint/2 cups water
2 medium potatoes, peeled and cut into pieces

^{1}/$_2$ cauliflower, cut into small florets
4 medium carrots, peeled and sliced
3 green chillies, finely chopped
fresh coriander (cilantro) leaves
1 tbsp lemon juice

1 Heat the oil in a large saucepan. Add the mustard, onion and white cumin seeds along with the curry leaves and fry until they turn a shade darker.

2 Add the onions to the pan and fry over a medium heat until golden.

3 Add the tomatoes and (bell) peppers and stir-fry for about 5 minutes.

4 Add the ginger, garlic, chilli powder, turmeric and salt and mix well.

5 Add 300 ml/^{1}/$_2$ pint/ 1^1/$_4$ cups of the water, cover and leave to simmer for 10-12 minutes.

6 Add the potatoes, cauliflower, carrots, green chillies and coriander (cilantro) leaves and stir-fry for about 5 minutes.

7 Add the remaining 150 ml/^{1}/$_4$ pint/^{2}/$_3$ cup of water and the lemon juice, stirring to combine. Cover and leave to simmer for about 15 minutes, stirring occasionally.

8 Transfer the mixed vegetables to serving plates and serve at once.

Dry Split Okra

Serves 4

INGREDIENTS

450 g/1 lb okra
150 ml/¼ pint/⅔ cup oil
100 g/3½ oz/½ cup dried onions

2 tsp aamchoor (dried mango powder)
1 tsp ground cumin

1 tsp chilli powder
1 tsp salt

1 Prepare the okra by cutting the ends off and discarding them. Using a sharp knife, carefully split the okra down the middle without cutting through them completely.

2 Heat the oil in a large saucepan. Add the dried onions and fry until they are crisp.

3 Remove the fried onions from the pan with a perforated spoon and leave them to drain thoroughly on sheets of paper towel.

4 When cool enough to handle, roughly tear the dried onions and place in a large bowl.

5 Add the aamchoor (dried mango), ground cumin, chilli powder and salt to the dried onions and blend well together.

6 Spoon the onion and spice mixture into the split okra.

7 Re-heat the oil in the saucepan.

8 Gently add the okra to the hot oil and cook over a low heat for about 10-12 minutes.

9 Transfer the cooked okra to a serving dish and serve immediately.

COOK'S TIP

Ground cumin has a warm, pungent aromatic flavour and is used extensively in Indian cooking. It is a good storecupboard standby.

Tomato Curry

Serves 4

INGREDIENTS

400 g/14 oz can tomatoes
1 tsp fresh ginger root, chopped finely
1 tsp fresh garlic, crushed
1 tsp chilli powder
1 tsp salt
1/2 tsp ground coriander

1/2 tsp ground cumin
4 tbsp oil
1/2 tsp onion seeds
1/2 tsp mustard seeds
1/2 tsp fenugreek seeds
1 pinch white cumin seeds
3 dried red chillies

2 tbsp lemon juice
3 eggs, hard-boiled (hard-cooked)
fresh coriander (cilantro) leaves

1 Place the tomatoes in a large mixing bowl.

2 Add the ginger, garlic, chilli powder, salt, ground coriander and ground cumin to the tomatoes and blend well.

3 Heat the oil in a saucepan. Add the onion, mustard, fenugreek and white cumin seeds, and the dried red chillies, and stir-fry for about 1 minute. Remove the pan from the heat.

4 Add the tomato mixture to the spicy oil mixture and return to the heat. Stir-fry the mixture for about 3 minutes, then reduce the heat and cook with the lid ajar for 7-10 minutes, stirring occasionally.

5 Sprinkle over the lemon juice sparingly.

6 Transfer the tomato curry to a serving dish, set aside and keep warm until required.

7 Shell and halve the hard-boiled (hard-cooked) eggs, then gently add them, yolk end down, to the tomato curry.

8 Garnish with fresh coriander (cilantro) leaves and serve hot.

COOK'S TIP

This tomato curry can be made in advance and frozen, as it freezes particularly well.

Mussel & Red Pepper Salad

Serves 4

INGREDIENTS

2 large red (bell) peppers
350 g/12 oz cooked shelled
   mussels, thawed if frozen
1 head of radicchio
25 g/1 oz rocket (arugula) leaves
8 cooked New Zealand mussels
   in their shells

TO SERVE:
lemon wedges
crusty bread

DRESSING:
1 tbsp olive oil
1 tbsp lemon juice
1 tsp finely grated lemon rind
2 tsp clear honey
1 tsp French mustard
1 tbsp snipped fresh chives
salt and pepper

1 Preheat the grill (broiler) to hot. Halve and deseed the (bell) peppers and place them skin-side up on the rack. Cook for 8–10 minutes until the skin is charred and blistered and the flesh is soft. Cool for 10 minutes, then peel off the skin.

2 Slice the (bell) pepper flesh into thin strips and place in a bowl. Gently mix in the shelled mussels and set aside.

3 To make the dressing, mix all of the ingredients until well blended. Mix into the (bell) pepper and mussel mixture until coated.

4 Remove the central core of the radicchio and shred the leaves. Place in a serving bowl with the rocket (arugula) leaves and toss together.

5 Spoon the mussel mixture into the centre of the leaves and arrange the large New Zealand mussels round the edge of the dish. Serve with lemon wedges and crusty bread.

VARIATION

Replace the shelled mussels with peeled prawns (shrimp) and the New Zealand mussels with large crevettes, if you prefer. Lime could be used instead of lemon for a different citrus flavour.

Sweet & Sour Fish Salad

Serves 4

INGREDIENTS

225 g/8 oz trout fillets
225 g/8 oz white fish fillets
   (such as haddock or cod)
300 ml/¹/₂ pint/1¹/₄ cups water
1 stalk lemon grass
2 lime leaves
1 large red chilli
1 bunch spring onions (scallions),
   trimmed and shredded

115 g/4 oz fresh pineapple
   flesh, diced
1 small red (bell) pepper,
   deseeded and diced
1 bunch watercress, washed and
   trimmed
fresh snipped chives, to garnish

DRESSING:
1 tbsp sunflower oil
1 tbsp rice wine vinegar
pinch of chilli powder
1 tsp clear honey
salt and pepper

1 Rinse the fish, place in a frying pan (skillet) and pour over the water. Bend the lemon grass in half to bruise it and add to the pan with the lime leaves. Prick the chilli with a fork and add to the pan. Bring to the boil and simmer for 7–8 minutes. Let cool.

2 Drain the fish fillet, discarding the lemon grass, lime leaves and chilli.

Flake the flesh away from the skin of the fish and place in a bowl. Gently stir in the spring onions (scallions), pineapple and (bell) pepper.

3 Arrange the washed watercress on 4 serving plates, spoon the cooked fish mixture on top and set aside.

4 To make the dressing, mix all the ingredients together and season well. Spoon over the fish and serve garnished with chives.

VARIATION

This recipe also works very well if you replace the fish with 350 g/12 oz white crab meat. Add a dash of Tabasco sauce if you like it hot!

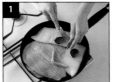

Beef & Peanut Salad

Serves 4

INGREDIENTS

¹/₂ head Chinese leaves
1 large carrot
115 g/4 oz radishes
100 g/3¹/₂ oz baby corn cobs
1 tbsp ground nut oil
1 red chilli, deseeded and
    chopped finely
1 clove garlic, chopped finely

350 g/12 oz lean beef (such as
    fillet, sirloin or rump),
    trimmed and shredded finely
1 tbsp dark soy sauce
25 g/1 oz fresh peanuts
    (optional)
red chilli, sliced, to garnish

DRESSING:
1 tbsp smooth peanut butter
1 tsp caster (superfine) sugar
2 tbsp light soy sauce
1 tbsp sherry vinegar
salt and pepper

1 Finely shred the Chinese leaves and arrange on a platter. Peel the carrot and cut into thin, matchstick-like strips. Wash, trim and quarter the radishes, and halve the baby corn cobs lengthwise. Arrange these ingredients around the edge of the dish and set aside.

2 Heat the oil in a non-stick wok or large frying pan (skillet) and stir-fry the chilli, garlic and beef for 5 minutes. Add the dark soy sauce and stir-fry for a further 1–2 minutes until tender and cooked through.

3 Meanwhile, make the dressing. Place all of the ingredients in a small bowl and blend them together until smooth.

4 Place the hot cooked beef in the centre of the salad ingredients. Spoon over the dressing and sprinkle with a few peanuts, if using. Garnish with slices of red chilli and serve immediately.

VARIATION

If preferred, use chicken, turkey, lean pork or even strips of venison instead of beef in this recipe. Cut off all visible fat before you begin.

Chicken & Spinach Salad

Serves 4

INGREDIENTS

4 boneless, skinless chicken
    breasts, 150 g/5¹/₂ oz each
450 ml/16 fl oz/2 cups fresh
    chicken stock
1 bay leaf
225 g/8 oz fresh young
    spinach leaves

1 small red onion, shredded
115 g/4 oz fresh raspberries
salt and freshly ground
    pink peppercorns
fresh toasted croûtons, to
    garnish

DRESSING:
4 tbsp low-fat natural
    (unsweetened) yogurt
1 tbsp raspberry vinegar
2 tsp clear honey

1 Place the chicken breasts in a frying pan (skillet). Pour over the fresh chicken stock and add the bay leaf. Bring to the boil, cover and simmer for 15–20 minutes, turning half-way through, until the chicken is cooked through. Leave the chicken to cool in the liquid.

2 Arrange the spinach leaves on 4 serving plates and top with the onion. Cover and leave to chill.

3 Drain the cooked chicken and pat dry on absorbent kitchen paper. Slice the chicken breasts thinly and arrange, fanned out, over the spinach and onion. Sprinkle with the raspberries.

4 To make the dressing, mix all the ingredients together in a small bowl.

5 Drizzle a spoonful of dressing over each chicken breast and season with salt and ground pink peppercorns to taste. Serve with freshly toasted croûtons.

VARIATION

This recipe is delicious with smoked chicken, but it will be more expensive and richer, so use slightly less. It would make an impressive starter for a dinner party.

Pasta Provençale

Serves 4

INGREDIENTS

225 g/8 oz penne (quills)
1 tbsp olive oil
25 g/1 oz pitted black olives, drained and chopped
25 g/1 oz dry-pack sun-dried tomatoes, soaked, drained and chopped
400 g/14 oz can artichoke hearts, drained and halved

115 g/4 oz baby courgettes (zucchini), trimmed and sliced
115 g/4 oz baby plum tomatoes, halved
100 g/3½ oz assorted baby salad leaves
salt and pepper
shredded basil leaves, to garnish

DRESSING:
4 tbsp passata (sieved tomatoes)
2 tbsp low-fat natural fromage frais (unsweetened yogurt)
1 tbsp unsweetened orange juice
1 small bunch fresh basil, shredded

1 Cook the penne (quills) according to the instructions on the packet. Do not overcook the pasta – it should still have 'bite'. Drain well and return to the pan. Stir in the olive oil, salt and pepper, olives and sun-dried tomatoes. Leave to cool.

2 Gently mix the artichokes, courgettes (zucchini) and plum tomatoes into the cooked pasta. Arrange the salad leaves in a serving bowl.

3 To make the dressing, mix all the ingredients together and toss into the vegetables and pasta.

4 Spoon the mixture on top of the salad leaves and garnish with shredded basil leaves.

VARIATION

For a non-vegetarian version, stir 225 g/8 oz canned tuna in brine, drained and flaked, into the pasta together with the vegetables. Other pasta shapes can be included – look out for farfalle (bows) and rotelle (spoked wheels).

Root Vegetable Salad

Serves 4

INGREDIENTS

350 g/12 oz carrots
225 g/8 oz mooli (white radish)
115 g/4 oz radishes
350 g/12 oz celeriac
1 tbsp orange juice
2 sticks celery with leaves,
    washed and trimmed

100 g/3^1/$_2$ oz assorted salad
    leaves
25 g/1 oz chopped walnuts

DRESSING:
1 tbsp walnut oil
1 tbsp white wine vinegar

1 tsp wholegrain mustard
^{1}/$_2$ tsp finely grated orange rind
1 tsp celery seeds
salt and pepper

1 Using a sharp knife, peel and coarsely grate or very finely shred the carrots, mooli (white radish) and radishes. Set aside in separate bowls.

2 Using a sharp knife, peel and coarsely grate or finely shred the celeriac and mix with the orange juice.

3 Remove the celery leaves and reserve them for garnishing. Finely chop the celery sticks.

4 Divide the salad leaves among 4 serving plates and arrange the vegetables in small piles on top. Set aside while you make the dressing.

5 To make the dressing, mix the walnut oil, wine vinegar, mustard, orange rind, celery seeds and season with salt and pepper to taste. Drizzle a little over each salad. Shred the reserved celery leaves and sprinkle over the salad with the chopped walnuts.

COOK'S TIP

Also known as Chinese white radish and daikon, mooli resembles a large white parsnip. It has crisp, slightly pungent flesh, which can be eaten raw or cooked. It is a useful ingredient in stir-fries. Fresh mooli tend to have a stronger flavour

Beetroot & Orange Rice Salad

Serves 4

INGREDIENTS

225 g/8 oz/1⅓ cups long-grain
  and wild rices (see Cook's Tip,
  below)
4 large oranges
450 g/1 lb cooked beetroot,
  peeled
2 heads of chicory

salt and pepper
fresh snipped chives, to garnish

DRESSING:
4 tbsp low-fat natural fromage
  frais (unsweetened yogurt)
1 garlic clove, crushed

1 tbsp wholegrain mustard
½ tsp finely grated orange rind
2 tsp clear honey

1 Cook the rices according to the instructions on the packet. Drain and set aside to cool.

2 Slice the top and bottom off each orange and remove the skin and pith. Holding the orange over a bowl to catch the juice, slice between each segment. Place the segments in a separate bowl. Cover the juice and leave to chill in the refrigerator until required.

3 Drain the beetroot if necessary and dice into cubes. Mix with the orange segments, cover and leave to chill.

4 When the rice has cooled, mix in the reserved orange juice and season with salt and pepper.

5 Line 4 serving bowls or plates with the chicory leaves. Spoon over the rice and top with the beetroot and orange segments.

6 Mix all the dressing ingredients together and spoon over the salad, or serve separately in a bowl, if preferred. Garnish with fresh snipped chives.

COOK'S TIP

Look out for boxes of ready-mixed long-grain and wild rices. Alternatively, cook 175 g/6 oz/1 cup white rice and 60 g/2 oz/¼ cup wild rice separately.

Red Hot Slaw

Serves 4

INGREDIENTS

½ small red cabbage	TO GARNISH:	3 tbsp low-fat natural
1 large carrot	red chilli strips	(unsweetened) yogurt
2 red-skinned apples	carrot strips	1 garlic clove, crushed
1 tbsp lemon juice		1 tsp paprika
1 medium red onion	DRESSING:	1–2 tsp chilli powder
100 g/3 ½ oz reduced-fat	3 tbsp reduced-calorie	pinch cayenne pepper (optional)
Cheddar cheese, grated	mayonnaise	salt and pepper

1 Cut the red cabbage in half and remove the central core. Finely shred the leaves and place in a large bowl. Peel and coarsely grate or finely shred the carrot and mix into the cabbage.

2 Core the apples and dice, leaving on the skins. Place in another bowl and toss in the lemon juice to prevent the apple browning. Mix the apple into the cabbage and carrot.

3 Peel and finely shred or grate the onion. Stir into the other vegetables along with the cheese and mix together.

4 To make the dressing, mix together the mayonnaise, yogurt, garlic and paprika in a small bowl. Add chilli powder according to taste, and the cayenne pepper, if using – remember this will add more spice to the dressing. Season well.

5 Toss the dressing into the vegetables and mix well. Cover and leave to chill in the refrigerator for 1 hour to allow the flavours to develop. Serve garnished with strips of red chilli and carrot.

Pasta Niçoise Salad

Serves 4

INGREDIENTS

225 g/8 oz farfalle (bows)

175 g/6 oz French (green) beans, topped and tailed

350 g/12 oz fresh tuna steaks

115 g/4 oz baby plum tomatoes, halved

8 anchovy fillets, drained on absorbent kitchen paper

2 tbsp capers in brine, drained

25 g/1 oz pitted black olives in brine, drained

fresh basil leaves, to garnish

salt and pepper

DRESSING:

1 tbsp olive oil

1 garlic clove, crushed

1 tbsp lemon juice

$\frac{1}{2}$ tsp finely grated lemon rind

1 tbsp shredded fresh basil leaves

1 Cook the pasta in lightly salted boiling water according to the instructions on the packet until just cooked. Drain well, set aside and keep warm.

2 Bring a small saucepan of lightly salted water to the boil and cook the French (green) beans for 5–6 minutes until just tender. Drain well and toss into the pasta. Set aside and keep warm.

3 Preheat the grill (broiler) to medium. Rinse and pat the tuna steaks dry on absorbent kitchen paper. Season on both sides with black pepper. Place the tuna steaks on the grill (broiler) rack and cook for 4–5 minutes on each side until cooked through.

4 Drain the tuna on absorbent kitchen paper and flake into bite-sized pieces. Toss the tuna into the pasta along with the tomatoes, anchovies, capers and olives. Set aside and keep warm.

5 Meanwhile, prepare the dressing. Mix all the ingredients together and season with salt and pepper to taste. Pour the dressing over the pasta mixture and mix carefully. Transfer t o a warmed serving bowl and serve sprinkled with fresh basil leaves.

Coconut Couscous Salad

Serves 4

INGREDIENTS

350 g/12 oz precooked couscous
175 g/6 oz no-need-to-soak
   dried apricots
1 small bunch fresh chives
2 tbsp unsweetened desiccated
   (shredded) coconut

1 tsp ground cinnamon
salt and pepper
shredded mint leaves, to garnish

DRESSING:
1 tbsp olive oil

2 tbsp unsweetened orange juice
$\frac{1}{2}$ tsp finely grated orange rind
1 tsp wholegrain mustard
1 tsp clear honey
2 tbsp chopped fresh mint leaves

1 Soak the couscous according to the instructions on the packet.

2 Bring a large saucepan of water to the boil. Transfer the couscous to a steamer or large sieve (strainer) lined with muslin (cheesecloth) and place over the pan of water. Cover and steam according to the instructions on the packet. Remove from the heat, place in a heatproof bowl and set aside to cool.

3 Meanwhile, slice the apricots into thin strips and place in a small bowl. Using scissors, snip the chives over the apricots.

4 When the couscous is cool, mix in the apricots, chives, coconut and cinnamon. Season well.

5 To make the dressing, mix all the ingredients together and season. Pour over the couscous and mix until well combined. Cover and leave to chill for 1 hour to allow the flavours to develop. Serve garnished with mint leaves.

COOK'S TIP

To serve this salad hot, when the couscous has been steamed, mix in the apricots, chives, coconut, cinnamon and seasoning along with 1 tbsp olive oil. Transfer to a warmed serving bowl and serve.

Bulgur Pilau

Serves 4

INGREDIENTS

75 g/2³/₄ oz/6 tbsp butter or
    vegetarian margarine
1 red onion, halved and sliced
2 garlic cloves, crushed
350 g/12 oz/2 cups bulgur wheat
175 g/6 oz tomatoes, seeded
    and chopped
50 g/1³/₄ oz baby corn cobs,

halved lengthwise
75 g/2³/₄ oz small
    broccoli florets
850 ml/1 ¹/₂ pints/3³/₄ cups
    vegetable stock
2 tbsp clear honey
50 g/1³/₄ oz/¹/₃ cup sultanas
    (golden raisins)

50 g/1³/₄ oz/¹/₃ cup pine
    kernels (nuts)
¹/₂ tsp ground cinnamon
¹/₂ tsp ground cumin
salt and pepper
sliced spring onions (scallions),
    to garnish

1 Melt the butter or margarine in a large flameproof casserole dish.

2 Add the onion and garlic and sauté for 2–3 minutes, stirring occasionally.

3 Add the bulgur wheat, tomatoes, corn cobs, broccoli and stock and bring to the boil. Reduce the heat, cover and cook for 15–20 minutes, stirring occasionally

4 Stir in the honey, sultanas (golden raisins), pine kernels (nuts), ground cinnamon, cumin and salt and pepper to taste, mixing well. Remove the casserole from the heat, cover and leave for 10 minutes.

5 Spoon the bulgur pilau into a warm serving dish.

6 Garnish the bulgur pilau with sliced spring onions (scallions) and serve immediately.

COOK'S TIP

The dish is left to stand for 10 minutes in order for the bulgur to finish cooking and the flavours to mingle.

Caesar Salad

Serves 6-8

INGREDIENTS

2 thick slices of white bread	1 clove garlic	DRESSING:
2 tbsp sunflower oil	50 g/1¾ oz fresh Parmesan	1 small egg
2 rashers streaky bacon or 6	cheese	juice 1 lemon
chopped anchovies	1 large cos (romaine) lettuce	6 tbsp olive oil
		salt and white pepper

1 To make the croûtons, remove the crusts from the bread and discard. Cut the bread into small cubes. Heat the oil in a frying pan (skillet) and fry the bread cubes until golden-brown. Drain on absorbent kitchen paper.

2 Remove the rind from the bacon and discard. Chop the bacon and fry until crisp. Drain on absorbent kitchen paper.

3 Cut the garlic in half and rub all around the inside of a serving dish.

This will give the salad just a hint of garlic.

4 Wash the lettuce, tear into bite-size pieces and then place in the serving dish.

5 Using a potato peeler, shave peelings off the Parmesan.

6 To make the dressing, whisk the egg in a small bowl. Gradually whisk in the lemon juice and oil. Season with a little salt and pepper to taste.

7 Pour the salad dressing over the lettuce and toss to coat. Serve sprinkled with the croûtons, bacon and Parmesan shavings.

COOK'S TIP

Pregnant women, children and people with weak immune systems may wish to avoid eating recipes containing raw egg.

Coleslaw

Serves 10–12

INGREDIENTS

150 ml/5 fl oz/²⁄₃ cup
   mayonnaise
150 ml/5 fl oz/²⁄₃ cup low-fat
   natural yogurt

dash of Tabasco sauce
1 medium head white cabbage
4 carrots
1 green (bell) pepper

2 tbsp sunflower seeds
salt and pepper

1 To make the dressing, combine the mayonnaise, yogurt, Tabasco sauce and salt and pepper to taste in a small bowl. Leave to chill in the refrigerator until required.

2 Cut the cabbage in half and then into quarters. Remove and discard the tough centre stalk. Shred the cabbage leaves finely. Wash the leaves and dry them thoroughly.

3 Peel the carrot and shred in a food processor. Alternatively, coarsely grate the carrot.

4 Quarter and deseed the (bell) pepper and cut the flesh into thin strips.

5 Combine the vegetables in a large serving bowl and toss. Pour over the dressing and toss until well coated then chill.

6 Just before serving, place the sunflower seeds on a baking tray and toast them in the oven or under the grill (broiler) until golden brown.

7 Scatter the sesame seeds over the coleslaw and serve.

COOK'S TIP

You can make coleslaw a few days in advance. To ensure that the sunflower seeds are crispy, add them just before serving.

VARIATION

For a slightly different taste, try the following ingredients in the coleslaw: raisins, grapes, grated apple, chopped walnuts, cubes of cheese or roasted peanuts.

Green Bean & Carrot Salad

Serves 4

INGREDIENTS

350 g/12 oz green (French) beans
225 g/8 oz carrots
1 red (bell) pepper
1 red onion

DRESSING:
2 tbsp extra virgin olive oil
1 tbsp red wine vinegar
2 tsp sun-dried tomato paste

¼ tsp caster (superfine) sugar
salt and pepper

1 Top and tail the beans and blanch them in boiling water for 4 minutes, until tender. Drain the beans and rinse under cold water until cooled. Drain again.

2 Transfer the beans to a large salad bowl.

3 Peel the carrots and cut them into thin matchsticks, using a mandolin if you have one.

4 Halve and deseed the (bell) pepper and cut the flesh into thin strips.

5 Peel the onion and cut it into thin slices.

6 Add the carrot, (bell) pepper and onion to the beans and toss to mix.

7 To make the dressing, place the oil, wine vinegar, sun-dried tomato paste, sugar and salt and pepper to taste in a screw-top jar and shake well.

8 Pour the dressing over the vegetables and serve immediately or leave to chill in the refrigerator until required.

COOK'S TIP

Use canned beans if fresh ones are unavailable. Rinse off the salty liquid and drain well. There is no need to blanch canned beans.

Spinach & Orange Salad

Serves 4-6

INGREDIENTS

225 g/8 oz baby spinach leaves
2 large oranges
½ red onion

DRESSING:
3 tbsp extra virgin olive oil
2 tbsp freshly squeezed orange
    juice

2 tsp lemon juice
1 tsp clear honey
½ tsp wholegrain mustard
salt and pepper

1 Wash the spinach leaves under cold running water and then dry them thoroughly on absorbent kitchen paper. Remove any tough stalks and tear the larger leaves into smaller pieces.

2 Slice the top and bottom off each orange with a sharp knife, then remove the peel.

3 Carefully slice between the membranes of the orange to remove the individual segments.

4 Using a sharp knife, finely chop the onion.

5 Mix together the salad leaves and orange segments and arrange in a serving dish. Scatter the chopped onion over.

6 To make the dressing, whisk together the olive oil, orange juice, lemon juice, honey, mustard and salt and pepper to taste.

7 Pour the dressing over the salad just before serving. Toss the salad well to coat the leaves with the dressing.

COOK'S TIP

Tear the spinach leaves into bite-sized pieces rather than cutting them because cutting bruises the leaves.

VARIATION

Use a mixture of spinach and watercress leaves, if you prefer a slightly more peppery flavour.

Potato Salad

Serves 4

INGREDIENTS

700 g/1 lb 9 oz tiny new
   potatoes
8 spring onions (scallions)
1 hard-boiled (hard-cooked) egg
   (optional)

250 ml/9 fl oz/1 cup mayonnaise
1 tsp paprika
salt and pepper

TO GARNISH:
2 tbsp chives, snipped
pinch of paprika

1 Bring a large pan of lightly salted water to the boil. Add the potatoes to the pan and cook for 10–15 minutes or until they are just tender.

2 Drain the potatoes in a colander and rinse them under cold running water until they are completely cold. Drain them again thoroughly. Transfer the potatoes to a mixing bowl and set aside until required.

3 Using a sharp knife, trim and slice the spring onions (scallions) thinly on the diagonal.

4 Chop the hard-boiled (hard-cooked) egg.

5 Combine the mayonnaise, paprika and salt and pepper to taste in a bowl. Pour the mixture over the potatoes.

6 Add the spring onions (scallions) and egg (if using) to the potatoes and toss together.

7 Transfer the potato salad to a serving bowl, sprinkle with snipped chives and a pinch of paprika. Cover and leave to chill in the refrigerator.

VARIATION

To make a lighter dressing, use a mixture of half mayonnaise and half natural yogurt.

VARIATION

Add cubes of cheese to the potato salad, if liked.

Tabouleh

Serves 4

INGREDIENTS

225 g/8 oz/2 cups cracked wheat
225 g/8 oz tomatoes
1 small onion
1/4 cucumber
1/2 red (bell) pepper

4 tbsp chopped, fresh parsley
3 tbsp chopped, fresh mint
2 tbsp pine nuts
4 tbsp lemon juice
4 tbsp extra virgin olive oil

2 cloves garlic, crushed
salt and pepper

1 Place the cracked wheat in a large bowl and cover with plenty of boiling water. Leave to stand for about 30 minutes or until the grains are tender and have swelled in size.

2 Drain the wheat through a large sieve. Press down with a plate in order to remove as much water as possible. Transfer the wheat to a large bowl.

3 Cut the tomatoes in half, scoop out the seeds and discard them. Chop the flesh into fine dice. Using a sharp knife, finely chop the onion.

4 Scoop out the seeds from the cucumber and discard them. Finely dice the cucumber flesh.

5 Deseed the (bell) peppers and chop the flesh. Add the prepared vegetables to the wheat with the herbs and pine nuts. Toss until mixed.

6 Mix together the lemon juice oil, garlic and salt and pepper to taste in a small bowl.

7 Pour the mixture over the wheat and vegetables and toss together. Leave to chill in the refrigerator until required.

COOK'S TIP

This salad is best made a few hours before it is required to allow time for the flavours to develop and blend together. It can even be made a few days ahead, if wished.

Hot Lentil Salad
with Balsamic Dressing

Serves 6-8

INGREDIENTS

175 g/6 oz Puy lentils, cooked	125 g/4½ oz green (French)	1 tsp Dijon mustard
4 tbsp olive oil	beans, trimmed and cut into	1 tbsp balsamic vinegar
1 small onion, sliced	short lengths	salt and pepper
4 sticks celery, sliced	½ red (bell) pepper, deseeded	
2 cloves garlic, crushed	and diced	
2 courgettes (zucchini), trimmed	½ yellow (bell) pepper, deseeded	
and diced	and diced	

1 Place the lentils in a large mixing or serving bowl. The lentils can still be warm, if wished.

2 Heat the oil in a pan and fry the onion and celery for 2–3 minutes until softened.

3 Stir the garlic, courgettes (zucchini) and green (French) beans into the pan and cook for a further 2 minutes.

4 Add the (bell) peppers to the pan and cook for 1 minute.

5 Stir the mustard and the balsamic vinegar into the pan and mix until warm and well combined.

6 Pour the warm mixture over the lentils and toss together to mix well. Season with salt and pepper to taste and serve at once.

COOK'S TIP

To cook the lentils, rinse them well and place in a large saucepan. Cover with plenty of cold water and bring to the boil. Boil rapidly for 10 minutes, then reduce the heat and simmer for 35 minutes until the lentils are tender. Drain well.

Italian Mozzarella Salad

Serves 6

INGREDIENTS
---

200 g/7 oz baby spinach	225 g/8 oz cherry tomatoes	salt and freshly ground black
125 g/4 ½ oz watercress	2 tsp balsamic vinegar	pepper
125 g/4 ½ oz Mozzarella cheese	1 ½ tbsp extra virgin olive oil	

1 Wash the spinach and watercress and drain thoroughly on absorbent kitchen paper. Remove any tough stalks. Place the spinach and watercress leaves in a serving dish.

2 Cut the Mozzarella into small pieces and scatter them over the spinach and watercress leaves.

3 Cut the cherry tomatoes in half and scatter them over the salad.

4 Sprinkle over the balsamic vinegar and oil, and season with salt and pepper to taste. Toss the mixture together to coat the leaves. Serve at once or leave to chill in the refrigerator until required.

VARIATION

Include Feta or Halloumi cheese instead of Mozzarella for a change, and use sherry vinegar instead of balsamic vinegar, if preferred.

COOK'S TIP

Mozzarella is a highly popular cheese. It is a soft, fresh cheese with a piquant flavour, traditionally made from water buffalo's milk. It is usually sold surrounded by whey to keep it moist. Buffalo milk is now scarce, and so nowadays this cheese is often made with cow's milk. Mozzarella combines well with tomatoes, and this combination is now a classic.

Artichoke & Prosciutto Salad

Serves 4

INGREDIENTS

275 g/9 ½ oz can artichoke
    hearts in oil, drained
4 small tomatoes
25 g/1 oz sun-dried tomatoes
    in oil
40 g/1 ½ oz Parma ham
    (prosciutto)

25 g/1 oz pitted black olives,
    halved
few basil leaves

DRESSING:
3 tbsp olive oil
1 tbsp white wine vinegar

1 clove garlic, crushed
½ tsp mild mustard
1 tsp clear honey
salt and pepper

1 Make sure the artichokes hearts are thoroughly drained, then cut them into quarters and place in a bowl until required.

2 Cut each fresh tomato into wedges. Slice the sun-dried tomatoes into thin strips. Cut the Parma ham (prosciutto) into thin strips and add to the bowl with the tomatoes and olive halves.

3 Keeping a few basil leaves whole for garnishing, tear the remainder of the leaves into small pieces and add to the bowl containing the other salad ingredients.

4 Put the oil, wine vinegar, garlic, mustard, honey and salt and pepper to taste in a screw-top jar and shake vigorously until well blended.

5 Pour the dressing over the salad and toss.

6 Serve the salad garnished with a few whole basil leaves.

COOK'S TIP

Use bottled artichokes in oil as they have a better flavour. Rinse canned artichokes to remove the salty liquid.

Pear & Roquefort Salad

Serves 4

INGREDIENTS

50 g/1 ³/₄ oz Roquefort cheese
150 ml/5 fl oz/²/₃ cup low-fat
    natural yogurt
2 tbsp snipped chives

few leaves of lollo rosso
few leaves of radiccio
few leaves of lamb's lettuce
    (corn salad)

2 ripe pears
pepper
whole chives, to garnish

1 Place the cheese in a bowl and mash with a fork. Gradually blend the yogurt into the cheese to make a smooth dressing. Add the chives and season with a little pepper according to taste.

2 Tear the lollo rosso, radiccio and lamb's lettuce leaves into manageable pieces. Arrange the salad leaves on a serving platter or on individual serving plates.

3 Quarter and core the pears and then cut them into slices.

4 Arrange the pear slices over the salad leaves.

5 Drizzle the dressing over the pears and garnish with a few whole chives. Serve at once.

COOK'S TIP

Arrange the Pear and Roquefort Salad on individual plates for an attractive starter, or on one large serving platter for a side salad.

COOK'S TIP

Look out for bags of mixed salad leaves as these are generally more economical than buying lots of different leaves separately. If you are using leaves that have not been prewashed, rinse them well and dry them thoroughly on absorbent paper kitchen towels or in a salad spinner. Alternatively, wrap the leaves in a clean tea towel (dish cloth) and shake dry.

Pasta Salad with Basil Vinaigrette

Serves 4

INGREDIENTS

225 g/8 oz fusilli (pasta spirals)
4 tomatoes
50 g/1 ³/4 oz black olives
25 g/1 oz sun-dried tomatoes
   in oil
2 tbsp pine nuts

2 tbsp grated Parmesan cheese
fresh basil, to garnish

VINAIGRETTE:
15 g/¹/2 oz basil leaves
1 clove garlic

2 tbsp grated Parmesan cheese
4 tbsp extra virgin olive oil
2 tbsp lemon juice
salt and pepper

1 Cook the pasta in lightly salted boiling water for 10–12 minutes until just tender, or according to the instructions on the packet. Drain the pasta, rinse under cold water, then drain again thoroughly. Place the pasta in a large bowl.

2 To make the vinaigrette, place the basil leaves, garlic, cheese, oil and lemon juice in a food processor. Season with salt and pepper to taste. Process until the leaves are well chopped and the ingredients are combined. Alternatively, finely chop the basil leaves by hand and combine with the other vinaigrette ingredients. Pour the vinaigrette over the pasta and toss to coat.

3 Cut the tomatoes into wedges. Pit and halve the olives. Slice the sun-dried tomatoes. Toast the pine nuts on a baking tray under the grill (broiler) until golden.

4 Add the tomatoes (fresh and sun-dried) and the olives to the pasta and mix until combined.

5 Transfer the pasta to a serving dish, scatter over the Parmesan and pine nuts and garnish with a few basil leaves.

Mango & Wild Rice Salad

Serves 6

INGREDIENTS

75 g/2³/₄ oz/¹/₂ cup wild rice
150 g/5 ¹/₂ oz/1 cup Basmati rice
3 tbsp hazelnut oil
1 tbsp sherry vinegar
1 ripe mango

3 sticks celery
75 g/2³/₄ oz ready-to-eat dried
   apricots, chopped
75 g/2³/₄ oz flaked (slivered)
   almonds, flaked

2 tbsp chopped, fresh coriander
   (cilantro) or mint
salt and pepper
sprigs of fresh coriander
   (cilantro) or mint, to garnish

1 Cook the rice in separate saucepans in lightly salted boiling water. Cook the wild rice for 45–50 minutes and the Basmati rice for 10–12 minutes. Drain, rinse well and drain again. Place in a large bowl.

2 Mix the oil, vinegar and seasoning together. Pour the mixture over the rice and toss well.

3 Cut the mango in half lengthwise, as close to the stone as possible. Remove and discard the stone.

4 Peel the skin from the mango and cut the flesh into slices.

5 Slice the celery thinly and add to the cooled rice with the mango, apricots, almonds and chopped herbs. Toss together and transfer to a serving dish. Garnish with sprigs of of fresh herbs.

COOK'S TIP

To toast almonds, place them on a baking sheet in a preheated oven 180°C/350°F/Gas Mark 4 for 5–10 minutes. Alternatively, toast them under the grill (broiler), turning frequently and keeping a close eye on them because they will quickly burn.

Mixed Bean Salad

Serves 6-8

INGREDIENTS

400 g/14 oz can flageolet
(small navy) beans, drained

400 g/14 oz can red kidney
beans, drained

400 g/14 oz can butter beans,
drained

1 small red onion, thinly sliced

175 g/6 oz dwarf green beans,
topped and tailed

1 red (bell) pepper, halved and
deseeded

DRESSING:

4 tbsp olive oil

2 tbsp sherry vinegar

2 tbsp lemon juice

1 tsp light muscovado sugar

1 tsp chilli sauce (optional)

1 Put the canned beans in a large mixing bowl. Add the sliced onion and mix together.

2 Cut the dwarf green beans in half and cook in lightly salted boiling water for about 8 minutes until just tender. Refresh under cold water and drain again. Add to the mixed beans and onions.

3 Place the (bell) pepper halves, cut side down, on a grill (broiler) rack and cook until the skin blackens and chars. Leave to cool slightly then pop them into a plastic bag for about 10 minutes. Peel away the skin from the (bell) peppers and discard. Chop the (bell) pepper flesh and add to the beans.

4 To make the dressing, place the oil, sherry vinegar, lemon juice, sugar and chilli sauce (if using) in a screw-top jar and shake vigorously.

5 Pour the dressing over the mixed bean salad and toss well. Leave to chill in the refrigerator until required.

VARIATION

You can use any combination of beans in this salad. For a distinctive flavour, add 1 teaspoon of curry paste instead of the chilli sauce.

Mediterranean Pepper Salad

Serves 4

2 red (bell) peppers, halved and deseeded

2 yellow (bell) peppers, halved and deseeded

3 tbsp extra virgin olive oil

1 onion, cut into wedges

2 large courgettes (zucchini), sliced

2 garlic cloves, sliced

1 tbsp balsamic vinegar

50 g/1¾ oz anchovy fillets, chopped

25 g/1 oz pitted black olives, quartered

fresh basil leaves

1 Place the (bell) pepper halves, cut side down, on a grill (broiler) pan and cook until the skin blackens and chars. Leave to cool slightly then pop them into a plastic bag for about 10 minutes.

2 Peel away the skin from the (bell) peppers and discard. Cut the flesh into thick strips.

3 Heat the oil in a large frying pan (skillet), add the onion and cook gently for 10 minutes or until softened. Add the

courgette (zucchini) slices, garlic and (bell) pepper strips to the pan and cook, stirring occasionally, for a further 10 minutes.

4 Add the vinegar, anchovies and olives to the pan. Season to taste. Mix well and leave to cool.

5 Reserve a few basil leaves for garnishing, then tear the remainder into small pieces. Stir them into the salad.

6 Transfer the salad to a serving dish and

garnish with a few whole basil leaves.

COOK'S TIP

Balsamic vinegar is made in and around Modena in Italy. Its rich, mellow flavour is perfect for Mediterranean-style salads, but if it is unavailable, use sherry vinegar or white wine vinegar instead.

Hot Salad

Serves 4

| INGREDIENTS |

½ medium-sized cauliflower	½ cucumber	2 tbsp butter
1 green (bell) pepper	4 carrots	salt and pepper
1 red (bell) pepper		

1 Rinse the cauliflower and cut into small florets, using a sharp knife.

2 Cut the (bell) peppers into thin slices.

3 Cut the cucumber into thin slices.

4 Peel the carrots and cut them into thin slices.

5 Melt the butter in a large saucepan, stirring constantly so that it doesn't burn.

6 Add the cauliflower, (bell) peppers, cucumber and carrots and stir-fry for 5-7 minutes. Season with salt and pepper to taste, cover the pan with a lid, reduce the heat and leave to simmer for about 3 minutes.

7 Transfer the vegetables to a serving dish, toss to mix, and serve immediately.

COOK'S TIP

In India, you can buy snacks and accompaniments along the roadside while elsewhere you can either buy them from Indian or Pakistani grocers. However, they are fresher and more satisfying made at home.

VARIATION

You can replace the vegetables in this recipe with those of your choice, if you prefer.

Cool Cucumber Salad

Serves 4

INGREDIENTS
---

225 g/8 oz cucumber
1 green chilli (optional)
fresh coriander (cilantro) leaves,
   finely chopped

2 tbsp lemon juice
½ tsp salt
1 tsp sugar

fresh mint leaves and red (bell)
   pepper strips, to garnish

---

1 Using a sharp knife, slice the cucumber thinly. Arrange the cucumber slices on a round serving plate.

2 Using a sharp knife, chop the green chilli (if using).

3 Scatter the chopped chilli over the cucumber.

4 To make the dressing, place the chopped coriander (cilantro) leaves, lemon juice, salt and sugar into a bowl, mix together and set aside.

5 Place the cucumber in the refrigerator and leave to chill for at least 1 hour, or until required.

6 Transfer the cucumber to a serving dish.

7 Pour the dressing over the cucumber just before serving and garnish with fresh mint leaves.

COOK'S TIP

To store fresh coriander (cilantro), put the roots in a glass of water and keep in a cool place for up to 4 days.

COOK'S TIP

Much of the heat in Indian dishes comes from fresh green chillies, although dried and ground red chillies are also commonplace. In southern India, with its searingly hot temperatures, large quantities of chillies are used because they cause the body to perspire, which has a cooling effect. Numerous varieties of fresh chilli grow in India.. As a general rule, the smaller the chilli, the hotter it will be. Fresh chillies will keep for about 5 days in the refrigerator.

Indian-Style Omelette

Serves 2-4

INGREDIENTS

1 small onion, very finely chopped	fresh coriander (cilantro) leaves, finely chopped	1 tsp salt
2 green chillies, finely chopped	4 medium eggs	2 tbsp oil

1 Place the onion, chillies and coriander (cilantro) in a large mixing bowl. Mix together, ideally with your fingers.

2 Place the eggs in a separate bowl and whisk together.

3 Add the onion mixture to the eggs and mix together well.

4 Add the salt to the egg and onion mixture and whisk together well.

5 Heat 1 tbsp of the oil in a large frying pan (skillet). Place a ladleful of the omelette batter into the heated pan.

6 Fry the omelette, turning once and pressing down with a flat spoon to make sure that the egg is cooked right through, until the omelette is a golden brown colour.

7 Repeat the same process for the remaining batter. Set the omelettes aside and keep warm while you make the remaining batches of omelettes.

8 Serve the omelettes immediately with Paratas or toasted bread. Alternatively, simply serve the omelettes with a crisp green salad for a light lunch.

COOK'S TIP

Indian cooks use a variety of vegetable oils, and groundnut or sunflower oils make good alternatives for most dishes, although sometimes more specialist ones, such as coconut oil, mustard oil and sesame oil, are called for.

Sweet & Sour Fruit

Serves 4

INGREDIENTS

400 g/14 oz can mixed fruit
   cocktail
400 g/14 oz can guavas
2 large bananas

3 apples
1 tsp ground black pepper
1 tsp salt

2 tbsp lemon juice
$\frac{1}{2}$ tsp ground ginger
fresh mint leaves, to garnish

1 Drain the can of fruit cocktail and pour the fruit pieces into a deep mixing bowl.

2 Mix the guavas and their syrup with the drained fruit cocktail.

3 Peel the bananas and cut into slices.

4 Peel and core the apples (optional) and cut into dice.

5 Add the pieces of fresh fruit to the bowl containing the canned fruit and mix together.

6 Add the ground black pepper, salt, lemon juice and ginger and stir well to mix.

7 Serve as a snack garnished with a few fresh mint leaves.

COOK'S TIP

The lemon juice in this recipe serves to add a sharp flavour to the dish but it also prevents the banana and apple from dicolouring and turning brown when the flesh is exposed to the air.

COOK'S TIP

Ginger is one of the most popular spices in India and also one of the oldest. It can be bought as fresh ginger root in most large supermarkets. It should always be peeled before use and can be finely chopped or puréed. Ground ginger is also useful to have in your storecupboard.

Baking & Desserts

The ideal ending to a meal is fresh fruit, topped with low-fat yogurt or fromage frais. Fruit contains no fat and is sweet enough not to need extra sugar, and it is also a valuable source of vitamins and fibre – ideal in every way for anyone who cares about their own and their family's health.

There are, however, dozens of other ways in which fruit can be used as the basis for desserts and bakes, and thanks to modern transportation systems the range of unusual and exotic fruits available in supermarkets seems to expand every week. Experiment with some of these unfamiliar fruits in delicious warm desserts, sophisticated mousses and fools, and satisfying cakes, and use old favourites in enticing new ways.

Paper-Thin Fruit Pies

Serves 4

INGREDIENTS

1 medium eating (dessert) apple
1 medium ripe pear
2 tbsp lemon juice
60 g/2 oz low-fat spread

4 rectangular sheets of filo
pastry, thawed if frozen
2 tbsp low-sugar apricot jam
1 tbsp unsweetened orange juice

2 tsp icing (confectioner's) sugar,
for dusting
low-fat custard, to serve

1 Preheat the oven to 200°C/400°F/Gas Mark 6. Core and thinly slice the apple and pear and toss them in the lemon juice to prevent discoloration.

2 Melt the low-fat spread over a gentle heat.

3 Cut the sheets of pastry into 4 and cover with a clean, damp tea towel (dish cloth). Brush 4 non-stick Yorkshire pudding tins (large muffin pans), measuring 10 cm/ 4 inch across, with a little of the low-fat spread.

4 Working on each pie separately, brush 4 sheets of pastry with the melted low-fat spread. Press a small sheet of pastry into the base of one tin (pan). Arrange the other sheets of pastry on top at slightly different angles. Repeat with the other sheets of pastry to make another 3 pies.

5 Arrange the apple and pear slices alternately in the centre of each pastry case and lightly crimp the edges of the pastry of each pie.

6 Mix the apricot jam and orange juice together until smooth and generously brush over the fruit. Bake for 12–15 minutes. Dust with icing (confectioner's) sugar and serve hot with low-fat custard.

VARIATION

Other combinations of fruit are equally delicious. Try peach and apricot, raspberry and apple, or pineapple and mango.

Almond Trifles

Serves 4

INGREDIENTS

8 Amaretti di Saronno biscuits	300 ml/¹/₂ pint/1¹/₄ cups	1 tsp almond essence (extract)
4 tbsp brandy or Amaretti liqueur	low-fat custard	15 g/¹/₂ oz toasted almonds,
225 g/8 oz raspberries	300 ml/¹/₂ pint/1¹/₄ cups low-fat	flaked (slivered)
	natural fromage frais	1 tsp cocoa powder
	(unsweetened yogurt)	

1 Place the biscuits in a mixing bowl and using the end of a rolling pin, carefully crush the biscuits into small pieces.

2 Divide the crushed biscuits among 4 serving glasses. Sprinkle the brandy or liqueur over the crushed biscuits and leave to stand for about 30 minutes to allow the biscuits to soften.

3 Top the layer of crushed biscuits with a layer of raspberries, reserving a few raspberries for decoration, and spoon over enough custard to just cover.

4 Mix the fromage frais (unsweetened yogurt) with the almond essence (extract) and spoon over the custard. Leave to chill in the refrigerator for about 30 minutes.

5 Just before serving, sprinkle over the toasted almonds and dust with cocoa powder. Decorate with the reserved raspberries and serve at once.

VARIATION

Try this trifle with assorted summer fruits. If they are a frozen mix, use them frozen and allow them to thaw so that the juices soak into the biscuit base – it will taste truly delicious.

Cheese Hearts with Strawberry Sauce

Serves 4

INGREDIENTS

150 g/5¹/₂ oz low-fat cottage
cheese
150 ml/5 fl oz/²/₃ cup low-fat
natural fromage frais
(unsweetened yogurt)

1 medium egg white
2 tbsp caster (superfine) sugar
1–2 tsp vanilla essence (extract)
rose-scented geranium leaves,
to decorate (optional)

SAUCE:
225 g/8 oz strawberries
4 tbsp unsweetened orange juice
2–3 tsp icing (confectioner's)
sugar

1 Line 4 heart-shaped moulds (molds) with clean muslin (cheesecloth). Place a sieve (strainer) over a mixing bowl and using the back of a metal spoon, press through the cottage cheese. Mix in the fromage frais (yogurt).

2 Whisk the egg white until stiff. Fold into the cheeses, with the caster (superfine) sugar and vanilla essence (extract).

3 Place the moulds (molds) on a wire rack set over a roasting tin (pan). Spoon the the cheese mixture into the moulds (molds) and smooth over the tops. Leave to chill for 1 hour or until firm and well drained.

4 To make the sauce, wash the strawberries under cold running water. Reserving a few strawberries for decoration, hull and chop the remainder. Place the strawberries in a blender or food processor with the orange juice and process until smooth. Alternatively, push through a sieve (strainer) to purée. Mix with the icing (confectioner's) sugar to taste. Cover and leave to chill until required.

5 Remove the cheese hearts from the moulds (molds) and transfer to serving plates. Remove the muslin (cheesecloth), decorate with the reserved strawberries and geranium leaves (if using) and serve with the sauce.

Almond & Sultana Cheesecakes

Serves 4

INGREDIENTS

12 Amaretti di Saronno biscuits
1 medium egg white, beaten
225 g/8 oz skimmed-milk soft
   cheese
$\frac{1}{2}$ tsp almond essence (extract)
$\frac{1}{2}$ tsp finely grated lime rind

25 g/1 oz ground almonds
25 g/1 oz caster (superfine) sugar
60 g/2 oz sultanas
2 tsp powdered gelatine
2 tbsp boiling water
2 tbsp lime juice

TO DECORATE:
25 g/1 oz flaked (slivered)
   toasted almonds
strips of lime rind

1 Preheat the oven to 180°C/350°F/Gas Mark 4. Place the biscuits in a clean plastic bag, seal the bag and using a rolling pin, crush them into small pieces. Place the crumbs in a bowl and bind together with the egg white.

2 Arrange 4 non-stick pastry rings or poached egg rings, 9 cm/3½ inches across, on a baking sheet (cookie sheet) lined with baking parchment. Divide the biscuit mixture into 4

equal portions and spoon it into the rings, pressing down well. Bake for 10 minutes until crisp and leave to cool in the rings.

3 Beat together the soft cheese, almond essence (extract), lime rind, ground almonds, sugar and sultanas until well mixed.

4 Dissolve the gelatine in the boiling water and stir in the lime juice. Fold into the cheese mixture and spoon over the biscuit

bases. Smooth over the tops and chill for 1 hour until set.

5 Loosen the cheesecakes using a small palette knife (spatula) and transfer to serving plates. Decorate with toasted almonds and lime rind, and serve.

VARIATION

If you prefer, substitute chopped no-need-to-soak dried apricots for the sultanas.

Red Fruits with Foaming Sauce

Serves 4

INGREDIENTS

225 g/8 oz redcurrants, washed
 and trimmed, thawed if frozen
225 g/8 oz cranberries
75 g/3 oz light muscovado sugar

200 ml/7 fl oz/³/₄ cup
 unsweetened apple juice
1 cinnamon stick, broken
300 g/10¹/₂ oz small strawberries,
 washed, hulled and halved

SAUCE:
225 g/8 oz raspberries, thawed
 if frozen
2 tbsp fruit cordial
100 g/3¹/₂ oz marshmallows

1 Place the redcurrants, cranberries and sugar in a saucepan. Pour in the apple juice and add the cinnamon stick. Bring the mixture to the boil and simmer gently for 10 minutes until the fruit has just softened.

2 Stir the strawberries into the cranberry and sugar mixture and mix well. Transfer the mixture to a bowl, cover and leave to chill for about 1 hour. Remove and discard the cinnamon stick.

3 Just before serving, make the sauce. Place the raspberries and fruit cordial in a small pan, bring to the boil and simmer for 2–3 minutes until the fruit is just beginning to soften. Stir the marshmallows into the raspberry mixture and heat through, stirring, until the marshmallows begin to melt.

4 Transfer the fruit salad to serving bowls. Spoon over the raspberry and marshmallow sauce and serve.

VARIATION

This sauce is delicious poured over low-fat ice cream. For an extra-colourful sauce, replace the raspberries with an assortment of summer berries.

Brown Bread Ice Cream

Serves 4

INGREDIENTS

175 g/6 oz fresh wholemeal
breadcrumbs
25 g/1 oz finely chopped walnuts
60 g/2 oz caster (superfine)
sugar

$\frac{1}{2}$ tsp ground nutmeg
1 tsp finely grated orange rind
450 ml/16 fl oz/2 cups low-fat
natural (unsweetened) yogurt
2 large egg whites

TO DECORATE:
walnut halves
orange slices
fresh mint leaves

1 Preheat the grill (broiler) to medium. Mix the breadcrumbs, walnuts and sugar together and spread over a sheet of foil in the grill (broiler) pan. Grill (broil), stirring frequently, for 5 minutes until crisp and evenly browned. (Take care that the sugar does not burn.) Remove from the heat and leave to cool.

2 When cool, transfer to a mixing bowl and mix in the nutmeg, orange rind and yogurt. In another bowl, whisk the egg whites until stiff. Gently fold into the breadcrumb mixture, using a metal spoon.

3 Spoon the mixture into 4 mini-basins, smooth over the tops and freeze for 1$\frac{1}{2}$–2 hours until firm.

4 To serve, hold the bases of the moulds (molds) in hot water for a few seconds, then turn out on to serving plates. Serve immediately, decorated with walnut halves, orange slices and fresh mint leaves.

COOK'S TIP

If you don't have mini-basins, use ramekins or teacups or, if you prefer, use one large bowl. Alternatively, spoon the mixture into a large, freezing container to freeze and serve the ice cream in scoops.

Chocolate Cheese Pots

Serves 4

INGREDIENTS

300 ml/^{1}/₂ pint/1^1/₄ cups low-fat
  natural fromage frais
  (unsweetened yogurt)
150 ml/5 fl oz/^{2}/₃ cup low-fat
  natural (unsweetened) yogurt
25 g/1 oz icing (confectioner's)
  sugar

4 tsp low-fat drinking
  chocolate powder
4 tsp cocoa powder
1 tsp vanilla essence (extract)
2 tbsp dark rum (optional)
2 medium egg whites
4 chocolate cake decorations

TO SERVE:
pieces of kiwi fruit, orange and
  banana
strawberries and raspberries

1 Combine the fromage
  frais (unsweetened
yogurt) and low-fat yogurt
in a mixing bowl. Sift in
the sugar, drinking
chocolate and cocoa
powder and mix well. Add
the vanilla essence (extract)
and rum, if using.

2 In another bowl,
  whisk the egg whites
until stiff. Using a metal
spoon, fold the egg whites
into the fromage frais
(unsweetened yogurt) and
chocolate mixture.

3 Spoon the fromage
  frais (unsweetened
yogurt) and chocolate
mixture into 4 small china
dessert pots and leave to
chill for about 30 minutes.
Decorate each chocolate
cheese pot with a chocolate
cake decoration.

4 Serve each chocolate
  cheese pot with an
assortment of fresh fruit,
such as pieces of kiwi fruit,
orange and banana, and a
few whole strawberries
and raspberries.

VARIATION

*This chocolate mixture
would make an excellent
filling for a cheesecake.
Make the base out of
crushed Amaretti di
Saronno biscuits and egg
white, and set the filling
with 2 tsp powdered
gelatine dissolved in 2 tbsp
boiling water. Make sure
you use biscuits made from
apricot kernels, which are
virtually fat free.*

Citrus Meringue Crush

Serves 4

INGREDIENTS

8 ready-made meringue nests
300 ml/$\frac{1}{2}$ pint/1$\frac{1}{4}$ cups low-fat
   natural (unsweetened) yogurt
$\frac{1}{2}$ tsp finely grated orange rind
$\frac{1}{2}$ tsp finely grated lemon rind
$\frac{1}{2}$ tsp finely grated lime rind
2 tbsp orange liqueur or
   unsweetened orange juice

TO DECORATE:
sliced kumquat
lime rind, grated

SAUCE:
60 g/2 oz kumquats
8 tbsp unsweetened orange juice
2 tbsp lemon juice

2 tbsp lime juice
2 tbsp water
2–3 tsp caster (superfine) sugar
1 tsp cornflour (cornstarch)
   mixed with 1 tbsp water

1 Place the meringues in a clean plastic bag, seal the bag and using a rolling pin, crush the meringues into small pieces. Transfer to a mixing bowl.

2 Stir the yogurt, grated citrus rinds and the liqueur or juice into the crushed meringue. Spoon the mixture into 4 mini-basins, smooth the tops and freeze for 1$\frac{1}{2}$–2 hours until firm.

3 To make the sauce, thinly slice the kumquats and place them in a small pan with the fruit juices and water. Bring gently to the boil and then simmer over a low heat for 3–4 minutes until the kumquats have just softened.

4 Sweeten with sugar to taste, stir in the cornflour (cornstarch) mixture and cook, stirring, until thickened. Pour into a small bowl, cover the surface with a layer of cling film (plastic wrap) and leave to cool – the film will help prevent a skin forming. Leave to chill.

5 To serve, dip the meringue basins in hot water for 5 seconds or until they loosen, and turn on to serving plates. Spoon over a little sauce, decorate with slices of kumquat and lime rind and serve immediately.

Tropical Fruit Fool

Serves 4

INGREDIENTS

1 medium ripe mango

2 kiwi fruit

1 medium banana

2 tbsp lime juice

$\frac{1}{2}$ tsp finely grated lime rind,
   plus extra to decorate

2 medium egg whites

425 g/15 oz can low-fat custard

$\frac{1}{2}$ tsp vanilla essence (extract)

2 passion fruit

1 To peel the mango, slice either side of the smooth, flat central stone. Roughly chop the flesh and blend the fruit in a food processor or blender until smooth. Alternatively, mash the chopped mango flesh with a fork.

2 Peel the kiwi fruit, chop the flesh into small pieces and place in a bowl. Peel and chop the banana and add to the bowl. Toss all of the fruit in the lime juice and rind and mix well to prevent discoloration.

3 In a grease-free bowl, whisk the egg whites until stiff and then gently fold in the custard and vanilla essence (extract) until thoroughly mixed.

4 In 4 tall glasses, alternately layer the chopped fruit, mango purée and custard mixture, finishing with the custard on top. Leave to chill in the refrigerator for 20 minutes.

5 Halve the passion fruits, scoop out the seeds and spoon the passion fruit over the fruit fools.

6 Decorate each serving with the extra lime rind and serve.

VARIATION

Other tropical fruits to try include papaya purée, with chopped pineapple and dates, and tamarillo or pomegranate seeds to decorate. Or make a summer fruit fool by using strawberry purée, topped with raspberries and blackberries, with cherries to finish.

Brown Sugar Pavlovas

Serves 4

INGREDIENTS

2 large egg whites
1 tsp cornflour (cornstarch)
1 tsp raspberry vinegar
100 g/3½ oz light muscovado
    sugar, crushed free of lumps

2 tbsp redcurrant jelly
2 tbsp unsweetened orange juice
150 ml/5 fl oz/¾ cup low-fat
    natural fromage frais
    (unsweetened yogurt)

175 g/6 oz raspberries, thawed
    if frozen
rose-scented geranium leaves,
    to decorate (optional)

1 Preheat the oven to 150°C/300°F/Gas Mark 2. Line a large baking sheet (cookie sheet) with baking parchment. In a large, grease-free bowl, whisk the egg whites until very stiff and dry. Fold in the cornflour (cornstarch) and vinegar.

2 Gradually whisk in the sugar, a spoonful at a time, until the mixture is thick and glossy.

3 Divide the mixture into 4 and spoon on to the baking sheet (cookie sheet), spaced well apart. Smooth each into a round, about 10 cm/4 inch across, and bake in the oven for 40–45 minutes until lightly browned and crisp; let cool.

4 Place the redcurrant jelly and orange juice in a small pan and heat, stirring, until melted. Leave to cool for 10 minutes.

5 Using a palette knife (spatula), carefully remove each pavlova from the baking parchment and transfer to a serving plate. Top with fromage frais (unsweetened yogurt) and raspberries. Spoon over the redcurrant jelly mixture to glaze. Decorate and serve.

VARIATION

Make a large pavlova by forming the meringue into a round, measuring 18 cm/ 7 inches across, on a lined baking sheet (cookie sheet) and bake for 1 hour.

Apricot & Orange Jellies

Serves 4

INGREDIENTS

225 g/8 oz no-need-to-soak
    dried apricots
300 ml/¹/₂ pint/1 ¹/₄ cups
    unsweetened orange juice
2 tbsp lemon juice
2–3 tsp clear honey
1 tbsp powdered gelatine

4 tbsp boiling water

CINNAMON 'CREAM':
115 g/4 oz medium fat ricotta
    cheese
1 tsp ground cinnamon
1 tbsp clear honey

115 g/4 oz low-fat natural
    fromage frais (unsweetened
    yogurt)

TO DECORATE:
orange segments
sprigs of mint

1 Place the apricots in a saucepan and pour in the orange juice. Bring to the boil, cover and simmer for 15–20 minutes until plump and soft. Leave to cool for 10 minutes.

2 Transfer the mixture to a blender or food processor and blend until smooth. Stir in the lemon juice and add the honey. Pour the mixture into a measuring jug and make up to 600 ml/1 pint /2 ¹/₂ cups with cold water.

3 Dissolve the gelatine in the boiling water and stir into the apricot mixture.

4 Pour the mixture into 4 individual moulds (molds), each 150 ml/5 fl oz/²/₃ cup, or 1 large mould (mold), 600 ml/1 pint/2 ¹/₂ cups. Chill until set.

5 Meanwhile, make the cinnamon 'cream'. Mix all the ingredients together and place in a small bowl. Cover and leave to chill.

6 To turn out the jellies, dip the moulds (molds) in hot water for a few seconds to loosen and invert on to serving plates. Decorate and serve with the cinnamon 'cream' dusted with extra cinnamon.

VARIATION

Other fruits that would work well in this recipe instead of the apricots are dried peaches, mangoes and pears.

Sticky Sesame Bananas

Serves 4

INGREDIENTS

4 ripe medium bananas
3 tbsp lemon juice
115 g/4 oz caster (superfine)
    sugar
4 tbsp cold water

2 tbsp sesame seeds
150 ml/5 fl oz/²/₃ cup low-fat
    natural fromage frais
    (unsweetened yogurt)

1 tbsp icing (confectioner's)
    sugar
1 tsp vanilla essence (extract)
lemon and lime rind, shredded,
    to decorate

1 Peel the bananas and cut into 5 cm/2 inch pieces. Place the banana in a bowl, spoon over the lemon juice and stir well to coat – this will prevent the bananas from discoloring.

2 Place the sugar and water in a small pan and heat gently, stirring, until the sugar dissolves. Bring to the boil and cook for 5–6 minutes until the mixture caramelizes.

3 Drain the bananas and blot with absorbent kitchen paper to dry. Line a baking sheet (cookie sheet) or board with parchment and arrange the bananas, well spaced out, on top.

4 Dizzle the caramel over the bananas, working quickly because the caramel sets almost instantly. Sprinkle over the sesame seeds and leave to cool for 10 minutes.

5 Meanwhile, mix the fromage frais (unsweetened yogurt) with the icing (confectioner's) sugar and vanilla essence (extract).

6 Peel the bananas away from the paper and arrange on serving plates. Serve the fromage frais (unsweetened yogurt) as a dip, decorated with the lemon and lime rind.

COOK'S TIP

For best results, use a cannelle knife or a potato peeler to peel away thin strips of rind from the fruit, taking care not to include any bitter pith. Blanch the shreds in boiling water for 1 minute, then refresh in cold water.

Mocha Swirl Mousse

Serves 4

INGREDIENTS

1 tbsp coffee and chicory
   essence (extract)
2 tsp cocoa powder, plus extra
   for dusting
1 tsp low-fat drinking chocolate
   powder

150 ml/5 fl oz/²⁄₃ cup half-fat
   crème fraîche, plus 4 tsp to
   serve (see Cook's Tip, below)
2 tsp powdered gelatine
2 tbsp boiling water
2 large egg whites

2 tbsp caster (superfine) sugar
4 chocolate coffee beans, to
   serve

1 Place the coffee and chicory essence (extract) in one bowl, and 2 tsp cocoa powder and the drinking chocolate in another bowl. Divide the crème fraîche between the 2 bowls and mix both until well combined.

2 Dissolve the gelatine in the boiling water and set aside. In a grease-free bowl, whisk the egg whites and sugar until stiff and divide this mixture evenly between the coffee and chocolate mixtures.

3 Divide the dissolved gelatine between the 2 mixtures and, using a large metal spoon, gently fold until well mixed.

4 Spoon small amounts of the 2 mousses alternately into 4 serving glasses and swirl together gently. Chill for 1 hour or until set.

5 To serve, top each mousse with 1 tbsp of crème fraîche, a chocolate coffee bean and a light dusting of cocoa powder.

COOK'S TIP

Traditional crème fraîche is soured cream and has a fat content of around 40 per cent. It is thick and has a slightly sour and nutty flavour. Lower fat versions have a reduced fat content and are slightly looser in texture, but they should be used in a low-fat diet only occasionally. If you want to use a lower fat alternative, a reduced fat, unsweetened yogurt or fromage frais would be more suitable.

Fruit & Fibre Layers

Serves 4

INGREDIENTS

115 g/4 oz no-need-to-soak
    dried apricots
115 g/4 oz no-need-to-soak
    dried prunes
115 g/4 oz no-need-to-soak
    dried peaches

60g /2 oz dried apple
25 g/1 oz dried cherries
450 ml/16 fl oz/2 cups
    unsweetened apple juice
6 cardamom pods
6 cloves

1 cinnamon stick, broken
300 ml/½ pint/1¼ cups
    low-fat natural yogurt
115 g/4 oz crunchy oat cereal
apricot slices, to decorate

1 To make the fruit compote, place the dried apricots, prunes, peaches, apples and cherries in a saucepan and pour in the apple juice.

2 Add the cardamom pods, cloves and cinnamon stick to the pan, bring to the boil and simmer for 10–15 minutes until the fruits are plump and tender.

3 Leave the mixture to cool completely in the pan. Remove and discard the spices from the fruits, then transfer the mixture to a bowl and leave to chill in the refrigerator for 1 hour.

4 Spoon the compote into 4 dessert glasses, layering it alternately with yogurt and oat cereal, finishing with the oat cereal on top.

5 Decorate each dessert with slices of apricot and serve at once.

COOK'S TIP

There are many dried fruits available, including mangoes and pears, some of which need soaking, so read the instructions on the packet before use. Also, check the ingredients label, because several types of dried fruit have added sugar or are rolled in sugar, and this will affect the sweetness of the dish that you use them in.

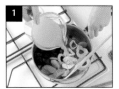

Pan-Cooked Apples in Red Wine

Serves 4

INGREDIENTS

4 eating (dessert) apples
2 tbsp lemon juice
40 g/1½ oz low-fat spread
60 g/2 oz light muscovado sugar

1 small orange
1 cinnamon stick, broken
150 ml/5 fl oz/⅔ cup red wine

225 g/8 oz raspberries, hulled
   and thawed if frozen
sprigs of fresh mint, to decorate

1 Peel and core the apples, then cut them into thick wedges. Place the apples in a bowl and toss in the lemon juice to prevent the fruit from discoloring.

2 In a frying pan (skillet), gently melt the low-fat spread over a low heat, add the sugar and stir to form a paste.

3 Stir the apple wedges into the pan and cook, stirring occasionally, for 2 minutes until well coated in the sugar paste.

4 Using a vegetable peeler, pare off a few strips of orange rind. Add the orange rind to the pan along with the cinnamon pieces. Extract the juice from the orange and pour into the pan with the red wine. Bring to the boil, then simmer for 10 minutes, stirring.

5 Add the raspberries to the pan and cook for 5 minutes until the apples are tender.

6 Discard the orange rind and cinnamon pieces. Transfer the apple

and raspberry mixture to a serving plate together with the wine sauce. Decorate with a sprig of fresh mint and serve hot.

VARIATION

For other fruity combinations, cook the apples with blackberries, blackcurrants or redcurrants. You may need to add more sugar if you use currants as they are not as sweet as raspberries.

Mixed Fruit Brûlées

Serves 4

INGREDIENTS

450 g/1 lb prepared, assorted
  summer fruits (such as
  strawberries, raspberries,
  blackcurrants, redcurrants
  and cherries), thawed if
  frozen

150 ml/5 fl oz/³⁄₄ cup half-fat
  double (heavy) cream
  alternative
150 ml/5 fl oz/³⁄₄ cup low-fat
  natural fromage frais
  (unsweetened yogurt)

1 tsp vanilla essence (extract)
4 tbsp demerara (brown crystal)
  sugar

1 Divide up each of
  the strawberries,
raspberries, blackcurrants,
redcurrants and cherries
evenly among 4 small,
heatproof ramekin dishes.

2 Mix together the half-
  fat cream alternative,
fromage frais (unsweetened
yogurt) and vanilla essence
(extract). Generously spoon
the mixture over the fruit.

3 Preheat the grill (broiler)
  to hot. Top each
serving with 1 tablespoon
demerara (brown crystal)
sugar and grill (broil) the
desserts for 2–3 minutes,
until the sugar melts and
begins to caramelize.
Serve hot.

VARIATION

*If you are making this
dessert for a special occasion,
soak the fruits in 2–3 tbsp
fruit liqueur before topping
with the cream mixture.*

COOK'S TIP

*Look out for half-fat creams,
in single and double (light
and heavy) varieties. They
are good substitutes for
occasional use. Alternatively,
in this recipe, omit the
cream and double the
quantity of fromage frais
(yogurt) for a lower
fat version.*

Grilled Fruit Platter with Lime Butter

Serves 4

INGREDIENTS

1 baby pineapple	4 tbsp dark rum	LIME 'BUTTER':
1 ripe papaya	1 tsp ground allspice	60 g/2 oz low-fat spread
1 ripe mango	2 tbsp lime juice	$\frac{1}{2}$ tsp finely grated lime rind
2 kiwi fruit	4 tbsp dark muscovado sugar	1 tbsp icing (confectioner's)
4 apple (finger) bananas		sugar

1 Quarter the pineapple, trimming away most of the leaves, and place in a shallow dish. Peel the papaya, cut it in half and scoop out the seeds. Cut the flesh into thick wedges and place in the same dish as the pineapple.

2 Peel the mango, cut either side of the smooth, central flat stone and remove the stone. Slice the flesh into thick wedges. Peel the kiwi fruit and cut in half. Peel the bananas. Add all of these fruits to the dish.

3 Sprinkle over the rum, allspice and lime juice, cover and leave at room temperature for 30 minutes, turning occasionally, to allow the flavours to develop.

4 Meanwhile, make the 'butter'. Place the low-fat spread in a small bowl and beat in the lime rind and sugar until well mixed. Leave to chill in the refrigerator until required.

5 Preheat the grill (broiler) to hot. Drain the fruit, reserving the juices, and arrange in the grill (broiler) pan. Sprinkle with the sugar and grill (broil) for 3–4 minutes until hot, bubbling and just beginning to char.

6 Transfer the fruit to a serving plate and spoon over the juices. Serve with the lime 'butter'.

VARIATION

Serve with a light sauce of 300 ml/ $\frac{1}{2}$ pint/1$\frac{1}{4}$ cups tropical fruit juice thickened with 2 tsp arrowroot.

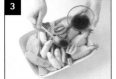

Baked Pears with Cinnamon & Brown Sugar

Serves 4

INGREDIENTS

4 ripe pears	1 tsp ground cinnamon	lemon rind, finely grated, to
2 tbsp lemon juice	60 g/2 oz low-fat spread	decorate
4 tbsp light muscovado sugar	low-fat custard, to serve	

1 Preheat the oven to 200°C/400°F/Gas Mark 6. Core and peel the pears, then slice them in half lengthwise and brush all over with the lemon juice to prevent the pears from discoloring. Place the pears, cored side down, in a small non-stick roasting tin (pan).

2 Place the sugar, cinnamon and low-fat spread in a small saucepan and heat gently, stirring, until the sugar has melted. Keep the heat low to stop too much water evaporating from the low-fat spread as it gets hot. Spoon the mixture over the pears.

3 Bake for 20–25 minutes or until the pears are tender and golden, occasionally spooning the sugar mixture over the fruit during the cooking time.

4 To serve, heat the custard until it is piping hot and spoon over the bases of 4 warm dessert plates. Arrange 2 pear halves on each plate. Decorate with grated lemon rind and serve.

VARIATION

This recipe also works well if you use cooking apples. For alternative flavours, replace the cinnamon with ground ginger and serve the pears sprinkled with chopped stem ginger in syrup. Alternatively, use ground allspice and spoon over some warmed dark rum to serve.

Baked Apples with Blackberries

Serves 4

INGREDIENTS

4 medium-sized cooking apples
1 tbsp lemon juice
100 g/3 ½ oz prepared
   blackberries, thawed if frozen
15 g/½ oz flaked (slivered)
   almonds

½ tsp ground allspice
½ tsp finely grated lemon rind
2 tbsp demerara (brown crystal)
   sugar
300 ml/½ pint/1 ¼ cups ruby
   port

1 cinnamon stick, broken
2 tsp cornflour (cornstarch)
   blended with 2 tbsp
   cold water
low-fat custard, to serve

1 Preheat the oven to 200°C/400°F/Gas Mark 6. Wash and dry the apples. Make a shallow cut through the skin around the middle of each apple – this will help the apples to cook through.

2 Core the apples, brush the centres with the lemon juice to prevent browning and stand in a shallow ovenproof dish.

3 In a bowl, mix together the blackberries, almonds, allspice, lemon rind and sugar. Using a teaspoon, spoon the mixture into the centre of each apple.

4 Pour the port into the dish, add the cinnamon stick and bake the apples in the oven for 35–40 minutes or until tender and soft. Drain the cooking juices into a pan and keep the apples warm.

5 Discard the cinnamon and add the cornflour (cornstarch) mixture to the cooking juices. Heat, stirring, until thickened.

6 Heat the custard until piping hot. Pour the sauce over the apples and serve with the custard.

VARIATION

Use raspberries instead of blackberries and, if you prefer, replace the port with unsweetened orange juice.

White Lace Crêpes with Oriental Fruits

Serves 4

INGREDIENTS

3 medium egg whites	FRUIT FILLING:	1 cm/½ inch piece root (fresh)
4 tbsp cornflour (cornstarch)	350 g/12 oz fresh lychees	ginger
3 tbsp cold water	¼ Galia melon	2 pieces stem ginger in syrup
1 tsp vegetable oil	175 g/6 oz seedless green grapes	2 tbsp ginger wine or dry sherry

1 To make the fruit filling, peel the lychees and remove the stones. Place the lychees in a bowl. Scoop out the seeds from the melon and remove the skin. Cut the melon flesh into small pieces and place in the bowl.

2 Wash and dry the grapes, remove the stalks and add to the bowl. Peel the ginger and cut into thin shreds or grate finely. Drain the stem ginger pieces, reserving the syrup, and chop the ginger pieces quite finely.

3 Mix the gingers into the bowl along with the ginger wine or sherry and the reserved stem ginger syrup. Cover and set aside.

4 Meanwhile, prepare the crêpes. In a small jug, mix together the egg whites, cornflour (cornstarch) and cold water until very smooth.

5 Brush a small non-stick crêpe pan with oil and heat until hot. Drizzle the surface of the pan with a quarter of the cornflour (cornstarch) mixture to give a lacy effect. Cook for a few seconds until set, then carefully lift out and transfer to absorbent kitchen paper to drain. Set aside and keep warm. Repeat with the remaining mixture to make 4 crêpes in total.

6 To serve, place a crêpe on each serving plate and top with the fruit filling. Fold over the pancake and serve hot.

Fruit Loaf with Strawberry & Apple Spread

Serves 8

INGREDIENTS

175 g/6 oz porridge oats
(oatmeal)
100 g/3 $\frac{1}{2}$ oz light muscovado
sugar
1 tsp ground cinnamon
125 g/4 $\frac{1}{2}$ oz sultanas
175 g/6 oz seedless raisins
2 tbsp malt extract

300 ml/$\frac{1}{2}$ pint/1 $\frac{1}{4}$ cups
unsweetened apple juice
175 g/6 oz self-raising
wholemeal (whole wheat)
flour
1 $\frac{1}{2}$ tsp baking powder
strawberries and apple wedges,
to serve

FRUIT SPREAD:
225 g/8 oz strawberries, washed
and hulled
2 eating (dessert) apples, cored,
chopped and mixed with
1 tbsp lemon juice to prevent
browning
300 ml/$\frac{1}{2}$ pint/1 $\frac{1}{4}$ cups
unsweetened apple juice

1 Preheat the oven to 180°C/350°F/Gas Mark 4. Grease and line a 900 g/2 lb loaf tin (pan). Place the porridge oats (oatmeal), sugar, cinnamon, sultanas, raisins and malt extract in a bowl. Pour in the apple juice, stir well and leave to soak for 30 minutes.

2 Sift in the flour and baking powder, adding any husks that remain in the sieve, and fold in using a metal spoon. Spoon the mixture into the tin (pan) and bake for 1 $\frac{1}{2}$ hours until firm or until a skewer inserted into the centre comes out clean. Cool for 10 minutes, then turn on to a rack and cool completely.

3 To make the fruit spread, place the strawberries and apples in a pan and pour in the apple juice. Bring to the boil, cover and simmer for 30 minutes. Beat the sauce well and spoon into a clean, warmed jar. Leave to cool, then seal and label.

4 Serve the loaf with 1–2 tbsp of the fruit spread and an assortment of apples and strawberries.

Banana & Lime Cake

Serves 10

INGREDIENTS

300 g/10½ oz plain (all-
 purpose) flour
1 tsp salt
1½ tsp baking powder
175 g/6 oz light muscovado
 sugar
1 tsp lime rind, grated
1 medium egg, beaten

1 medium banana, mashed with
 1 tbsp lime juice
150 ml/5 fl oz/⅔ cup low-fat
 natural fromage frais
 (unsweetened yogurt)
115 g/4 oz sultanas
banana chips and finely grated
 lime rind, to decorate

TOPPING:
115 g/4 oz icing (confectioner's)
 sugar
1–2 tsp lime juice
½ tsp lime rind, finely grated

1 Preheat the oven to
180°C/350°F/Gas
Mark 4. Grease and line a
deep 18 cm/7 inch round
cake tin (pan) with baking
parchment. Sift the flour,
salt and baking powder
into a bowl and stir in the
sugar and lime rind.

2 Make a well in the
centre of the dry
ingredients and add the
egg, banana, fromage frais
(yogurt) and sultanas. Mix
well until incorporated.

3 Spoon the mixture into
the tin and smooth the
surface. Bake for 40–45
minutes until firm to the
touch or until a skewer
inserted in the centre
comes out clean. Leave to
cool for 10 minutes, then
turn out on to a wire rack.

4 For the topping, sift the
icing (confectioner's)
sugar into a bowl and mix
with the lime juice to form
a soft, but not too runny,
icing. Stir in the lime rind.

Drizzle the icing over the
cake, letting it run down
the sides.

5 Decorate with banana
chips and lime rind.
Let stand for 15 minutes so
that the icing sets.

VARIATION

*Replace the lime rind
and juice with orange and
the sultanas with
chopped apricots.*

Crispy Sugar-Topped Blackberry & Apple Cake

Serves 10

INGREDIENTS

350 g/12 oz cooking apples
3 tbsp lemon juice
300 g/10½ oz self-raising
  wholemeal (whole wheat)
  flour
½ tsp baking powder

1 tsp ground cinnamon, plus
  extra for dusting
175 g/6 oz prepared blackberries,
  thawed if frozen, plus extra
  to decorate
175 g/6 oz light muscovado sugar
1 medium egg, beaten

200 ml/7 fl oz/¾ cup low-fat
  natural fromage frais
  (unsweetened yogurt)
60 g/2 oz white or brown sugar
  cubes, lightly crushed
sliced eating (dessert) apple,
  to decorate

1 Preheat the oven to 190°C/375°F/Gas Mark 5. Grease and line a 900 g/ 2 lb loaf tin (pan). Core, peel and dice the apples. Place them in a pan with the lemon juice, bring to the boil, cover and simmer for 10 minutes until soft. Beat well and let cool.

2 Sift the flour, baking powder and 1 tsp cinnamon into a bowl, adding any husks that remain in the sieve. Stir in 115 g/4 oz blackberries and the sugar.

3 Make a well in the centre of the ingredients and add the egg, fromage frais (yogurt) and cooled apple purée. Mix well. Spoon the mixture into the prepared loaf tin (pan) and smooth over the top.

4 Sprinkle with the remaining blackberries, pressing them down into the cake mixture, and top with the crushed sugar lumps. Bake for 40–45 minutes. Leave to cool in the tin (pan).

5 Remove the cake from the tin and peel away the lining paper. Serve dusted with cinnamon and decorated with extra fruit.

Rich Fruit Cake

Serves 12

INGREDIENTS

175 g/6 oz unsweetened
  pitted dates
115 g/4 oz no-need-to-soak
  dried prunes
200 ml/7 fl oz/³/₄ cup
  unsweetened orange juice
2 tbsp treacle (molasses)
1 tsp finely grated lemon rind
1 tsp finely grated orange rind

225 g/8 oz self-raising
  wholemeal (whole wheat)
  flour
1 tsp mixed spice
115 g/4 oz seedless raisins
115 g/4 oz golden sultanas
115 g/4 oz currants
115 g/4 oz dried cranberries
3 large eggs, separated

icing (confectioner's) sugar, to
  dust

TO DECORATE:
1 tbsp apricot jam, softened,
175 g/6 oz sugarpaste
strips of orange rind
strips of lemon rind

1 Preheat the oven to 170°C/325°F/Gas Mark 3. Grease and line a deep 20.5 cm/8 inch round cake tin (pan). Chop the dates and prunes and place in a pan. Pour over the orange juice and bring to the boil. Simmer for 10 minutes until very soft. Remove the pan from the heat and beat the fruit mixture until puréed. Stir in the treacle (molasses) and citrus rinds. Let cool.

2 Sift the flour and mixed spice into a bowl, adding any husks that remain in the sieve. Mix in the dried fruits and make a well in the centre.

3 When the date and prune mixture is cool, whisk in the egg yolks. In a separate bowl, whisk the egg whites until stiff. Spoon the fruit and egg yolk mixture into the dry ingredients and mix.

4 Fold in the egg whites using a metal spoon. Transfer to the tin (pan) and bake for 1½ hours. Leave to cool in the tin (pan).

5 Remove the cake from the tin (pan) and brush the top with jam. Dust the work surface with icing (confectioner's) sugar and roll out the sugarpaste thinly. Lay the sugarpaste over the top of the cake and trim the edges. Decorate.

Carrot & Ginger Cake

Serves 10

INGREDIENTS

225 g/8 oz plain (all-purpose)
flour
1 tsp baking powder
1 tsp bicarbonate of soda
2 tsp ground ginger
1/2 tsp salt
175 g/6 oz light muscovado
sugar
225 g/8 oz carrots, grated

2 pieces stem ginger in syrup,
drained and chopped
25 g/1 oz root (fresh) ginger,
grated
60 g/2 oz seedless raisins
2 medium eggs, beaten
3 tbsp corn oil
juice of 1 medium orange

FROSTING:
225 g/8 oz low-fat soft cheese
4 tbsp icing (confectioner's)
sugar
1 tsp vanilla essence (extract)

TO DECORATE:
grated carrot
stem (fresh) ginger
ground ginger

1 Preheat the oven to 180°C/350°F/Gas Mark 4. Grease and line a 20.5 cm/8 inch round cake tin (pan).

2 Sift the flour, baking powder, bicarbonate of soda, ground ginger and salt into a bowl. Stir in the sugar, carrots, stem ginger, root (fresh) ginger and raisins. Make a well in the centre of the dry ingredients.

3 Beat together the eggs, oil and orange juice, then pour into the centre of the well. Combine the ingredients together.

4 Spoon the mixture into the tin and smooth the surface. Bake in the oven for 1–1¼ hours until firm to the touch, or until a skewer inserted into the centre comes out clean. Cool in the tin (pan).

5 To make the frosting, place the soft cheese in a bowl and beat to soften. Sift in the icing (confectioner's) sugar and add the vanilla essence (extract). Stir well to mix.

6 Remove the cake from the tin (pan) and smooth the frosting over the top. Decorate and serve.

Strawberry Roulade

Serves 8

INGREDIENTS

3 large eggs
115 g/4 oz caster (superfine)
   sugar
115 g/4 oz plain (all-purpose) flour
1 tbsp hot water

FILLING:
200 ml/7 fl oz/³/₄ cup low-fat
   natural fromage frais
   (unsweetened yogurt)
1 tsp almond essence (extract)

225 g/8 oz small strawberries
15 g/¹/₂ oz toasted almonds,
   flaked (slivered)
1 tsp icing (confectioner's sugar)

1 Preheat the oven to 220°C/425°F/Gas Mark 7. Line a 35 x 25 cm/14 x 10 inch Swiss roll tin (pan) with parchment. Place the eggs in a bowl with the caster (superfine) sugar. Place the bowl over a pan of hot water and whisk until pale and thick.

2 Remove the bowl from the pan. Sift in the flour and fold into the eggs with the hot water. Pour the mixture into the tin (pan) and bake for 8–10 minutes, until golden and set.

3 Transfer the mixture to a sheet of parchment. Peel off the lining paper and roll up the sponge along with the parchment. Wrap in a tea towel (dish towel) and let cool.

4 To make the filling, mix together the fromage frais (yogurt) and almond essence (extract). Reserving a few strawberries for decoration, wash, hull and slice the rest. Leave the filling mixture to chill until ready to assemble.

5 Unroll the sponge, spread the fromage frais (yogurt) mixture over the sponge and sprinkle with the strawberries. Roll the sponge up again. Sprinkle with the almonds and lightly dust with icing (confectioner's) sugar. Decorate with the reserved strawberries.

VARIATION

Serve the roulade with a fruit purée, sweetened with a little sugar.

Fruity Muffins

Makes 10

INGREDIENTS

225 g/8 oz self-raising
    wholemeal (whole wheat)
    flour
2 tsp baking powder
25 g/1 oz light muscovado sugar

100 g/3¹/₂ oz no-need-to-soak
    dried apricots, chopped finely
1 medium banana, mashed with
    1 tbsp orange juice
1 tsp orange rind, grated finely

300 ml/¹/₂ pint/1¹/₄ cups
    skimmed milk
1 medium egg, beaten
3 tbsp corn oil
2 tbsp porridge oats (oatmeal)
fruit spread, honey or maple
    syrup, to serve

1 Preheat the oven to 200°C/400°F/Gas Mark 6. Place 10 paper muffin cases in a deep patty tin (pan).

2 Sift the flour and baking powder into a bowl, adding any husks that remain in the sieve. Stir in the sugar and apricots.

3 Make a well in the centre of the dry ingredients and add the banana, orange rind, milk, beaten egg and oil. Mix to form a thick batter. Divide the batter evenly among the 10 paper cases.

4 Sprinkle with a few porridge oats (oatmeal) and bake for 25–30 minutes until well risen and firm to the touch, or until a skewer inserted into the centre comes out clean. Transfer to a wire rack to cool slightly.

5 Serve the muffins warm with a little fruit spread, honey or maple syrup.

VARIATION

If you like dried figs, they make a deliciously crunchy alternative to the apricots; they also go very well with the flavour of orange. Other no-need-to-soak dried fruits, chopped up finely, can be used as well. Store these muffins in an airtight container for 3-4 days. They also freeze well in sealed bags or in freezer containers for up to 3 months.

Chocolate Brownies

Makes 12

INGREDIENTS

60 g/2 oz unsweetened pitted dates, chopped

60 g/2 oz no-need-to-soak dried prunes, chopped

6 tbsp unsweetened apple juice

4 medium eggs, beaten

300 g/10½ oz dark muscovado sugar

1 tsp vanilla essence (extract)

4 tbsp low-fat drinking chocolate powder

2 tbsp cocoa powder

175 g/6 oz plain (all-purpose) flour

60 g/2 oz dark chocolate chips

ICING:

115 g/4 oz icing (confectioner's) sugar

1–2 tsp water

1 tsp vanilla essence (extract)

1 Preheat the oven to 180°C/350°F/Gas Mark 4. Grease and line a 18 x 28 cm/7 x 11 inch cake tin (pan) with parchment. Place the dates and prunes in a small pan and add the apple juice. Bring to the boil, cover and simmer for 10 minutes until soft. Beat to form a smooth paste, then set aside to cool.

2 Place the cooled fruit in a mixing bowl and stir in the eggs, sugar and vanilla essence. Sift in 4 tbsp drinking chocolate, the cocoa and the flour, and fold in along with the chocolate chips until well incorporated.

3 Spoon the mixture into the prepared tin (pan) and smooth over the top. Bake for 25–30 minutes until firm to the touch or until a skewer inserted into the centre comes out clean. Cut into 12 bars and leave to cool in the tin (pan) for

10 minutes. Transfer to a wire rack to cool completely.

4 To make the icing, sift the sugar into a bowl and mix with enough water and the vanilla essence (extract) to form a soft, but not too runny, icing.

5 Drizzle the icing over the chocolate brownies and allow to set. Dust with extra chocolate powder before serving.

Cheese & Chive Scones

Makes 10

INGREDIENTS

250 g/9 oz self-raising flour
1 tsp powdered mustard
½ tsp cayenne pepper
½ tsp salt

100 g/3½ oz low-fat soft cheese
    with added herbs
2 tbsp fresh snipped chives, plus
    extra to garnish

100 ml/3½ fl oz and 2 tbsp
    skimmed milk
60 g/2 oz reduced-fat Cheddar
    cheese, grated
low-fat soft cheese, to serve

1 Preheat the oven to 200°C/400°F/Gas Mark 6. Sift the flour, mustard, cayenne and salt into a mixing bowl.

2 Add the soft cheese to the mixture and mix together until well incorporated. Stir in the snipped chives.

3 Make a well in the centre of the ingredients and gradually pour in 100 ml/3½ fl oz milk, stirring as you pour, until the mixture forms a soft dough.

4 Turn the dough on to a floured surface and knead lightly. Roll out until 2 cm/¾ inch thick and use a 5 cm/2 inch plain pastry cutter to stamp out as many rounds as you can. Transfer the rounds to a baking sheet (cookie sheet).

5 Re-knead the dough trimmings together and roll out again. Stamp out more rounds – you should be able to make 10 scones in total.

6 Brush the scones with the remaining milk and sprinkle with the grated cheese. Bake in the oven for 15–20 minutes until risen and golden. Transfer to a wire rack to cool. Serve warm with low-fat soft cheese, garnished with freshly snipped chives.

VARIATION

For sweet scones, omit the mustard, cayenne pepper, chives and grated cheese and add 75g/3 oz currants or sultanas and 25 g/1 oz sugar, and use plain low-fat soft cheese.

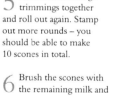

Savoury Tomato & Pepper Bread

Serves 8

INGREDIENTS

1 small red (bell) pepper

1 small green (bell) pepper

1 small yellow (bell) pepper

60 g/2 oz dry-pack sun-dried
  tomatoes

50 ml/2 fl oz/^{1}/$_4$ cup boiling
  water

2 tsp dried yeast

1 tsp caster (superfine) sugar

150 ml/5 fl oz/^{2}/$_3$ cup tepid water

450 g/1 lb/4 cups strong white
  bread flour

2 tsp dried rosemary

2 tbsp tomato purée (paste)

150 ml/5 fl oz/^{2}/$_3$ cup low-fat
  natural fromage frais
  (unsweetened yogurt)

1 tbsp coarse salt

1 tbsp olive oil

1 Preheat the oven to 220°C/425°F/Gas Mark 7 and the grill (broiler) to hot. Halve and deseed the (bell) peppers, arrange on the rack and cook until the skin is charred. Cool for 10 minutes, peel off the skin and chop the flesh.

2 Slice the tomatoes into strips and place in a bowl. Pour over the boiling water and set aside to soak.

3 Place the yeast and sugar in a small jug,

pour over the tepid water and leave for 10–15 minutes until frothy. Sift the flour into a bowl and add 1 tsp dried rosemary. Make a well in the centre and pour in the yeast mixture. Add the tomato purée (paste), the tomatoes and soaking liquid, the (bell) peppers, fromage frais (yogurt) and half the salt. Mix together to form a soft dough.

4 Turn the dough out on to a floured surface and knead for 3–4 minutes until

smooth and elastic. Place in a floured bowl, cover and leave in a warm room for about 40 minutes until doubled in size. Knead again and place in a greased 23 cm/9 inch round spring-clip cake tin (pan). Make 'dimples' in the surface. Cover for 30 minutes.

5 Brush with oil and sprinkle with rosemary and salt. Bake for 35–40 minutes, cool for 10 minutes and release from the tin (pan). Leave to cool.

Exotic Fruity Parcels

Serves 4

INGREDIENTS

1 pawpaw (papaya)	1 tbsp grenadine	single (light) cream or natural
1 mango	3 tbsp orange juice	yogurt, to serve
1 star fruit		

1 Cut the pawpaw (papaya) in half, scoop out the seeds and discard them. Peel the pawpaw (papaya) and cut the flesh into thick slices.

2 Prepare the mango by cutting it lengthwise in half either side of the central stone.

3 Score each mango half in a criss-cross pattern. Push each mango half inside out to separate the cubes and cut them away from the peel.

4 Using a sharp knife, slice the star fruit.

5 Place all of the fruit in a bowl and mix.

6 Mix the grenadine and orange juice together and pour over the fruit. Leave to marinate for at least 30 minutes.

7 Divide the fruit among 4 double thickness squares of kitchen foil and gather up the edges to form a parcel that encloses the fruit.

8 Place the foil parcel on a rack set over warm coals and barbecue (grill) the fruit for about 15–20 minutes.

9 Serve the fruit in the parcel, with single (light) cream or yogurt.

COOK'S TIP

Grenadine is a sweet syrup made from pomegranates. If you prefer you could use pomegranate juice instead of the grenadine for this recipe. To extract the juice, cut the pomegranate in half and squeeze gently with a lemon squeezer – do not press too hard or the juice may become bitter.